Internationalizing Higher Education in Korea:

Challenges and Opportunities
in Comparative Perspective

INTERNATIONALIZING HIGHER EDUCATION IN KOREA

Challenges and Opportunities

in Comparative Perspective

Edited by
Yeon-Cheon Oh,
Gi-Wook Shin, and
Rennie J. Moon

Stanford | **APARC** Walter H. Shorenstein Asia-Pacific Research Center   **FSI** *Freeman Spogli* Institute for International Studies

THE WALTER H. SHORENSTEIN ASIA-PACIFIC RESEARCH CENTER (Shorenstein APARC) is a unique Stanford University institution focused on the interdisciplinary study of contemporary Asia. Shorenstein APARC's mission is to produce and publish outstanding interdisciplinary, Asia-Pacific–focused research; to educate students, scholars, and corporate and governmental affiliates; to promote constructive interaction to influence U.S. policy toward the Asia-Pacific; and to guide Asian nations on key issues of societal transition, development, U.S.-Asia relations, and regional cooperation.

The Walter H. Shorenstein Asia-Pacific Research Center
Freeman Spogli Institute for International Studies
Stanford University
Encina Hall
Stanford, CA 94305-6055
tel. 650-723-9741 | fax 650-723-6530 | http://aparc.fsi.stanford.edu

Internationalizing Higher Education in Korea:
Challenges and Opportunities in Comparative Perspective
may be ordered from:
The Brookings Institution
c/o DFS, PO Box 50370, Baltimore, MD, USA
tel. 1-800-537-5487 or 410-516-6956 | fax 410-516-6998 | http://www.brookings.edu/press

Library of Congress Cataloging-in-Publication Data

Names: O, Yæon-ch'æon, editor. | Shin, Gi-Wook, editor. | Moon, Rennie, editor.
Title: Internationalizing higher education in Korea : challenges and opportunities in comparative perspective / edited by Gi-Wook Shin, Yeon-Cheon Oh, Rennie J. Moon.
Description: Baltimore, MD : Shorenstein Asia-Pacific Research Center, 2016. | Includes bibliographical references and index.
Identifiers: LCCN 2016019078 | ISBN 9781931368421 (paperback)
Subjects: LCSH: Education, Higher--Korea (South). | Education, Higher--Aims and objectives--Korea (South) | International education--Korea (South) | Student mobility--Korea (South) | Education, Higher--Asia. | International education--Asia. | BISAC: POLITICAL SCIENCE / Globalization. | EDUCATION / Educational Policy & Reform / General.
Classification: LCC LA1333 .I67 2016 | DDC 378.009519--dc23
LC record available at https://lccn.loc.gov/2016019078

First printing, 2016

ISBN 978-1-931368-42-1

Contents

Tables and Figures

Tables

Figures

Abbreviations

APAIE	Asia-Pacific Association for International Education
APEC	Asia-Pacific Economic Cooperation
APT	ASEAN Plus Three
ARF	ASEAN Regional Forum
ASEM	Asia-Europe Meeting
BK21	Brain Korea 21
BRIC	Brazil, Russia, India, and China
CAMPUS Asia	Collective Action for Mobility Program of University Students in Asia
CASE	Council for Advancement and Support of Education
CFCRS	Chinese-Foreign Cooperation in Running Schools
CUEP	Committee on University Education Pathways Beyond 2015
DIS	Division of International Studies
EAS	East Asian Summits
FEZ	free economic zone
FHRMS	Foreign Human Resources Management System
GATS	General Agreement on Trade in Services
GHC	Global Hub College
GKS	Global Korea Scholarship
GNI	gross national income
GSIS	graduate school of international studies
GSKA	Global Society of Korea America

GUISM	Globalizing Universities and International Student Mobilities in East Asia
HEI	higher education institution
HRD	health-related discipline
HSS	humanities and social sciences
ICA	Immigration & Checkpoints Authority
EQAS	International Education Quality Assurance System
IMD	International Institute of Management Development
IRO	International Relations Office
ISEP	International Student Exchange Program
KAFSA	Korean Association of Foreign Student Administrators
KAIT	Korea Association for ICT Promotion
KEDI	Korean Educational Development Institute
KGGIP	Korean Government Global Internship Program
KOCCA	Korea Creative Content Agency
KOICA	Korea International Cooperation Agency
KOTRA	Korea Trade-Investment Promotion Agency
KUBA	Korea University Buddy Assistants
MEXT	Ministry of Education, Science, Culture and Sports
MOU	memorandum of understanding
MSIP	Ministry of Science, ICT and Future Planning
NAFSA	Association of International Educators of America
NIIED	National Institute for International Education
NOC	NUS Overseas College
NSE	natural sciences and engineering
NUS	National University of Singapore
ODA	official development assistance
OECD	Organization for Economic Cooperation and Development
PCEI	Presidential Committee on Education Innovation
PR	permanent resident
QS	Quacquarelli Symonds
SETI	Samsung Economic Research Institute
SEZ	special economic zone
SNU	Seoul National University
STEM	science, technology, engineering, and mathematics

STEPI	Science and Technology Policy Institute
TNHE	transnational higher education
TOPIK	Test of Proficiency in Korean
TWC	The Washington Center
UR	Uruguay Round
UTOWN	University Town
WCU	World Class Universities
WTO	World Trade Organization

Contributors

SUN-GEUN BAEK is a professor in the Department of Education at Seoul National University. He has served in numerous positions at both the domestic and international levels, including: president of the Korean Educational Development Institute and president of the Korean Society for Educational Evaluation; dean of the Office of Admissions and vice dean of the College of Education, both at Seoul National University (SNU); member of the Presidential Council for Future & Vision under the Lee Myung-Pak administration; secretary general of the Korean Association of Academic Societies; a board member of the Korea Education & Research Information Service, the Center for Educational Research and Innovation at the Organization for Economic Cooperation and Development (OECD), and the Korean National Commission for the United Nations Educational, Scientific and Cultural Organization (UNESCO); a member of the Council for Korean University Accreditation at the Korean Council for University Education, and of the Finance Policy Advisory Committee of Korea's Ministry of Strategy and Finance. Baek received his BA and MA from SNU and PhD from the University of California at Berkeley.

HANAH CHO is a PhD candidate at the Graduate School of Public Administration at Seoul National University. She received her BA in biological science from Korea Advanced Institute of Science and Technology (KAIST), where she also completed her master's in science and technology policy. Her research interests include science and technology policy, science education, and research networks.

JOON NAK CHOI is the 2015–16 Koret Fellow in the Korea Program at Stanford University's Walter H. Shorenstein Asia-Pacific Research Center (Shorenstein APARC). A sociologist by training, Choi is an assistant professor at Hong Kong University of Science and Technology. His research and teaching areas include economic development, social networks, organizational theory, and global and transnational sociology, within the Korean context. Choi, a Stanford graduate, has worked jointly with Gi-Wook Shin to analyze the transnational bridges linking Asia and the United States. The research project explores how economic development links to foreign skilled workers and diaspora communities. Most recently, Choi coauthored *Global Talent: Skilled Labor as Social Capital in Korea* with Shin, who is also the director of the Korea Program. From 2010 to 11, Choi developed the manuscript while he was a William Perry Postdoctoral Fellow at Shorenstein APARC.

MICHELLE FOONG graduated from the master's program in geography at the National University of Singapore in 2013, supported by the Globalizing Universities and International Student Mobilities in East Asia project. She holds a postgraduate teaching diploma and has taught in public and private schools in Singapore and Japan. Her research interests include spatial and gendered youth mobility as well as the cosmopolitan practices of global youth. An avid traveler and volunteer, she has backpacked in more than thirty countries and participates in international volunteer work pertaining to youths with social anxieties. She teaches at an international school in Singapore.

JARED FURUTA is a doctoral candidate in sociology at Stanford University. His research interests focus on comparative and historical approaches to education and social stratification. He is currently pursuing projects that examine historical changes in college admissions policies in the United States, organizational changes in higher education in the United States, and cross-national and historical changes in tracking and high stakes examination regimes.

MOTOHISA KANEKO received his BA and EdM from the University of Tokyo and his PhD from the University of Chicago. He has been a professor since 2012 at Tsukuba University's Research Center for University Studies, where he was named a Distinctive Service Professor in 2015. Kaneko joined the Institute of Economic Development in Japan after graduating from the University of Tokyo. He served as a consultant for the World Bank and as a visiting assistant professor at the State University of New York at Albany before joining the Research Institute for Higher Education at Hiroshima

University. He became a professor of higher education at the University of Tokyo's Graduate School of Education, where he also served as dean. In 2010, he became the director of research at the Center for National University Finance and Management.

Kaneko is currently a member of a number of public committees and councils, including the Central Education Council, a major government organ delineating educational policies in Japan. He is a member of the Science Council of Japan and until 2015 served as president of the Japan Society for Higher Education Studies. His academic interests cover higher education, the economics of education, and development and education, on which he has published extensively.

HOON-HO KIM is a research fellow at the Korean Educational Development Institute (KEDI) and is currently working in the Higher Education Division. He received his BA, MA, and PhD from Seoul National University. Before joining KEDI, he worked as a trainee in the Directorate of Education and Skills at the OECD in Paris for the Assessment of Higher Education Learning Outcomes (AHELO) project. His major research interest area is educational administration and higher education, with specific focus on the relationship between finance structure and university performance.

JUNKI KIM is a professor at the Graduate School of Public Administration at Seoul National University and currently represents the chief of the National Assembly Budget Office in Korea. He received his BA in economics from the London School of Economics and Political Science and completed his master's and PhD in public policy from the Kennedy School of Government at Harvard University. Kim served as dean of the Graduate School of Public Administration at Seoul National University from 2012 to 2014. His main research areas include financial administration, government-business relations, public enterprise, the quasi-public sector, and information communication policy.

KILKON KO is an associate professor at the Graduate School of Public Administration at Seoul National University. He received his PhD in public and international affairs from the University of Pittsburgh. Ko is an editor-in-chief of the *Asian Journal of Political Science*. His research interests are administrative ethics, methodologies in public policy and management, and theories in public administration. He is currently working on book projects about efficiency analysis and causal theory in public policy.

DAE BONG KWON is a professor and former dean of the College of Education, Korea University. He was an assistant professor of the Educational Administration, and evaluator for the Kellogg Leadership and Local Government Education Project at Michigan State University. He was a visiting professor in the Centre for Policy Studies in Higher Education and Training at the University of British Columbia. He served as the fifth president of the Korea Research Institute for Vocational Education & Training (KRIVET), a Korean national think tank, and as a consultant for the World Bank. He has served on the board of the Korea National Commission for UNESCO and advisory committees for the prime minister's office, the Ministry of Education and Human Resource Development, and the Ministry of Employment and Labor in Korea.

Kwon's research interests lie in the areas of international and comparative education, continuing higher education leadership, and education for national development. He has presented at numerous conferences, including those organized by the OECD, UNESCO, World Bank, Global HR Forum, World Knowledge Forum, Asian Productivity Organization, Stanford University, University of British Columbia, Nagoya University, and Hokkaido University.

KA HO MOK is vice president and concurrently Chair Professor of Comparative Policy at Lingnan University, Hong Kong. Before joining Lingnan, he was the vice president (research and development) and Chair Professor of Comparative Policy at the Hong Kong Institute of Education, and associate dean and professor of social policy of the Faculty of Social Sciences at the University of Hong Kong. Prior to this, Mok was appointed as the Founding Chair Professor in East Asian Studies and established the Centre for East Asian Studies at the University of Bristol, United Kingdom.

Mok has worked creatively across the academic worlds of sociology, political science, and public and social policy while building up his knowledge of China and the region. He has published extensively in the fields of comparative education policy, comparative development and policy studies, and social development in contemporary China and East Asia. In particular, he has contributed to the field of social change and education policy in a variety of ways, not the least of which has been his leadership and entrepreneurial approach to the organization of the field. He is the founding editor-in-chief of the *Journal of Asian Public Policy* and *Asian Education and Development Studies* as well as a book series editor for Routledge and Springer.

RENNIE J. MOON is an assistant professor at the Underwood International College at Yonsei University. With a background in international comparative education and sociology, her main research and teaching interests have concentrated on globalization and higher education, global talent and brain flows, cultural diversity and social tolerance, and international cooperation and development (with a focus on Asia, especially Korea). Her articles have appeared in academic journals including *Comparative Education Review*, *Comparative Education*, and the *Australian Journal of International Affairs*. Moon is currently working on several projects, including talent flows in Asia, Korea's official development assistance in higher education, and diversity in Japanese higher education.

YEON-CHEON OH has had an extensive career as a university administrator and professor, and in leadership positions in South Korea's civil service. He was the twenty-fifth president of Seoul National University (SNU) from 2010 to 2014 and chairman of its Board of Trustees. Before then, he taught at SNU's Graduate School of Public Administration from 1983 to 2010, and also served as the dean of that school from 2000 to 2004. His main areas of research and teaching include applied public economy and financial management. Oh is currently the president of Ulsan University in Korea.

FRANCISCO O. RAMIREZ is Professor of Education and (by courtesy) Sociology at Stanford University. He received his BA in social sciences from De La Salle University in the Philippines and his MA and PhD in sociology from Stanford University. His current research interests focus on the rise and institutionalization of human rights, on the worldwide rationalization of university structures and processes, and on gender and education issues. His work has contributed to the development of the world society perspective in the social sciences. Recent publications may be found in the *American Sociological Review*, *Social Forces*, *Sociology of Education*, *Comparative Education*, *Comparative Education Review*, and *Higher Education*. He is the coeditor of *Towards a Comparative Institutionalism: Forms, Dynamics, and Logics Across the Organizational Fields of Health Care and Higher Education* (2016).

GI-WOOK SHIN is the director of the Walter H. Shorenstein Asia-Pacific Research Center and a professor of sociology at Stanford University. As a historical-comparative and political sociologist, his research has concentrated on social movements, nationalism, development, and international relations. Shin is the author/editor of twenty books and numerous articles.

His recent books include *Global Talent: Skilled Labor as Social Capital in Korea* (2015); *New Challenges for Maturing Democracies in Korea and Taiwan* (2014); and *One Alliance, Two Lenses: U.S.-Korea Relations in a New Era* (2010). His new book, *Divergent Histories: National Opinion Leaders and Memories of the Asia-Pacific War,* will be published in summer 2016. He is currently engaged in a research project on brain flows and development in Asia.

BRENDA S.A. YEOH is Provost's Chair Professor in the Department of Geography, as well as dean of the Faculty of Arts and Social Sciences, at the National University of Singapore (NUS). She is the research leader of the Asian Migration Cluster at the Asia Research Institute, NUS. Her research interests include the politics of space in colonial and postcolonial cities as well as transnational migration in the Asian context. She has published widely on these topics, and her recent books include *Return: Nationalizing Transnational Mobility in Asia* (Duke University Press, 2013, with Xiang Biao and Mika Toyota) and *Transnational Labour Migration, Remittances and the Changing Family in Asia* (Palgrave Macmillan, 2015, with Lan Anh Hoang).

About the Koret Series on Korea

This volume is the fifth in a series of policy-related studies on contemporary Korea. The Koret Foundation of San Francisco made the project possible by a generous grant to the Korea Program at Stanford University. The Koret Foundation's gift allowed Stanford's Walter H. Shorenstein Asia-Pacific Research Center, of which the Korea Program is a part, to establish a Koret Fellowship to bring leading professionals in Asia and the United States to Stanford to study U.S.–Korean relations. Koret Fellows conduct their own research on Korea and the bilateral relationship, with the broad aim of fostering greater understanding and closer ties between the two countries.

Preface and Acknowledgements

Over the past fifty years, (South) Korea has undergone immense changes. Its economic rise paired with its social and political development is well known to the outside world, and now places Korea in pace with other advanced industrialized nations. Among many contributing factors, education has provided the critical foundation for Korea's rise and development. However, in an increasingly globalized and digital world, higher education faces an array of new challenges. At its core, the challenge facing every country is how to cultivate relatively immobile assets—national populations—to capture increasingly mobile jobs with transforming skill requirements. Korea is no exception. Despite having an abundant supply of college graduates, for instance, Korea is hard-pressed to fill the immense demand in certain key sectors of business and technology. Such a situation is likely to get worse in the coming years as the country faces a serious demographic crisis due to its low birth rate and aging population.

Apparently, higher education systems today are under increasing pressure to internationalize and to produce global citizens with skills for fast-paced change. Historically, universities used to function more or less as isolated entities, but now it is necessary for them to actively engage in international exchange and cross-cultural collaboration if they are to remain competitive. Settler countries with advanced higher education systems such as the United States, Australia, and Canada have been effective in attracting and retaining top talent, but ethnically homogenous societies like Korea and Japan have historically not been as successful in attracting, accommodating, and retaining foreigners. In Korea, social policies and institutions in key areas such as higher education and immigration policy are still lacking, despite its status as an advanced industrialized nation.

To address the main challenges and opportunities associated with internationalizing higher education in Korea, we convened the seventh annual Koret conference on February 27, 2015, at the Walter H. Shorenstein Asia-Pacific Research Center (Shorenstein APARC) at Stanford University. The international conference examined programs that help develop an international faculty and student body, and the types of synergies necessary to create university collaborations in research and teaching. The conference participants also discussed the structure and forms of student exchange programs, and how these and other initiatives work to enhance narratives of tolerance and diversity in universities and beyond. They debated how Korea can attract global talent and if current policies of multiculturalism are adequate to do so. We then looked at Singapore, Japan, China, and the United States to offer a comparative context for Korea, and critically assessed the ways in which countries could learn from one another's experiences. This edited volume is primarily based on the collection of papers presented at this conference.

As always, we are indebted to the many people who made the convening of the conference and publication of this book possible. We are particularly grateful to the Koret Foundation and its chairwoman, Susan Koret, for generous support of both the conference and this publication. The seventh Koret Fellow at the Center's Korean Studies Program, Yeon Cheon Oh, former president of Seoul National University and currently president of the University of Ulsan (in Korea), played a leading role in all aspects of the conference and book publication. Twelve of the conference participants were from outside the Stanford community, and from countries including Korea, Singapore, China, and Japan. We would also like to thank all those who contributed to the conference as discussants: Jean Oi, Takeo Hoshi, Yong Lee, Yumi Moon, Dafna Zur, David Straub, Karen Eggleston, and Sook Kim.

Finally, we appreciate the dedication and hard work of all Shorenstein APARC staff members who contributed to this project, especially Heather Ahn and George Krompacky, who were responsible, respectively, for the arrangement of an efficient and pleasant conference and for the professional editing of this publication.

The Editors

Internationalizing Higher Education in Korea:

Challenges and Opportunities
in Comparative Perspective

Introduction

CHALLENGES AND OPPORTUNITIES IN INTERNATIONALIZING
HIGHER EDUCATION: KOREA IN COMPARATIVE PERSPECTIVE

Rennie J. Moon and Gi-Wook Shin

In the past few decades, many countries around the world have actively pursued the "internationalization" of higher education. While the concept has many definitions and has taken many forms, a major feature of this so-called internationalization of higher education is increased student mobility around the world. This book examines the realities, consequences, and challenges of such student (and to a lesser extent, faculty) mobility, with a focus on South Korea and Asia, where mobility patterns are undergoing dramatic changes. In particular, we direct attention to the recent trends in inbound and outbound student mobility and the twin challenges created by this mobility—growing diversity in host (receiving) countries and brain drain (and circulation) for home (sending) countries—challenges that are becoming major barriers to achieving broader socioeconomic goals and that have significant implications for growing intraregional mobility, competition, and cooperation within Northeast Asia. Most importantly, the empirical and theoretical chapters in this book seek to explore and propose unconventional ideas and related policies that might better address such challenges in the Asian higher education context.

Student Mobility in Higher Education: Global and Regional Trends

Over the past three decades, the global population of internationally mobile students increased more than fivefold, from 0.8 million worldwide in 1975 to 4.5 million in 2012 (OECD 2014). The rate of that increase has also accelerated, with the number of internationally mobile students enrolled worldwide doubling from 2000 to 2010 (Institute of International Education

2015). Within East Asia and the Pacific,[1] this change has been even more dramatic, with enrollment figures almost tripling during the same 2000–10 period (see figure I.1). In 2012, 53 percent of all internationally mobile students originated from Asia, up from 41 percent in 2000 and a figure that continues to rise (OECD 2002, 2014).

Traditionally, the flow of students has been toward study destinations in developed countries in North America and Europe. While those destinations remain the dominant providers of education for international students, this pattern has changed as more students choose to study in non-Western, non-core countries. Student mobility patterns over the past few decades show a fundamental shift from a periphery-to-core to a periphery-to-semi-periphery (i.e., to emerging economies) movement.[2] In addition, the intensity of flows and exchanges to and within Asia and the development of several education hubs in the region are relatively recent and notable developments (British Council 2008). Australia and Japan, traditional destinations in this region, are now rivaled by newcomers such as South Korea, China, and Singapore (OECD 2014). In 2004, only 46,142 students studying in China were from Asia; just five years later, this number had more than tripled to 161,605 in 2009. From 2004 to 2014, the number of foreign students from Asia studying in Japan increased 1.6 times while in Korea the number increased more than fivefold. At the same time, in both Korea and Japan, the proportion of local students choosing Asian destinations has increased significantly. In 2001, 33 percent of Koreans chose to study in Asian countries, but in 2013, this percentage reached 52 percent (see table I.1). Korean students form the largest international student group in China. Even for Japan, the most developed Asian country, only 7.6 percent of Japanese students chose to study in other Asian countries in 2001, but in 2011, as many as 13 percent decided to do so. Overall, as figure I.1 shows, student mobility within Asia as a percentage of total outbound students has increased continuously from 27 percent in 2000 to 44 percent in 2010. This is consistent with broader trends in intraregional social, cultural, and economic exchanges in Northeast Asia, along with the rise of China.

1 Countries in this region are Australia, Brunei Darussalam, Cambodia, China, Hong Kong, Macao, Cook Islands, the Democratic People's Republic of Korea, Fiji, Indonesia, Japan, Kiribati, the Lao People's Democratic Republic, Malaysia, Marshall Islands, Micronesia, Myanmar, Nauru, New Zealand, Niue, Palau, Papua New Guinea, Philippines, the Republic of Korea, Samoa, Singapore, Solomon Islands, Thailand, Timor-Leste, Tokelau, Tonga, Vanuatu, and Vietnam.

2 The share of international student enrollment of the top five destination countries (United States, United Kingdom, France, Australia, and Germany) declined from 55 percent in 2000 to 47 percent in 2012 (OECD 2014).

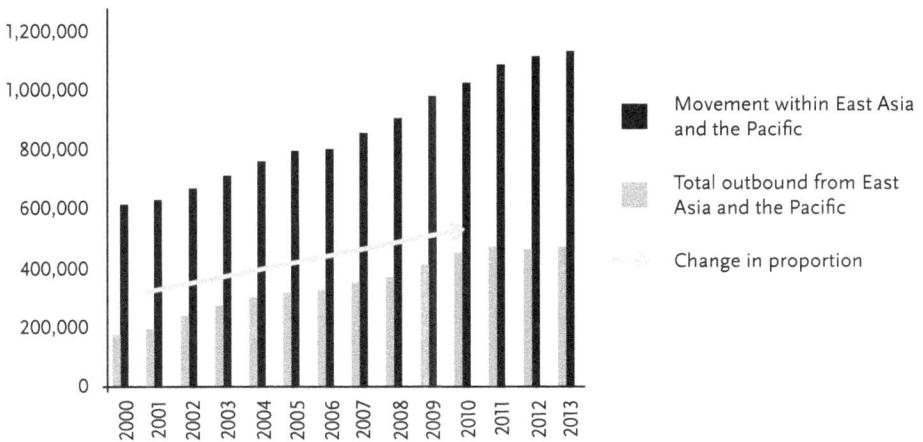

FIGURE I.1 Proportion of within-Asia student mobility, 2000–13
Source: UNESCO Institute for Statistics.

TABLE I.1
Inbound and outbound student mobility in China, Japan, and Korea

	Inbound from Asia					
	2004			2014		
	Inbound from Asia	Inbound total	Percent	Inbound from Asia	Inbound total	Percent
China	46,142	61,869	74.6*	161,605	238,184	67.8†
Japan	109,520	117,302	93.4‡	170,720	184,155	92.7§
Korea	14,563	16,832	86.5ǀ	73,229	84,491	86.0ǀ
	Outbound to Asia					
	2001			2013		
	Outbound to Asia	Outbound total	Percent	Outbound to Asia	Outbound total	Percent
China	72,580	165,648	43.8#	287,865	712,157	40.4
Japan	4,367	57,132	7.6#	4,708	35,731	13.0**
Korea	50,053	149,933	33.0††	113,130	219,543	52.0

Sources: *UNESCO (2013), 21 (figures are for 2001); †UNESCO (2013) (figures are for 2009); ‡JASSO (2004); §JASSO (2015); ǀStatistics of foreign students in Korea, Ministry of Education, Republic of Korea (2014a); #Outbound internationally mobile students by host region, UNESCO Institute for Statistics; **figures are for 2011; ††Statistics of Korean students abroad, Ministry of Education, Republic of Korea (2014b).

One of the major concerns related to greater student mobility in the region is the prospect of losing human capital ("brain drain") as many students studying abroad, especially those from China and South Korea, remain in their host countries after their studies (see table I.4 and more details below). That is, study abroad can be an excellent way of enhancing human capital capacity, but less developed countries may lose their brightest students to more advanced countries, resulting in brain drain. The same concerns arise when foreign students perceive their Asian hosts as "stepping-stones" to more advanced educational and career opportunities in the West, with few deciding to stay and work in their initial host countries.

Another growing concern has to do with increasing student diversity and how this might impact local students and host societies. Foreign students bring human capital to their host societies, but they also bring new backgrounds, experiences, perspectives, and ideas to their classrooms and campuses. These students serve as important resources for local students by offering opportunities for them to enhance their intercultural skills, key to producing global citizens. However, their presence may not necessarily lead to a tolerance of diversity; rather, it may become a source of tension, leading instead to a culturally divisive environment. Sometimes, countries fail to recognize the value of greater diversity in higher education, hampering efforts to successfully attract human capital and enhance internationalized student learning for local students (discussed below).

Both issues are closely interrelated and have important policy implications. Brain drain and declines in domestic student populations lead countries to attract more foreign students. This will make college campuses more diverse but may also bring disruptive changes to host societies, often resulting in tensions between local and foreign students. For countries and universities that embrace diversity, the returns are high. But for those that do not, they will fail to attract and retain global talent in the long term. These are particularly important research and policy topics for ethnically homogeneous countries such as Korea and Japan.

Why Korea?

South Korea, a major player in the internationalization of higher education in Asia, serves as a good reference point for examining these issues. First, Korea, as a rapidly aging society with a record-low fertility rate, is facing a dramatic decline in its domestic student population. As Baek and Kim describe in chapter 1, the population of high school graduates dropped by approximately 17 percent from 2000 to 2013 (760,000 in 2000 to 630,000 in 2013) and is projected to fall by another 37 percent (to 450,000) by the year 2023 (see figure 1.2 in chapter 1). As a result, Korea will have to rely on foreign students more than ever for its higher education industry as well as human capital needs. Two decades ago, only 1,879 foreign students were studying in Korean universities. Already over the past decade, the number of foreign students increased more than sevenfold, from 12,314 in 2003 to 86,878 in 2012 (see figure 2.1 in chapter 2), and recently the Korean government announced an ambitious new goal to attract two hundred thousand more foreign students by 2020. Yet Korea is not alone in this undertaking and will be competing with neighboring Asian countries in attracting foreign students from the same pool of (mostly Chinese) students.

Second, Korea experiences brain drain more severely than many other advanced economies, with many Korean students studying abroad and decreasing numbers returning home. Despite its relatively small population of approximately fifty million, Korea continues to be a major sending country, with about 4 percent of its college-age population studying abroad (as of 2010). Koreans comprise the largest source of students in China and the third largest in the United States (after Chinese and Indian students). When adjusted for population (of the source country), Korea sends the largest number of students among the top five sources of international students in the United States. Almost half of all Korean PhD graduates in science and engineering fields of study in the United States decide to stay in the United States (see table I.4). As a result, converting this brain drain into brain circulation (i.e., bringing students educated abroad back home) has been a major policy agenda for the Korean government.

Third, Korea, unsurprisingly, scores consistently low in its ability to attract top-tier global talent. The vast majority of foreign students studying in Korea return to their home countries upon graduation, failing to counterbalance Korean talent lost abroad. It is an ethnically homogenous country, with little appetite for diversity, which makes it even more difficult to replenish its labor shortages with foreign skilled talent. These shortages will only worsen over the next few years, reflecting one of the most rapid demographic changes ever recorded.

Fourth, Korea has been a leader in government-led internationalization reforms, starting in the early 1990s. Despite its ethnic parochialism and linguistic resistance, Korean universities implemented drastic and wide-scale Anglicization reforms before other countries in the region that had an earlier start with internationalization (e.g., Japan). As Kwon shows in chapter 2, international colleges, graduate schools of international studies, and other programs in English that were established throughout the 2000s were considered highly experimental at the time. As part of a broader globalization strategy, the Korean government has devoted substantial resources to recruiting foreign students to Korean universities through ambitious schemes such as Study Korea (designed to attract international students and aimed at bridging developed and developing countries), by globalizing domestic higher education to improve its competitiveness, providing scholarships, and marketing a foreigner-friendly image of Korea (see chapter 1). These and other dynamic reforms helped Korean universities build prestige and improve their reputations overseas in a very short period of only two decades, with many now ranking among the top one hundred universities in Asia and known to offer excellent education in engineering and the sciences, with a highly organized system of research, experiment-based training, and an established research network (see Kim, Cho and Ko, chapter 3).

Accordingly, the Korean case can effectively illustrate the many issues and challenges associated with the internationalization of higher education noted above—from inbound/outbound student mobility trends to issues of brain drain, global talent, and cultural diversity in higher education.

Comparison Cases

However, this book is not limited to examining the Korean experiences of the internationalization of higher education. Rather, we draw on the experiences of other key players in the region and beyond to engage in a comparative discussion of Korea's successes, failures, and ongoing challenges, with a focus on the issues outlined above (brain drain, global talent, and diversity).

Our comparative cases of interest include Japan, China, Singapore, and the United States. Korea and Japan share many similarities—both are ethnically homogenous, face similar demographic crises—but are also very different. Japan is much more resistant to internationalization because of its history of indigenous higher education and deeply embedded cultural history of particularism and parochialism (Agawa 2011). China is an important player in the region, supplying the majority of foreign students in both Japan and Korea and representing the most promising source of human capital for both countries. Also, China and Korea, two leading providers of international students worldwide, face similar challenges of brain drain as many of their outgoing students decide to stay in their host countries after graduation. On the other hand, many in Japan are concerned that the number of Japanese students studying abroad has been on the decline in recent decades. Singapore is an English-speaking, ethnically diverse Asian city-state that recognizes the limitations of its small and open economy and has been a leader in internationalizing higher education in Asia. Its experiences can offer important perspectives for middle powers such as Korea struggling with human capital generation imperatives. The United States is the most popular destination for foreign students from Asia, but some are concerned by the lack of American students going to study abroad for global experiences—a sharp contrast to China, which will be competing with the United States in the global market. This imbalance in U.S.-China student flows has been the motivation behind recent initiatives to send more American students to China (Onsman 2013). Also, the top-down, centralized Asian systems of higher education contrast sharply with the decentralized nature of U.S. higher education, where government intervention is minimal. Lastly, both Singapore and the United States are ethnically diverse societies, and their differing approaches to embracing diversity can be contrasted with the cases of China, Korea, and Japan.

Inbound- versus Outbound-Driven Countries

We begin by outlining some key comparative statistics on inbound and outbound student numbers that provide the basis for our discussion. Figure I.2 shows that the United States, Japan, and Singapore tend to be inbound-driven, while China and Korea are both outbound-driven.

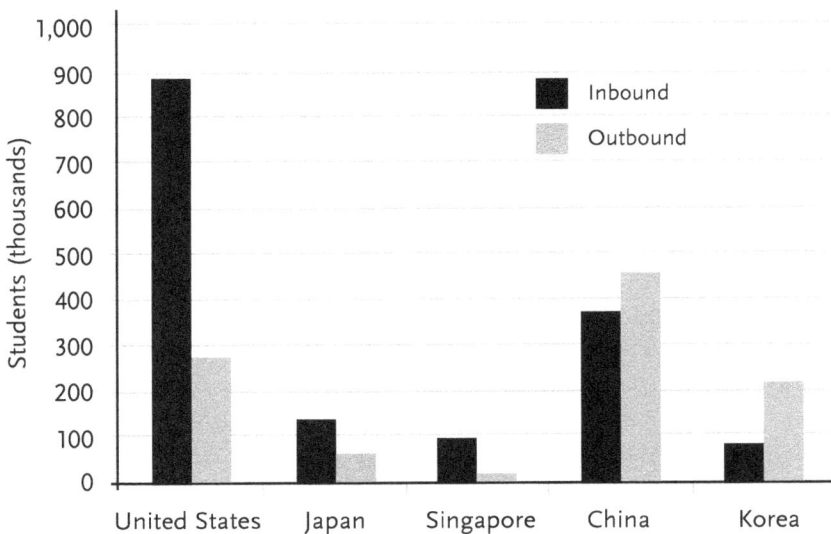

FIGURE I.2 Number of inbound and outbound students (as of April 2014)

Source: Statistics for United States, Japan, and China are from the Institute of International Education, Center for Academic Mobility Research; inbound numbers for Singapore are 2009 figures from UNESCO (2013), 57; outbound numbers for Singapore are from UNESCO Institute for Statistics; outbound internationally mobile students by host region, http://data.uis.unesco.org; statistics for Korea are from the Ministry of Education, Republic of Korea (2014b).

The United States is a traditional destination country, with international students comprising 4 percent of total U.S. higher education enrollment, accounting for 20 percent of international students worldwide (Institute of International Education 2015). As an immigrant country, the United States is known to welcome and harness the talent of foreign students and professionals. The United States is not as revenue-focused as the United Kingdom or Australia, where the figures are much higher (international students comprise 20 percent of total higher education enrollment in both countries), although second- and third-tier American universities that are struggling financially increasingly view foreign students (especially Chinese students from wealthy families) as a source of revenue (Svoboda 2015). Singaporean universities, on the other hand, draw foreign students through concerted marketing efforts (including through overseas recruitment drives and generous scholarships) because attracting overseas talent is seen as central to its national agenda for human capital generation, given the limitations of its small, open, and natural-resource–poor economy. In Japan, attracting foreign students is a part of overall efforts to globalize Japanese universities, many of which are also struggling with under-enrollment due to a shrinking college-age population (the population of eighteen-year-olds has decreased by 40 percent since the 1990s) (Kazuyoshi 2015), as well as part of Japanese efforts to introduce more bilingual foreign graduates to the labor market (Tanikawa 2012). Japan also has a long history of foreign student recruitment through official development assistance since the 1950s, as Motohisa Kaneko notes in chapter 6, and currently has the largest government grant program in Asia (the Government Scholarship Grant program). At the same time, there is a growing concern in Japan about the declining number of Japanese students going to study abroad (Sugimoto 2014), as Japanese corporations need more graduates capable of helping them globalize.

As outbound-driven countries, China and Korea are major sending countries whose students make up the first- and third-largest number of international students in the United States, respectively, as shown in table I.2.

The large numbers of Chinese and Korean students studying abroad is often attributed to the high value placed on higher and international education by students and parents due to perceived enhanced career prospects and/or dissatisfaction with the quality of local higher education provision. But in recent years, China and Korea, two leaders of outbound student mobility and traditional source markets, have also become active recruiters of foreign students. Interestingly, Chinese are the largest group of international students in Korea while Koreans are the largest in China (table I.2). As Korea develops economically and improves its higher education sector, it will be

TABLE I.2
Top sources of foreign students in select countries, 2014

Rank	China*		Korea		Japan		Singapore†	United States	
1	Korea	17.7	China	64.3	China	55.9	China	China	31.0
2	United States	7.1	Mongolia	4.2	Korea	10.0	India	India	11.6
3	Thailand	6.5	Vietnam	4.0	Vietnam	8.0	Southeast Asian countries	Korea	7.7
4	Japan	4.8	United States	3.4	Nepal	3.8	—	Saudi Arabia	6.1

Source: Project Atlas; Ministry of Education, Korea (2014a).

Notes: *China data is from 2013; †percentages unavailable for Singapore.

interesting to see if Korea's student mobility patterns will follow the path of Japan, or what Motohisa Kaneko calls the "transitional trap" in chapter 6.

Growing Diversity in Host Countries

Internationalization of higher education brings both opportunities and challenges. One such challenge that the influx of foreign students poses for host countries is the issue of growing student diversity. While diversity has been embraced as a major normative agenda in North America and Western Europe, this is a new issue for most Asian countries. Even in Singapore, where cultural diversity has been actively promoted in some universities (NUS 2013), integrating foreign students and addressing local and foreign tensions on campus have become major policy issues (Tan 2013). For example, every year the Singaporean government struggles with how many students to admit in order not to arouse local resentment. In 2011, the government announced that it would decrease the foreign student quota from 18 percent to 11 percent in 2015 in response to local discontent about the state's policy of attracting and retaining foreign talent and the rising competition for limited university places, scholarships, and professional jobs. As a result of this policy, the number of foreign students dropped from 84,000 in 2012 to 75,000 in 2014 (Davie 2014).

In ethnically homogenous countries like Korea and Japan, embracing diversity is even more challenging. When local populations fail to appreciate the value of incoming foreign student populations, it can impact the experience those students have abroad. For instance, in a recent survey conducted in 2013 by the Gyeonggi Research Institute of Chinese students residing in Gyeonggi-do, the most populous province in South Korea, 66.1 percent expressed significantly reduced levels of satisfaction relative to their expectations before arriving in Korea (Ui, Shin, and Yoon 2013). In another survey of 302 foreign students in Korea conducted by the University Tomorrow Research Laboratory for the Twenties (2013), 62.6 percent of Asian students, who comprise the vast majority of foreign students, stated having come to Korea with high expectations of Korean higher education but only 41.4 percent of Asian students stated that their current experience met their initial expectations. This is in stark contrast to European and North American students, who are more satisfied than they expected, as shown in figure I.3, although they comprise only a minority of foreign students in Korea.

Many foreign students also report having experienced discrimination in their classroom and social activities. In the same survey (University Tomorrow Research Laboratory for the Twenties 2013; Nam 2013), 31 percent of foreign students said they experienced discrimination, with Asian students experiencing the most when broken down by continental origin (Asians 36.5 percent, versus Europeans 20.7 percent and North American students 32.1 percent). In a 2010 survey conducted by the National Research Council for Economics, Humanities, and Social Sciences, 40 percent of 1,200 Chinese students attending Korean universities said they had developed anti-Korean sentiments during their studies (Ui, Shin, and Yoon 2013). In addition, Korean students often complain about perceived government tax spending on scholarships for "substandard" foreign students from

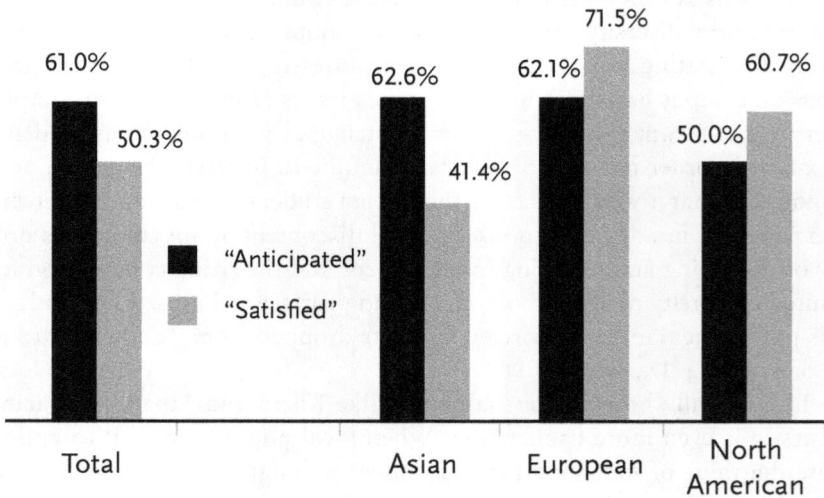

FIGURE I.3. Expectations and satisfaction of foreign students before and after studying in Korea

Source: University-Tomorrow Research Laboratory for the Twenties (2013).

Note: n=302.

developing countries while they themselves must pay full tuition fees (Moon 2016), reflecting the general tendency to think of diversity in Korean higher education as "assistance" rather than as a strength, as Moon and Shin elaborate in chapter 4. Perhaps as a result of this, the proportion of foreign students wanting to continue their education in Korea decreases dramatically over the college years (see below and figure I.4). The same trend can be seen in the proportion of foreign students wanting to find a job in Korea. In fact, it is estimated that approximately only 1 percent of foreign students who graduate from Korean universities find employment in Korea (Min et al. 2014, 27). That is, among the approximately ten thousand foreign students who graduate from Korean universities every year, it is estimated that only around one hundred are hired to work in Korea, though the actual number is unknown and may be higher. In Japan, intercultural interaction between local and foreign students is low, and so are opportunities for contact. Foreign students at Japanese universities often feel isolated among themselves within their international programs (Shin and Moon 2015), suggesting that Japanese, like Koreans, may be reluctant to embrace diversity and perhaps reflecting the traditional conception in Japanese higher education of foreign students as primarily recipients of development aid (Ninomiya, Knight, and Watanabe 2009).

As Moon and Shin discuss in chapter 4, this is a very different picture from that of settler societies such as the United States and the United Kingdom (British Council 2014) where diversity is valued, embraced, and actively encouraged as vital to achieving both educational (e.g., enhancing intercultural skills) and socioeconomic goals (e.g., innovation).[3] Asian universities seem to disregard inclusive ideals compared to those in Europe, where at least "intercultural learning in individuals and organisations tends to occur accidentally and haphazardly" (Hermans 2005, 113; Nilsson and Otten 2003), while both Asian and European universities fall far behind American universities, where a culture of valorizing diversity is highly institutionalized and implemented at various levels (Jayakumar 2008), given the United States' longer history of intercultural studies (Wächter 2003; de Wit 2011). Models of education such as cultural diversity that validate the identities and rights of individuals have become highly legitimate and widely adopted (Sutton 2005) and such inclusive ideals have been increasingly emphasized in the discourse on the internationalization of higher education (Turner and Robson 2008; Van der Wende 2001; Brown and Jones

3 Even in the United States, the influx of foreign students to local campuses can create a challenging environment. For a recent story about Chinese students in a Midwestern university, see Drash (2015).

2007), as well as reflected in curricula and organizational commitments (Leask 2009; Hermans 2005), especially in Western contexts. Thus, cultural diversity has emerged and spread globally as a key discourse, as seen in various international declarations and conventions such as the Universal Declaration on Cultural Diversity (2001) and regional initiatives in Latin America, Southeast Asia, Africa, the Middle East, and Europe—all focused on respecting cultural diversity and increasingly linked to educational reforms.[4] Ramirez and Furuta, in their chapter on American higher education, describe this as the "valorization of diversity" where "the ideal university incorporates a broad range of people and perspectives, and all are culturally enriched in the process." This kind of thinking is reflected at many levels of American universities—in university mission statements, in student admissions and faculty hiring quotas, in the curriculum ("diversity courses" are a requirement), and in institutional and organizational commitments (32 percent of four-year colleges and universities in the United States have "diversity administrators") (see Ramirez and Furuta, chapter 9).

In many ways, international students should be considered an even more valuable resource for Asian countries than they are for settler societies such as the United States. This is because for non-immigrant societies, where massive immigration of faculty and students is not the norm and there is only a small proportion of foreigners, international students are a critical source of ethnic diversity and talent. Also, for local students who might never have the experience of studying abroad, foreign students are the best available resource at home for learning and developing global, intercultural skills. This is clearly the case in Japan, with its large domestic market and relatively closed economy, where its local students have little incentive to learn English and obtain degrees abroad. As Foong and Yeoh describe in chapter 8 on foreign student experiences in Singapore, university campuses act as "contact zones" where "cultures meet, clash, and grapple with each other" (Pratt 1997, 63) and students of different backgrounds interact and experience disequilibrium, a learning process that helps them negotiate changing identities and develop their global competencies. Lastly, for aging societies with declining birth rates and rising labor shortages, foreign students are potentially one of the most significant sources of diversity for driving innovation and economic growth (Ramirez 2015). Much research demonstrates the positive effects of diversity on various academic and social outcomes (e.g., the ability to form out-group friendship networks, increased

4 For example, the 1993 Recommendation on the Recognition of Studies and Qualifications in Higher Education, which is aimed at promoting better understanding between cultures and peoples, including mutual respect for their diversity.

cultural awareness, acquisition of global citizenship skills, improvement of the campus climate, increased innovation, etc.)(Jayakumar 2008; Page 2008). Facilitating diversity and recognizing its long-term effects for innovation and development should be a major goal of higher education in Asian countries.

Asian countries, however, find it challenging to transition from diversity in numbers, or "structural diversity," to a meaningful diversity of interaction and inclusion, or "intercultural diversity" (Moon 2016). In Asian universities, the population of foreign students has diversified, but foreign-local cross-cultural interaction remains low, and Asian campuses are still far from becoming inclusive places of learning. In Korea, identity-related factors play a particularly significant role in creating barriers to interaction with foreigners in Korea, in many instances preceding or exacerbating more commonly cited barriers of language and culture, highlighting a lasting legacy of ethnic nationalism in Korea (Shin 2006). Consequently, foreign students often perceive and experience a strong sense of cultural chauvinism and ethnocentrism in their daily encounters with Korean peers and faculty (Park 2015). One study by Moon (2016) demonstrates that foreign students often comment that "Koreans are very nationalistic," "have a tendency to keep to themselves," and are "not very interested in foreigners." One Mongolian student's comment captures a sentiment commonly felt by other foreign students in Korea:

> Honestly speaking, although there are many Koreans who are friendly toward foreigners, I get the sense that there are also many people who don't want to mix with foreigners. They always designate us as "foreigner."

Another student, from Iran, explained that she didn't have many Korean friends because "in general, my Korean acquaintances are not interested in interacting and not very aggressive about getting to know other cultures. They seem to like to live among themselves in their own ways." Such barriers may make Korea a less attractive place for foreign students than settler societies; one student noted that he could live in Korea for perhaps a year but that "afterwards I prefer to go to [a] country like Canada where there are lots of immigrants and diverse ethnic groups where I think it'll be easier to adapt to the environment" (Moon 2016). Despite low cross-cultural interaction and high foreign-local tensions, most Korean universities do not offer mentoring programs and support services to foreign students and, even if they do, such services tend to be superficially managed (Ui, Shin, and Yoon 2013). Few courses encourage local students to critically think about diversity, and Korean professors are poorly trained in managing diversity in the classroom (Moon 2016).

As a more developed country with a longer history of attracting foreign students, Japan and many of its universities are known to offer decent institutional support for foreign students. However, in Japan too, while some foreign students report positive interpersonal experiences, interactions between foreign students and Japanese students for the most part remain infrequent and superficial (Murphy-Shigematsu 2002). This is despite the fact that many foreign students are motivated to learn Japanese, and come to Japan expecting to interact with Japanese students. Foreign students find it very challenging to interact with Japanese students at a certain, non-superficial level that they would consider to be personally and socially meaningful. One recently conducted study of fifty-five foreign students in Japan (Shin and Moon 2015) reveals a sentiment typically shared by foreign students studying in Japan: regardless of fluency in Japanese, they feel they are viewed primarily as visitors and guests by Japanese, rather than as friends or peers. A Nepalese student's response exemplified this sentiment: "It's kind of interesting because Japanese people see you as a guest when you first come. And they'll treat you very, very nicely but because you are a guest. Not because you are a friend." Even students such as Vi, a Taiwanese student studying economics who had spent several years in Japan, found her interpersonal experiences to be socially frustrating: "What I felt during these four years is that they seemed pretty long and it gets boring, especially when you have difficulty making friends with the people around you." Furthermore, Shin and Moon's study shows that foreign and Japanese students misunderstand each other to a great extent. For example, foreign students are disappointed that not many Japanese are willing to approach them, but Japanese students are afraid to inconvenience their foreign visitors with their "poor" English. Foreign students are tired of guessing what their Japanese counterparts really feel and think (their *honne* [本音]), but Japanese students think it is rude and impolite to be too frank and direct even among other Japanese, let alone foreign students (Shin and Moon 2015).

To reduce these and other misgivings and gaps in cultural understanding, Japanese and Korean universities need to put in place more cross-cultural programs and opportunities for both sides to come into natural contact and create a campus environment and culture that appreciates and respects diversity. To achieve such goals, universities need to establish institutional frameworks or programs to promote interaction between local and foreign students. For example, they should offer more courses that both local and foreign students can take together. Rather than just focusing on teaching local languages and cultures to foreign students, local students should be encouraged to take more courses in English and also those on other cultures and societies, ideally together with foreign students. These courses can instill values of cultural diversity in higher education in ethnically homogenous countries. Japanese and Korean universities also need to ensure that structural segregation between programs, courses, dormitories, and campuses does not obstruct the promotion of greater interaction between foreign and local students (Shin and Moon 2015). In other words, the value of university spaces as "contact zones" should be maximized (see Foong and Yeoh, chapter 8).

More so for Japan than Korea and China, achieving intercultural diversity is an urgent task since Japan sends out only half the number of students than it receives, and the motivation for going overseas has largely lost its momentum. Japanese higher education may be experiencing a "transitional trap," as Motohisa Kaneko explains in chapter 6, because of a gap between the actual and immediate returns of studying abroad and the recognition of the potential benefits of studying abroad. Japanese students have little enthusiasm for going abroad and there is a lack of drive and commitment on the part of Japanese universities to internationalize their programs. In this context, foreign students present opportunities for increasingly inward-looking Japanese youths to learn and develop global, intercultural skills at home.

In sum, Asian countries have seen notable increases in "structural diversity" but not "intercultural diversity" and converting the former to the latter will be a major challenge as they seek to promote innovation and compete for global talent with advanced Western countries in the postindustrial period.

Brain Drain in Sending Countries

It might be argued that the ultimate goal of the internationalization of higher education and student mobility is the added ability to increase a country's stock of global talent, or "individuals with key technical or professional skills conferring valuable advantages for firms in competing global markets" (Shin and Choi 2015). In an era of economic globalization accompanied by bleak and irreversible demographic trends in most countries, the demand for individuals with globally competitive intercultural skills—that is to say, the "global war for talent"—is intensifying.

Countries perceive the internationalization of higher education as a key solution. Foreign students are seen as a vital source of talent that will help address the problems resulting from a shrinking working-age population in the host country (Tanikawa 2012). Their presence is also seen as a resource for endowing domestic students at home with more relevant global, intercultural skills, as well as a way to reduce too many students from studying abroad and prevent possible brain drain. Sending students abroad to develop a global outlook is also seen as a good source of global talent, when those students return home after being trained overseas (NUS 2009). Thus, the better a country can attract and retain foreign students (brain gain) and at the same time recruit back students studying abroad (brain circulation), the higher its stock of global talent, in turn enhancing global competitiveness for that country.

Three of the Asian countries we examine here—China, Korea, and Japan—all experience high brain drain and low brain gain, and thus also score low on global talent competitiveness, as shown in table I.3. They also score very low on overall indices of attracting and retaining talent (Lanvin and Evans 2014). The United States and Singapore are just the opposite; they experience low brain drain and high brain gain, and thus score high on global talent competitiveness. Immigrant countries receptive to foreigners have a natural advantage when it comes to attracting and retaining talent.

Despite the rapid improvement of Korean universities, Korean students still study abroad believing that they are receiving a better education in countries with more established higher education systems, such as the United States. The recent *joki yuhak* (pre-college study abroad) trend has further exacerbated this situation. Over the past decade, Koreans have begun sending their children overseas at a younger age to avoid secondary education in Korea, notorious for the stress it puts not only on students but also on parents. Coming from middle- and upper-class backgrounds, *joki yuhak* students go abroad to elite private institutions on the way to attending top colleges or universities in the United States and Europe, even though they could have attended top universities in Korea. While they only represent a small portion of the total number of Koreans studying abroad, the number

TABLE I.3

Global talent competitiveness index

Country	Overall Rank	Brain Drain	Tolerance of Immigrants	Brain Gain	Attract	Retain
United States	4	4	13	5	11	3
Canada	5	14	1	7	7	5
Australia	9	25	4	12	5	4
Singapore	2	6	41	2	1	9
Japan	20	23	43	48	54	11
Korea	29	20	48	22	65	35
China	41	24	66	18	61	65

Source: Lanvin and Evans (2014).

of *joki yuhak* students has surpassed twenty thousand and has ignited the brain-drain debate within Korea.

The problem is that high numbers of Korean students studying abroad do not return to Korea (low brain circulation). To be sure, many of these students come back to Korea after receiving a first-rate education overseas; Korean students who receive PhDs in American universities return home at far higher rates than their Indian and Chinese peers return to India and China, respectively. Still, significant numbers of them remain in the host countries after their education. According to a survey by the Oak Ridge Associated Universities (Finn 2014), almost 70 percent of foreign PhD recipients in science and engineering in the United States from 2006 to 2009 reported that they would prefer to stay and work in the United States. In fact, as table I.4 shows, as of 2011, 42 percent of those Korean students stayed in the United States after obtaining their PhDs, a significant increase from 22 percent in 2001. As a result, stemming the tide of outbound students and converting brain drain into brain circulation has become a major point on the Korean policy agenda.

Chinese students often study abroad for the same reasons as Koreans. However, the brain-drain situation could be even worse in China, as 85 percent of Chinese science and engineering PhD recipients decide to stay in the United States. This has been the case despite the Chinese government implementing a wide range of top-tier talent recruitment programs such as the Thousand Foreign Experts Scheme and the Changjiang Professor Scheme,

TABLE I.4

Five-year stay rates for foreign students on temporary visas receiving science/engineering doctorates, 2001–11 (select countries)

Country/Region	2001	2003	2005	2007	2009	2011
China	98	93	95	94	89	85
India	89	90	89	83	79	82
Europe	53	63	67	67	60	62
Canada	66	63	60	56	53	55
South Korea	22	36	44	42	42	42
Japan	24	39	41	33	40	38
Taiwan	41	48	52	43	37	38
Mexico	31	22	32	33	35	39
Brazil	26	26	31	32	33	37
All Countries	58	64	67	63	62	66

Source: Finn (2014).

which together brought home only a little over two thousand returnees in 2012 (Kirby 2014).

Both China and Korea have made attempts to counterbalance their shortages of top-tier talent by attracting foreign students and providing alternatives to domestic students by expanding English language programs, foreign branch campuses, and joint programs with foreign partners, as Ka Ho Mok describes in chapter 7, and Dae Bong Kwon in chapter 2. China is well-known for its Sino-foreign initiatives, with the majority being Sino-foreign cooperation programs (1,052 total as of 2014) followed by Sino-foreign cooperation second-tier colleges (52 total) and Sino-foreign cooperation universities (eight total). Yet, for the three Sino-foreign cooperation universities with graduating classes, available statistics show that very high percentages (ranging from 50 to 90 percent) choose to continue their education abroad. For example, over 80 percent of University of Nottingham Ningbo graduates in 2013 chose to continue their education abroad. This suggests that domestic students may view these universities as a stepping-stone to other destinations and that such joint universities may not be particularly successful in retaining domestic students for advanced degrees.

Similarly, Korea has established branch campuses of foreign universities (currently five) in the Incheon Free Economic Zone. These branch campuses uphold satisfactory academic reputations, but it still remains to be seen whether they can compete with top Korean universities in attracting the brightest Korean students. Perhaps one of Korea's most representative efforts to absorb outbound domestic students has been the establishment of English-taught, international-studies-centered graduate and undergraduate departments at Korean universities (eleven graduate schools and seventeen undergraduate schools as of 2015), as Kwon describes in chapter 2. However, since most of the graduates are bachelor's and master's degree holders and their career trajectories are unknown, it is unclear whether such students can be considered top-tier talent for Korea.

Retaining inbound students has also been challenging in Korea, China, and Japan. According to one survey of a sample of 296 foreign students in Korea (see figure I.4), the percentages of those who said they planned to get a job in Korea (18.6 percent) or get a job in their country of origin (19.3 percent) are substantial. However, when analyzed by grade level (from freshmen to seniors), the percentage of those planning to get a job in Korea drops dramatically (from 29.8 percent to 9.4 percent) while the percentage planning to get a job in their country of origin increases (17 percent to 22 percent). The same inverse trends can be seen for the percentage of foreign students planning to continue their education in Korea (12.8 percent to 0 percent) and those planning to continue their education in their country of origin (12.8 percent to 22 percent) (University-Tomorrow Research Laboratory for the Twenties 2013). Another survey of only Chinese students shows that the percentage of Chinese students who choose to study in Japan with plans to work there after graduating is roughly three times the percentage of Chinese students who choose to study in Korea with plans to work there after graduating (only 6.5 percent) (Min et al. 2014).

Faced with strict work visa requirements, wage discrimination, a general preference for Koreans who can speak English rather than foreigners who can speak Korean, and social pressure to give employment priorities to Koreans rather than to foreigners, many foreign students have no choice but to return to their home countries right after graduation—and they do so with strong anti-Korean sentiments (Min et al. 2014). Neither Korean universities nor the Korean government even keep official statistics on foreign student employment after graduation; foreign students are altogether excluded from the national statistics on employment rates. This situation itself, beyond the poor efforts of Korean universities to help foreign students find employment (Ui, Shin, and Yoon 2013), demonstrates that Korean society shows little appreciation for the value of foreign students as skilled labor.

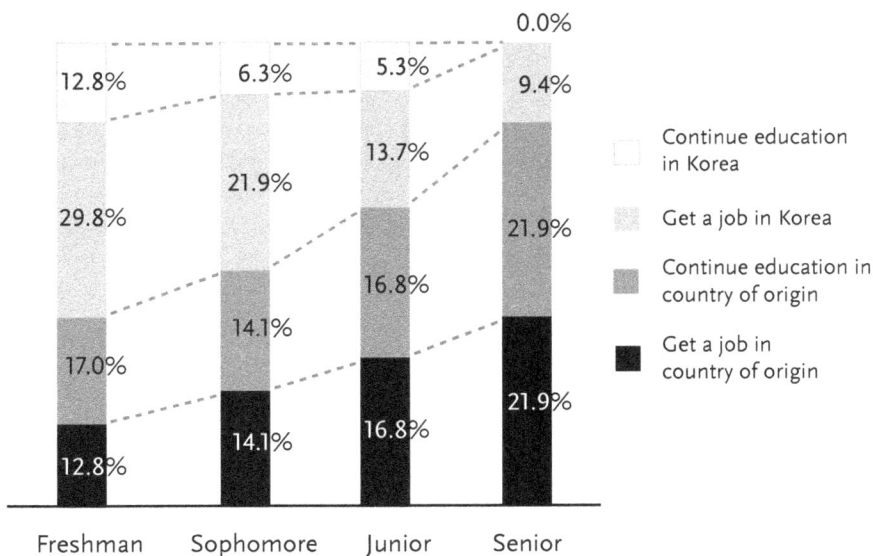

FIGURE I.4 Changing educational and career aspirations of foreign students

Source: University-Tomorrow Research Laboratory for the Twenties (2013).

Note: n=296.

Japan, as a more developed country with a much longer history of foreign student recruitment, fares better than Korea but is far behind many advanced countries in the West (Murai 2015). According to a 2013 survey by the Japan Student Services Organization, a government-funded organization that offers support programs for non-Japanese students, while as many as 65 percent of 39,650 students who graduated from an educational institution in Japan were looking for a job in Japan, only 24 percent found a position. However, even if a foreign student successfully lands a job, Japan's rigid corporate culture poses difficulties. Foreign students feel that Japanese firms are reluctant to embrace their full potential and largely expect them to assimilate (Murai 2015), often motivating them to stay in Japan only for the short term. In order to compete with North America and Western Europe, both Japan and Korea need to better appreciate the value of and promote cultural diversity across both campuses and corporations.

Singapore, interestingly, despite low levels of tolerance for immigrants (see table I.3), is able to attract and retain foreign students, most likely to due to strong incentives, including generous subsidies, scholarships, and loan schemes tied to employment after graduation, as well as fairly liberal immigration requirements (see chapter 8). Some parts of China, such as Shanghai, are taking similar measures. A new talent policy released there in July 2015 approved work permits for international students graduating from Chinese universities with a bachelor's degree or above and did away with a requirement that graduating master's students have two years' work experience to receive a work permit.[5]

Despite such efforts, however, the reality for countries such as Korea, China, and Japan is that students studying abroad will choose to remain overseas (especially in the United States) and most foreign students studying in those countries from abroad will decide to return to their home countries (or go elsewhere). These two tendencies have been major concerns for policymakers in these countries. However, Gi-Wook Shin and Joon Nak Choi in chapter 5 propose a creative solution to these concerns. They argue that these "lost brains" can generate "brain linkage" by becoming transnational bridges (a particular type of social capital that bridges geographic and cultural distance) between the different countries they form networks in. Seen this way, human capital flight need not be considered brain drain, but an opportunity to build powerful social capital for home and host societies, creating a win-win situation for both. The value of social capital, especially transnational bridges, will only become more important for firms and

5 "China Relaxes Rules for Foreign Students to Work," *Times of India*, July 26, 2015, http://toi.in/FoZfZY.

countries in an increasingly globalized economy. Shin and Choi show how Korean students studying abroad can potentially be an excellent source of transnational bridges. The same can be said of foreign students, regardless of whether or not they decide to leave their host countries.

This social capital perspective has important implications for government policies and student mobility in Asia beyond Korea. For countries with high outbound student mobility such as China and Korea, governments should continue to encourage study abroad while helping to ensure that students studying abroad can maintain their home identities and networks even if they don't return home, thus helping convert brain drain to brain linkage. These countries can learn from Israel, which has been effectively utilizing the outstanding talent within its diaspora community—without bringing them home—through a program called Birthright Israel. This program offers steady support to young overseas Jewish adults to stay in Israel for a short time and experience Jewish traditions and culture, thereby helping them establish their identity. Although they might not return to work in Israel, they can nevertheless be expected to act as intermediaries between Israel and the countries in which they reside.

For countries with high inbound student mobility such as Japan, governments should encourage foreign students to build networks while residing in their host country (like Singapore's bond for foreign students) and help them maintain these networks even after they leave. In fact, many foreign students come to Japan to learn about Japanese society and economy, with plans to become a bridge between Japan and their home countries after graduation. However, due to the lack of interpersonal interaction with Japanese students, foreign students often end up interacting primarily among themselves. Thus, they are also likely to bridge among themselves, rather than with the Japanese, and that is a loss, given that Japan has invested so much in attracting foreign students (Shin and Moon 2015).

Since Chinese students form the largest source of foreign students in the Asian region (and also in the United States), this group deserves special attention. In particular, given China's growing economic ties with its Asian neighbors, the role of Chinese students as bridges will become increasingly important. China is an important trading partner for Japan, with 18 percent of Japanese exports going to China in 2014 (Ministry of Finance 2014) and the most important trading partner for Korea, with 25.4 percent of Korea's exports going to China. Also, English-speaking Asian countries like Singapore, with globally ranked institutions that have been more successful as a hub for international students, will inevitably be able to attract and retain Chinese students better than others (Sharma 2014). As a result, countries such as Japan and Korea should consider an alternative strategy that appreciates the value of social capital (beyond human capital) by helping Chinese students build and maintain social ties with their host countries (i.e., Korea and Japan). In the opposite direction, the proportion of outbound Koreans students going to China has been growing (from 12 percent in 2008 to 17 percent in 2014) (see table 2.3 in Kwon) while the proportion going to Japan, Australia, Canada, and the United Kingdom has decreased over the same period, reflecting South Korea's strengthening economic ties with China. The growing preference of Korea's large firms for China-educated Koreans and the potential to tap their personal networks on the Chinese mainland demonstrate the increasing value of social capital and transnational bridges between Korea and China.[6]

What is Ahead?

The chapters that follow address those issues outlined above and are organized into three sections.

The first section provides a detailed portrait of internationalization in Korean higher education over the past twenty years. As the government has been a key player in such internationalization, Sun-Geun Baek and Hoon-Ho Kim begin with major government policies since the Kim Young-Sam administration in the early 1990s and end with a discussion of current and ongoing policy challenges. Dae Bong Kwon, in chapter 2, focuses on student mobility trends in Korea and how they have evolved since the introduction of internationalization policies in Korean higher education. Junki Kim, Hanah Cho, and Kilkon Ko evaluate and discuss Korea's growing research capacity and how networks might play a greater role in retaining high-skilled researchers and talent.

The second section seeks to address two of the challenges highlighted repeatedly in the first three chapters: the problem of brain drain and circulation in the form of (1) Korean students leaving Korea (and staying abroad) as well as (2) foreign students returning to their home countries rather than contributing human capital to Korea. Rennie Moon and Gi-Wook Shin, in chapter 4, view these issues in light of a more fundamental problem—the absence of a diversity-respecting culture of inclusion in Korean higher education and society—arguing that "diversity" can serve as a particularly useful policy discourse in the Korean context. The fifth chapter, by Gi-Wook

---

6 "South Korean Students Turn to China Colleges for Career Edge," *South China Morning Post*, September 6, 2013. http://www.scmp.com/news/china/article/1304268/south-korean-students-turn-china-colleges-career-edge.

Shin and Joon Nak Choi, presents empirical findings on Korean students studying in the United States to illustrate their potential as social capital for Korea. Shin and Choi move away from conventional arguments about brain drain and brain circulation from a human capital perspective and propose a more promising approach for Korea, which faces real limitations compared to settler societies when it comes to competing for global talent.

The third and last section includes chapters focusing on similar themes and issues in the United States, Singapore, Japan, and China. Francisco Ramirez and Jared Furuta, in chapter 9 on the United States, demonstrate how diversity has become a normative and policy agenda in American higher education. In a related vein, in chapter 8 Michelle Foong and Brenda Yeoh explore how greater student diversity has created spaces, or "contact zones," at Singaporean universities where students constantly negotiate their changing, transnational identities. In chapter 6 Motohisa Kaneko points out the strikingly low numbers of Japanese students studying abroad and an increasingly inward-looking Japan that stands in stark contrast to the current status of its Asian neighbors. Ka Ho Mok's chapter 7 on transnational higher education in China also addresses issues of brain drain and brain circulation while at the same time appropriately raising the important question of China's role in promoting regionalization and cooperation in Asia, given the scale and influence of Chinese higher education in the region and globally.

It is hoped that the chapters in this volume can offer critical perspectives on the internationalization of Korean higher education and suggest implications for other Asian countries that have pursued similar efforts and policies.

References

Agawa, Naoyuki. 2011. "The Internationalization of Japan's Higher Education: Challenges and Evolutions." *Repères* 10 (December).

British Council. 2008. *International Student Mobility in East Asia: Executive Summary*. Prepared by JWT Education, February.

———. 2014. *Integration of International Students: A UK Perspective.* September.

Brown, Sally, and Elspeth Jones. 2007. *Internationalising Higher Education*. London: Routledge.

Davie, Sandra. 2014."Singapore May Rue Fall in Foreign Student Numbers." *The Straits Times,* October 2. Accessed September 29, 2015. http://ifonlysingaporeans.blogspot.kr/2014/10/singapore-may-rue-fall-in-foreign.html.

de Wit, Hans. 2011. "Global Citizenship and Study Abroad: A European

Comparative Perspective." In *Trends, Issues and Challenges in Internationalisation of Higher Education*. Amsterdam: Centre for Applied Research on Economics and Management, 77–91.

Drash, Wayne. 2015. "Culture Clash in Iowa." *CNN*, July. Accessed September 29, 2015. http://www.cnn.com/interactive/2015/07/us/culture-clash-american-story.

Finn, Michael G. 2014. *Stay Rates of Foreign Doctorate Recipients from U.S. Universities, 2011*. Oak Ridge, TN: Oak Ridge Institute for Science and Education.

Hermans, Jeanine. 2005. "The X factor: Internationalization with a Small 'c.'" In *Internationalisation in Higher Education: European Responses to the Global Perspective*, edited by Barbara Kehm and Hans de Wit, 134–53. Amsterdam: European Association for International Education (EAIE).

Institute of International Education. 2015. *Project Atlas: Trends and Global Data 2014*. Center for Academic Mobility Research. Accessed September 28, 2015

Japan Student Services Organization (JASSO). 2004. "Result of an Annual Survey of International Students in Japan 2004." http://www.jasso.go.jp/statistics/intl_student/data04_e.html.

———. 2015. "Result of an Annual Survey of International Students in Japan 2014." http://www.jasso.go.jp/statistics/intl_student/data14_e.html.

Jayakumar, Uma M. 2008. "Can Higher Education Meet the Needs of a Increasingly Diverse and Global Society? Campus Diversity and Cross-Cultural Workforce Competencies." *Harvard Educational Review* 78 (4): 615–51.

Kazuyoshi, Harada. 2015. "Universities Struggle to Cope with Shrinking Population and Globalization." *Nippon.com*, March 16. Accessed October 1, 2015. http://www.nippon.com/en/features/h00095/.

Kirby, William C. 2014. "The Chinese Century? The Challenges of Higher Education." *Daedalus: The Journal of the American Academy of Arts & Sciences* 143 (2): 145–56.

Lanvin, Bruno, and Paul Evans, eds. 2014. *INSEAD: The Global Talent Competitiveness Index 2014*. Novus: Singapore.

Leask, Betty. 2009. "Using Formal and Informal Curricula to Improve Interactions Between Home and International Students." *Journal of Studies in International Education* 13 (2): 205–21.

Min, Gui Shik, Jung Sun Ki, Jo Bok Su, Kim Jiyoung, Kim Jinyoung, Yoo Dahyung, and Jung Chang Yoon. 2014. *Oegugin yuhaksaeng yuch'i chiwŏn hwaktaerŭl wihan chŏngch'aek yŏn'gu* [Policy study for the expansion of recruitment and support for foreign students]. Ministry of Education,

National Institute for International Education. http://www.prism.go.kr/homepage/many/retrieveManyDetail.do;jsessionid=%EA%B5%AD.node02?research_id=1342000-201400072.

Ministry of Education. 2014a. *Kungnae oegugin yuhaksaeng hyonhwang* [Statistics of foreign students in Korea]. Accessed October 1, 2015. http://www.moe.go.kr/web/100101/ko/board/view.do?bbsId=350&pageSize=10&currentPage=0&encodeYn=N&boardSeq=57449&mode=view.

———. 2014b. *Kukoe Hankukin yuhaksaeng hyonhwang* [Statistics of Korean students abroad]. Accessed October 1, 2015. http://www.moe.go.kr/web/100098/ko/board/view.do?bbsId=350&pageSize=10&currentPage=0&encodeYn=N&boardSeq=57736&mode=view.

Ministry of Finance. 2014. "Trade Statistics of Japan." *Japan Customs*. Accessed July 1, 2015. http://www.customs.go.jp/toukei/info/index_e.htm.

Moon, Rennie J. 2016. "Internationalization without Cultural Diversity? Higher Education in Korea." *Comparative Education* 52(1): 91–108

Murai, Shusuke. 2015. "International Students Face Job Hunting Hurdles in Japan." *The Japan Times,* June 10. Accessed September 28, 2015. http://www.japantimes.co.jp/news/2015/06/10/national/international-students-face-job-hunting-hurdles-japan.

Murphy-Shigematsu, Stephen. 2002. "Psychological Struggles for International Korean Students in Japan." *International Education Journal* 3(5): 75–84.

Nam, Hyun-woo. 2013. "3 out of 10 expat students experience discrimination." *The Korea Times,* November 12. Accessed September 20, 2015. http://www.koreatimes.co.kr/www/news/nation/2013/11/116_146078.html.

National University of Singapore (NUS). 2009. "International Exchange Day Offers International Mileage to Students." *Newshub—NUS' News Portal,* September 7. Accessed June 22, 2015. http://newshub.nus.edu.sg/headlines/0909/ied_07Sep09.php.

———. 2013. "Fostering Diversity on Campus." *Newshub—NUS' News Portal,* February 25. Accessed September 30, 2015. http://newshub.nus.edu.sg/headlines/1302/diversity_25Feb13.php.

Nilsson, Bengt, and Matthias Otten, eds. 2003. "Internationalisation at Home." Special Issue of the *Journal of Studies in International Education* 7, no. 1 (Spring).

Ninomiya, Akira, Jane Knight, and Aya Watanabe. "The Past, Present, and Future of Internationalization in Japan." *Journal of Studies in International Education* 13, no. 2 (2009): 117–24.

Organisation for Economic Co-operation and Development (OECD). 2002. *Education at a Glance 2002: OECD Indicators.* Paris: OECD Publishing.

———. 2014. *Education at a Glance 2014: OECD Indicators*. Paris: OECD Publishing.

Onsman, Andrys. 2013. "Why Do International Students Go to China?" *University World News*, October 25. Accessed September 28, 2015. http://www.universityworldnews.com/article.php?story=20131022125122189.

Page, Scott E. 2008. *The Difference: How the Power of Diversity Creates Better Groups, Firms, Schools, and Societies*. Princeton: Princeton University Press.

Park, Kwan Kyu. 2015. "Bye Korea, palgil tollinŭn oegugin yuhyaksaeng" [Bye Korea, foreign students turn back home]. *Hankook Ilbo*, May 16.

Pratt, Mary Louise. 1997. "Arts of the Contact Zone." In *Mass Culture and Everyday Life,* edited by Peter Gibian, 61–72. New York: Routledge.

Ramirez, Elaine. 2015. "Diversity Missing in Korea's Creative Economy Drive." *The Korea Herald*, May 7. Accessed September 28, 2015. http://www.koreaherald.com/view.php?ud=20150507000848.

Sharma, Yojana. 2014. "Internationally Mobile Students Head for Asia." *University World News,* January 31. Accessed September 28, 2014. http://www.universityworldnews.com/article.php?story=20140131102318847.

Shin, Gi-Wook. 2006. *Ethnic Nationalism in Korea: Genealogy, Politics, and Legacy*. Stanford, CA: Stanford University Press.

Shin, Gi-Wook and Joon Nak Choi. 2015. *Global Talent: Skilled Labor as Social Capital in Korea*. Stanford: Stanford University Press.

Shin, Gi-Wook, and Rennie J. Moon. 2015. "Japanese Education's Foreign Problem." *Nikkei Asian Review*, July 16.

Sugimoto, Akiko. 2014. "Japan's Top University Needs to Get with the Globalization Program," *Nikkei Asian Review*, October 2. Accessed October 1, 2015. http://s.nikkei.com/YTB14A.

Sutton, Margaret. 2005. "The Globalization of Multicultural Education." *Global Legal Studies* 12 (1): 97–108.

Svoboda, Sarah. 2015. "Why do so Many Chinese Students Choose US Universities?" *BBC News*, June 2. Accessed September 30, 2015. http://www.bbc.com/news/business-32969291.

Tan, Jason. 2013. "Introduction." In *The International Mobility of Students in Asia and the Pacific*. Bangkok: United Nations Educational, Scientific and Cultural Organization.

Tanikawa, Miki. 2012. "Japanese Universities Go Global, But Slowly." *New York Times*, July 29. Accessed October 1, 2015. http://nyti.ms/UdepsU.

Turner, Yvonne, and Sue Robson. 2008. *Internationalizing the University*. New York, NY: Continuum.

United Nations Education, Scientific and Cultural Organization (UNESCO). 2013. *The International Mobility of Students in Asia and the Pacific*. Bangkok: United Nations Educational, Scientific and Cultural Organization.

———. 2015. UNESCO Institute of Statistics (UIS.Stat). Accessed October 1, 2015. http://data.uis.unesco.org/#.

University Tomorrow Research Laboratory for the Twenties. 2013. *Survey of Satisfaction of Foreign Students in Korea*. Research Report No. 15.

Ui, Sung W., Jin Ho Shin, and Ho Jin Yoon. 2013. "Oegugin yuhaksaeng 9 man myŏng munŏjinŭn K'orian dream" [Ninety thousand foreign students: The fallen Korean dream]. *Joong-ang Ilbo*, June 5. Accessed September 28, 2015. http://article.joins.com/news/article/article.asp?total_id=11718334.

Van der Wende, Marijk. C. 2001. "Internationalisation Policies: About New Trends and Contrasting Paradigms." *Higher Education Policy* 14 (3): 249–59.

Wächter, Bernd. 2003. "An Introduction: Internationalisation at Home in Context." *Journal of Studies in International Education* 7 (1): 5–11.

1 Internationalizing Higher Education in Korea: Government Policies

Sun-Geun Baek and Hoon-Ho Kim

Over the last two decades, the higher education sector in many countries has undergone various reforms to meet the demands of the rapidly changing knowledge-based society. "Internationalization" has been pinpointed as one of the key driving forces underlying the transformation of higher education. The successful recruitment of high-quality foreign students and faculty members is believed to bring various economic and social benefits to the host country. In order to respond to these changes, many countries have introduced policies to enhance the competitiveness of their higher education sectors as well as to attract high-quality foreign talent. China, for example, introduced the Thousand Talents Program in 2008, which provides many benefits to study-abroad returnees and also actively welcomes foreign talent to increase China's global competitiveness (Kim 2012, 68–72; Gu et al. 2012; Gu et al. 2013). Japan, a country whose population is rapidly aging, has also actively attempted to attract foreign talent by introducing the 300,000 Foreign Students Plan in 2008, aimed at overcoming problems related to a declining student population. Singapore is also successfully building on its internationalization strategy by attracting world-class institutions from abroad (e.g., MIT) in order to establish itself as the "Boston of the East" (MEST 2012a, 1).

Following this trend, the Republic of Korea (hereafter Korea) has also introduced policies to promote the internationalization of higher education with the goal of becoming the region's new educational hub. In 2004, the introduction of the Study Korea Project, a state-led initiative, resulted in Korea later experiencing one of the highest rates of increase in international students among the Organization for Economic Cooperation and Development

(OECD) countries (OECD 2009). The internationalization of higher education in Korea not only produced an increase in international students, but also brought other structural changes to institutions, including the internationalization of faculty members and the introduction of English-exclusive lectures. The Korean government and universities have established special degree programs and curricula (e.g., graduate schools of international studies [GSISS] and international colleges for undergraduate degrees) to foster intercultural learning of both domestic and international students. Moreover, the Korean government has allocated significant financial resources to maximize the effect of internationalization in higher education and to increase the competitiveness of Korea as a study-abroad destination.

However, despite the government's and universities' attempts to increase global competitiveness, many domestic students still choose to study abroad. At the same time, the quality of higher education in many "student-sending" Asian countries, including China, has improved rapidly, and as a result, more students now choose to study at their local institutions. Since more than half of the international students in Korea come from China, the sustainability of internationalization strategies in Korean higher education is now facing challenges.

Therefore, this chapter aims to investigate internationalization policy changes made by past administrations, in particular exploring the changes made to government funding for internationalization. We also examine student mobility trends and government efforts to bring out institutional changes in university structure and educational programs so as to achieve the internationalization of Korean higher education. Lastly, we aim to identify current challenges and opportunities surrounding Korea's higher education internationalization strategy and accordingly offer policy recommendations.

Initiatives for the Internationalization of Higher Education

The Korean government's initiatives for the internationalization of higher education can be categorized into four major trends. First, the government has promoted an increase in the exchange of *students*, encouraging more domestic students to go abroad through student exchange programs or training and internship programs. At the same time, the Korean government has been implementing initiatives to attract international students to study in Korean institutions. The second trend can be defined as the mobility of *academics*, insofar as the Korean government has provided financial support to attract high-quality foreign academics to come to work in Korea, as well as to encourage more local academics to acquire research experience abroad. The third trend is the exchange of educational *programs*. The

Korean government has developed mutual joint curriculum programs, credit recognition, and joint degree programs with foreign governments and their institutions. The last trend is the mobility of educational *institutions*. The government has encouraged more local institutions to enter foreign countries and has sought to attract more high-quality foreign higher education institutions to open branch campuses in Korea.

Policy interest in the internationalization of higher education in Korea began in the 1990s; below we examine the core characteristics of the internationalization policies of Korean governments starting from 1993.[1]

Kim Young-sam Administration (1993–97)

During this period, countries around the globe loosened trade protections and aimed to realize trade liberalization following the Uruguay Round (UR) of Multilateral Trade Negotiations in 1993. As a result, the World Trade Organization (WTO) was established in 1995. The UR was closely related to education since WTO member countries were asked to gradually and selectively open up their higher education and adult education markets according to its terms and agreements. As a result, in order to respond to this change, the Kim Young-sam administration established a "master plan for the internationalization of higher education" and increased cooperation with international organizations and agencies. Moreover, the administration saw that opening up the education market could offer a major opportunity to increase the global competitiveness of Korean education.

Specifically, the Korean government requested that universities act as a major platform for the internationalization of education. The government provided financial support for universities' language research institutes to enhance foreign language training programs and also offered support for research activities. A number of universities established GSISs, which can effectively nurture a skilled labor force specifically trained for international negotiations and conferences. The government also requested international offices in universities to be created to support more international cooperation among local and foreign institutions.

During this period, the Korean government substantially increased support to encourage more human resource mobility (such as among academics, students, and researchers). First, it entered into a cultural agreement

1 Information and sources related to internationalization policy for each administration have been taken from documents of the "Annual Policy Briefing to the President," which can be retrieved from the Presidential Committee on Education Innovation (PCEI) (2006a, 2006b, 2006c, 2006d) and the Korean government's policy online briefing archive (http://www.korea.kr/archive/mainList.do).

with eight countries, including Singapore, Kazakhstan, and Slovenia, and introduced policies to support teaching and research activities for Korean studies in those countries. In addition, the Korean government aimed to enhance the research competencies of its higher education system by actively encouraging research collaboration with renowned overseas scholars and publishing journals that appeal to international audiences. The government prepared for globalization by encouraging universities to deliver courses in English and by establishing various structural facilitators to collaborate with foreign universities, such as creating ties with overseas institutions and promoting credit and student exchange programs.

Furthermore, the Kim Young-sam administration introduced policy tools to enhance internationalization, such as increasing the number of Korean government scholarships available to international students and establishing a website for international students providing information about studying in Korea. The Test of Proficiency in Korean (TOPIK), introduced in October 1997, was designed to increase Korean language dissemination and enhance Korean proficiency for international students studying in Korea.

Kim Dae-jung Administration (1998–2002)

The number of Korean students choosing to study abroad began to increase significantly during the Kim Dae-jung administration (see figure 1.1). As a result, the Korean government started to open up its higher education market, inviting foreign universities to set up branch campuses in Korea to absorb Korean students' demand for an international educational experience. The government revised the Public Educational Officials Act to increase the number of foreign faculty hired in national and public universities and also introduced government scholarship programs to attract more international students.

In 2000, the Korean government organized talks on education at the ministerial level with China and Japan and discussed measures to increase the exchange of academics and students. The Asia-Europe Meeting (ASEM), held in Korea in October 2000, served as a platform to discuss policy measures to increase human resource exchange among Asian and European countries. It was agreed that the ASEM-DUO Fellowship Program would be introduced, enabling over four thousand university students, faculty members, and teachers in primary and secondary education to have exchange experiences. Beginning in 2001, in order to attract a greater number of high-quality human resources from abroad, various policy measures, including the joint management of education programs with foreign institutions, were introduced. In particular, in that year the Korean government initiated a

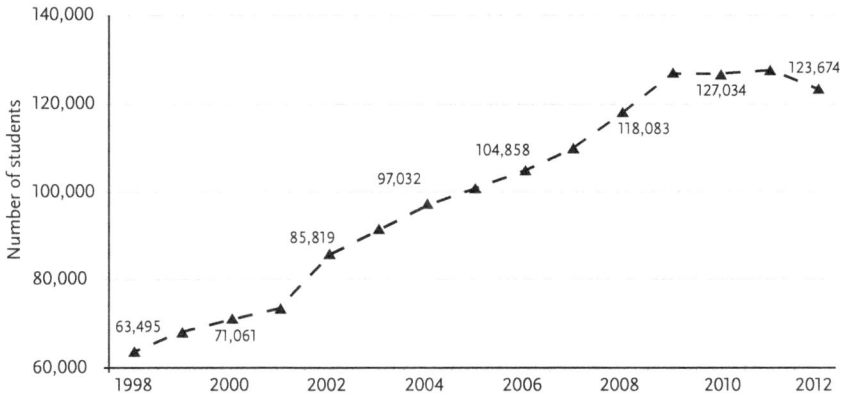

FIGURE 1.1 Korean outward mobile students, 1998–2012

Source: UNESCO Institute for Statistics (Retrieved on January 15, 2015, from http://data.uis.unesco.org).

Note: The data used for yearly outbound students have been extracted from UNESCO's Institute for Statistics. However, some countries may not have accurately reported the number of international students to UNESCO, which may result in underestimation of the total number of Korean students studying in foreign countries. The number of students represents Korean students abroad in *degree programs*; it does not include students in language programs or exchange students.

strategic policy to attract up to sixteen thousand international students by 2003 through collaborations with universities and industry.

Roh Moo-hyun Administration (2003–07)

A key characteristic of higher education internationalization policy during this period was the government's growing interest in improving the *quality* of Korean universities' education and research competencies relative to global standards, rather than simply increasing the number of international faculty members and students.

Under WTO influence, global trade barriers were diminished and the number of free trade agreements (FTAS) began to rapidly increase during this period. Education was no exception. The Korean government further promoted the expansion of human resource trade by implementing joint programs with foreign universities. Free economic zones (FEZS), a class of special economic zones (SEZS) (e.g., Songdo in Incheon), were established to more effectively attract high-quality foreign institutions. The government also initiated the Study Korea Project in 2004 to attract fifty thousand international students by 2010 (MEST 2008). A number of strategies were employed to meet this target. First, Korean government scholarship opportunities for international students, especially those from developing countries, were expanded. Second, measures to enhance employment opportunities for international students were introduced by creating linkages with domestic firms, and the visa issuance process was simplified in order to increase the competitiveness of Korea as a study abroad destination. Third, cooperation between central and local governments as well as universities in the same region was enhanced; as a result, joint projects such as communal dormitories for international students were established (e.g., Nuri Hall in Daejeon). Fourth, the international network for attracting more foreign students was strengthened, and the locations of student recruitment fairs were diversified and fairs were held more frequently. Moreover, the government initiated expansion of English-exclusive lectures and Korean language training courses in Korean universities, and linked institutions' level of support for international students to government subsidies.

Starting in 2006, the government lifted a number of restrictions in order to encourage more active cooperation between domestic and foreign institutions' joint curricula and credit recognition programs. Of particular importance, the restriction on establishing foreign branch campuses in FEZS was significantly relaxed, as were restrictions on curriculum management and tuition fees, etc. In 2007, the government began to concentrate on improving the education and research competencies of Korean universities relative to global standards. The government attempted to strengthen the research competencies of universities by supporting large-scale research projects related to academic exchange and global network establishment. Also, in part with the Brain Korea 21 (BK21) project, international internship programs and international campus projects were introduced to help in enhancing undergraduate and postgraduate students' global competencies.

Lee Myung-bak Administration (2008–12)

Attracting globally renowned foreign scholars to Korean universities was a key characteristic of the Lee Myung-bak administration's higher education internationalization policy. In 2008, the Korean government established action plans for the attraction and utilization of talent in science and technology, and endowed professorships, chairs, and research positions at the national level were introduced in order to attract one thousand high-quality academics by 2012. The World Class University (WCU) project was introduced in 2009, aimed at attracting world-class scholars to Korean universities, with the expectation that their presence would help to improve the quality of Korean universities' education and research competencies. The government concentrated not only on attracting foreign talent to the Korean academic community, but also on sending local researchers and faculty members abroad to enhance their global research competencies by establishing joint research centers with foreign institutions.

With regard to student mobility, the Lee Myung-bak administration actively supported both inbound and outbound students. The previous administration had hoped to attract fifty thousand international students through the launch of the Study Korea Project in 2004, but when this goal was met two years ahead of schedule, the Lee Myung-bak administration in 2008 announced a new target of one hundred thousand international students by 2012. To achieve this goal the government initiated various strategies, including in 2010 the Global Korea Scholarship (GKS), an extended scholarship program designed to attract more high-quality students from developing countries in Asia and the BRICS.[2] The GKS scholarship program included Korean government scholarships, which had existed since 1967, as well as other programs, including support structures for high-quality international exchange students and fee-paying international students. Moreover, the GKS program included scholarships for Korean students who went abroad. The International Education Quality Assurance System (IEQAS) was initiated in 2012 in an attempt to improve international students' learning environment in Korean universities. During this period, the Korean government aimed to offer "one-stop" service, taking care of international students' entire course of study in Korea (from admission to graduation) by operating the Information Service for International Students[3] beginning in 2011. In the same year, the government started to actively encourage universities to build joint dormitories for international students.

In 2012, the Study Korea Project (2004–12) initiated under the Roh administration was terminated, and the second phase of the original program, Study Korea Project 2020 (2013–20), was initiated. Under this new scheme, the Korean government announced its goal to attract two hundred thousand international students by 2020. The government further increased financial subsidies to promote the internationalization of Korean higher education.

Recent Higher Education Internationalization Policies

The current administration of Park Geun-hye (2013–17) has largely maintained and developed policies introduced by previous administrations. However, since all Korean universities are now under national evaluation for structural reform from 2015, each university's quality of education is

2 "BRICs" designates the world's four fastest growing economies: Brazil, Russia, India, and China.

3 http://www.studyinkorea.go.kr/en.

being used as one of the core components for evaluation. The section below briefly addresses the key internationalization policies of the current administration, with specific focus on the relationship between national evaluation of universities for structural reform and the internationalization of higher education.

The Background of the Higher Education Internationalization Policy

One of the critical challenges that Korea faces comes with the dramatic decline of its student population, which adds urgency to the government and universities' motivation to internationalize the student body (MEST 2012a; Ministry of Education 2014). According to Ministry of Education analyses, beginning in 2018 the number of high school graduates will fall below the college entrance quota, and the gap will start to increase sharply from 2020 (see figure 1.2). Such a dramatic decline in the college-age population will have a significant impact on universities located outside the Seoul metropolitan area and also on two-year colleges nationwide. The government expects that the decline of college students enrolled in regional universities will directly impact regional industries and economies (Ministry of Education 2014).

To avert this crisis, the Korean government introduced two main strategies: reduce the college entrance quota based on performance and attract international students by enhancing higher education's global competitiveness. First, the government enlisted the Korean Educational Development Institute (KEDI) to evaluate the performance of all universities and colleges

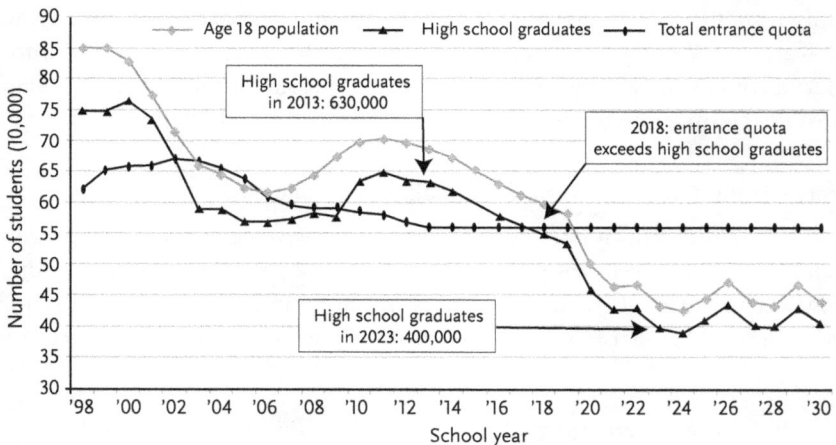

FIGURE 1.2 Predicted trend of Korean college enrollment capacity, 1998–2030

Source: Ministry of Education (2014, 1).

in Korea every three years; the evaluation results will be used to differentially reduce each institution's entrance quota and to restrict government subsidies for those institutions that are evaluated as below "average" (see table 1.1). The government plans to reduce the entrance quota by 160,000 by the 2023 academic year (Ministry of Education 2014, 2015a).

The first evaluation took place in 2015; the results, announced in August of the same year, included the percentage reduction of each university's entrance quota according to their evaluation results (see table 1.2). Of the 298 institutions that participated in the evaluation, all except for the forty-eight that received a grade of "A" are compelled to reduce their entrance quotas by between 3 and 15 percent based on their evaluation results, until the 2017 academic year. The government expects to reduce the total entrance quota

TABLE 1.1

Entrance quota reduction based on evaluation grades and related finance restriction measures

Evaluation grade	Entrance quota reduction	Government financial support program
A (Outstanding)	Can voluntarily reduce entrance quota	Able to participate
B (Good)	Must reduce by less than the average level*	Able to participate
C (Average)	Must reduce by the average level	Able to participate
D (Poor)	Must reduce by more than the average level	Able to partially participate†
E (Very Poor)‡	Must significantly reduce	Unable to participate

Source: Ministry of Education (2014, 9; 2015a, 25).

Notes: *The average level of reduction to the entrance quota is set by the government; †Included in the restriction are government scholarships and student loans; ‡If an institution receives the "Very Poor" grade consecutively, it will be weeded out.

TABLE 1.2

2015 evaluation results and entrance quota reduction rates by grades given

Evaluation grade		A	B	C	D	E	Special case*	No eval.*	Total
Number of institutions	University	34	56	36	26	6	5	29	192
	Junior College	14	26	58	27	7	3	2	137
Reduction rate	University	Voluntary†	4%	7%	10%	15%	7%		
	Junior College	Voluntary†	3%	5%	7%	10%	5%		

Source: Ministry of Education (2015b, 3).

Note: *Included in "Special case" and "Not evaluated" are institutions for training religious leaders; art, music and physical education institutions; and new institutions. †Institutions that receive the "A" grade may voluntarily reduce their entrance quotas.

by forty-seven thousand by 2017 based on the combined mandatory and voluntary quota reductions from each institution (Ministry of Education 2015b, 5).

The Korean government has been providing consulting services and encouraging each institution to establish a characterization plan based on the evaluation results and the context of the local environment since September 2015. Such a characterization plan would include providing lifelong vocational courses to adult learners, thus meeting the demands of local industries and economies.

Second, the government has also attempted to resolve problems associated with the decline in the student population by actively attracting international students. According to the government's August 2012 statement, if the recent increase rate (6–8 percent annually) of international students continues, the total number of international students is expected to reach approximately 160,000–180,000 by 2020, which will partially absorb the excessive supply of college entrance places (200,000–220,000 places) (MEST 2012b; Ha & Moon 2012).

Strategy for Higher Education Internationalization

The Korean government started to actively attract international students with the introduction of the Study Korea Project in 2004 (MEST 2012a, 2012b). When the project was first established, the government aimed to attract fifty thousand international students (including non-degree students) and introduced strategies to meet the goal, such as increasing its global network, promoting Korea as a study-abroad destination, and so on. As discussed above, the goal was accomplished two years earlier than originally planned and updated with a new goal—to attract one hundred thousand international students by 2012 (MEST 2008). However, the total number of international students peaked in 2011 and the goal was not met.

In order to stimulate more effective internationalization, the government announced the Higher Education Internationalization Strategy in August 2012, aiming to attract two hundred thousand international students by 2020 (MEST 2012a, 2012b). This framework has been consistent despite the change in administrations in 2013 (Ministry of Education 2014, 2015a). The government's revised strategies for internationalization are to establish infrastructure for global higher education in Korea, to attract international students, and to expand exchanges with foreign higher education and research institutions.[4] Below are more detailed descriptions of these strategies.

4 The policies related to attracting international students and establishing

Infrastructure

In order to establish the infrastructure needed to internationalize higher education in Korea, the government focused on the following areas. First, the government deregulated to allow greater autonomy (including admissions, tuition fees, faculty recruitment, etc.) to foreign institutions established in Korea's FEZS (e.g., Songdo in Incheon) in order to attract more foreign branch campuses.

To increase the effectiveness of the internationalization process, there has been a reorganization of government agencies. For instance, the National Institute for International Education (NIIED) was expanded and reorganized as a central-government–funded agency (formerly it was an affiliated organization of the Ministry of Education) that operates the Study Korea Project as well as other related programs such as GKS and TOPIK. In order to promote study-abroad opportunities in Korea, the government merged Korean Education Centers and Korean Cultural Centers located in foreign countries and established a flexible cooperation system with NIIED to attract prospective international students. The IEQAS, which was established to respond to ongoing criticisms regarding the quality of the internationalization of domestic universities, has been directly managed by the Ministry of Education since 2011. The IEQAS aims to improve domestic universities' management competency of international students by awarding accreditation to universities that have high competencies in attracting and supporting international students (MEST 2011). Universities that do not meet the standard are penalized, for instance by restricting visa issuances for international students attending those institutions.

Inbound Students and Researchers

The government adopted several strategies to attract high-quality international students, researchers, and institutions. These strategies include hosting study-abroad fairs in various countries. Through cooperation with the Korea Trade-Investment Promotion Agency (KOTRA), the government aims to retain high-quality international students who are interested in working in Korea after their studies. Also, the government has increased financial support for high-quality international students (through the GKS program) and undertaken large-scale projects such as WCU and BK21 to attract high-quality postgraduate students and researchers with strong research backgrounds from abroad. Moreover, the government offers more Korean language programs to international students and has simplified visa

infrastructure were specified in more detail in the Study Korea Project 2020 (2013–20), announced in October 2012 (MEST 2012b).

issuance procedures. Finally, the government seeks to attract high-profile foreign institutions to Korea so that it can absorb the needs of outbound students and promote greater research collaboration.

Outbound Korean Students and Universities

The Korean government is actively promoting the overseas experiences of its domestic students, such as through foreign internship programs, by utilizing KOTRA's network. The comprehensive system is operated by the Korean government in support of domestic university students' experiential learning. The NIIED leads diverse international educational exchange programs. For instance, the Korea-Japan Educational Exchange and Korea-China Educational Exchange were introduced to promote educational exchange and facilitate cooperation between participating students from two countries. Selected students are financially supported by the government; they engage in special lectures, visit historical and cultural sites, and experience local culture through staying with a host family for seven to ten days.

In order to assist student skills enhancement in preparation for employment, the Korean government also offers the Korean Government Global Internship Program (KGGIP).[5] This program sends Korean students to actual workplaces in the public and business sectors in a foreign country and lets them develop hands-on knowledge about their field or career interest. It also intends to foster Korean students' understanding of cultural diversity through the experience of living in foreign countries. The KGGIP was initiated in 2009 and about 2,500 students participated annually in its eleven to thirteen subprograms until 2015. In total, about thirteen thousand students had benefited from this program as of 2014. The eleven running subprograms in 2015 are based on major focus field areas such as business, education, international relations, and hospitality and tourism (see table 1.3).

For each subprogram, internship candidates are recruited by each implementing agency through a rigorous selection process that includes screening, written examinations, and interviews. Once selected, the participants receive intensive instruction from the agency. Depending on the position needs of host institutions, the internship period may last from two to eighteen months. Grants are awarded by the government and the host institution to all participating students, covering airfare, living expenses, insurance, and visa fees. Selection of participants from vulnerable or low-income groups has been prioritized and as of 2013, 746 of the 2,283 participants (32.6 percent) came from prioritized groups. Considering the cost of many

---

5 More information can be found on the official website (http://www.worldjob. or.kr/eng/).

TABLE 1.3

Subprograms under the Korean Government Global Internship Program

Program	Implementing Agency	Government Ministry
Global Internship for University Students	Korean Council for University Education	Ministry of Education
Global Workplace Training Program for Junior College Students	Korean Council for Junior College Education	
WEST (Work, English Study and Travel) Program	National Institute for International Education	
Teaching Abroad Project for Pre-Service Teachers	National Research Foundation of Korea	
Global Trade Experts Internship Program	Korea International Trade Association	Ministry of Employment and Labor
Exhibition Industry Internship Program	Association of Korea Exhibition Industry	
Overseas Korean Business Internship Program	World Federation of Overseas Korean Traders Associations	
Global Internship for Training International Export-Import Specialist	Korea Importers Association	
Global Internship for Logistics	Korea Integrated Logistics Association	
Textile and Fashion Industry Internship Program	Gyeonggi Small And Medium Business Center	
Global Internship Program for Tourism and Hospitality	Baekseok Culture University	

Source: Overseas Integrated information Network (http://www.worldjob.or.kr/).

student-supported exchange programs, this government program is particularly beneficial to those who would not otherwise have access to overseas opportunities. The program plans to expand the proportion of particpants from prioritized groups.

Another recently introduced project, a collaboration between Korea, Japan, and China, is Collective Action for Mobility Program of University Students in Asia (CAMPUS Asia). The initiative, modeled after the EU's Erasmus Program, promotes educational collaboration between these three countries to nurture a new generation of leaders in Asia through the operation of integrated joint degree programs in select areas of study. The project seeks to create new bonds in regional networks and improve the competitiveness of Korean, Japanese, and Chinese universities by educating students according to shared East Asian values and societal interests. The ten pilot programs are in table 1.4. The initial monitoring of the CAMPUS Asia project

TABLE 1.4

List of CAMPUS Asia Project pilot programs

Co-operational Graduate Education Program for the Development of Global Human Resources in Energy and Environmental Science and Technology	Training Human Resources for the Development of an Epistemic Community in Law and Political Science to Promote the Formation of *jus commune* (common law) in East Asia
TKT CAMPUS Asia Consortium	Asia Business Leaders Program (ABLP)
Northeast Asian Consortium for Policy Studies	Program for Careers in Risk Management with Experts in East Asia
Cooperative Asian Education Gateway for a Sustainable Society: Expanding the Frontiers in Science and Technology of Chemistry and Material Science	Program for Core Human Resources Development: For the Achievement of the Common Good and a Re-evaluation of Classical Culture in East Asia
Beijing-Seoul-Tokyo Dual Degree Master's Program in International and Public Policy Studies (BESETO DDMP)	Plan for a Joint Campus Representing Korea, China, and Japan to Foster Leaders in East Asian Humanities for the Next Generation

Source: Korea's CAMPUS Asia Project (http://www.campusasia.kr).

has reported satisfactory results; the project aims to expand its size into fifty consortia involving 1,500 students by 2020.

The government has also supported the overseas expansion of Korean universities by deregulating restrictions on overseas branch establishment and offering a consulting service to universities entering the overseas market. Since the mid-1990s, there has been a continuous debate over advancing the quality of higher education by opening the education market. In fact, the Korean government maintained a somewhat passive position in opening up the higher education market until it took an active step by introducing the Special Act on the Establishment and Operation of Foreign Educational Institutions in 2005. Some years afterward, the first foreign branch campus in Korea, named "Incheon Global Campus," opened in Songdo, the FEZ located in Incheon. With an investment of US$1 billion, the initial phase of construction started in 2009. Not only foreign universities but also international research institutions and manufacturing industries are to be clustered in the region, with the goal of enabling proactive collaboration. The Korean government expects that improvements to the educational system through this project will establish Korea as an innovative research hub in Northeast Asia.

So far, four foreign universities have launched campuses in Korea. Three are American universities: the State University of New York (SUNY), George Mason University, and the University of Utah. The last is Belgium's Ghent University. These branch campuses offer courses in selected fields— for example, SUNY offers undergraduate and graduate degree programs in computer science, mechanical engineering, and technological systems management. George Mason University offers undergraduate programs in economics, global affairs, and management.

Classes are taught in English by faculty members and specially employed academic staff from the home universities. The curricula and programs are designed to be identical to those of the home campuses; thus, a student who has successfully completed the program will receive the same degree as a student at the home campus. In addition, students have the opportunity to spend one academic year at the home campus.[6]

Incheon Global Campus is continuously growing. Currently, additional foreign universities including the University of Illinois and Alfred University, both American institutions; Moscow State University and Saint Petersburg State University of Russia have signed memoranda of understanding (MOUs) with Incheon Free Economic Zone Authority (Kim et al. 2013). Two Korean universities, Yonsei University and Hankuk University of Foreign Studies, have opened extended campuses in the zone as well. Incheon Catholic University and Inha University are likewise planning to open campuses to improve the educational environment and intensify global research networks. The Incheon Global Campus aims to recruit two hundred thousand international students by 2020.

Compared to the flurry of investments in foreign branch campuses, there has been significant indifference toward the promotion of outbound institutional mobility. That is to say, there is a lack of interest in encouraging Korean higher education institutions to collaborate with neighboring Asian countries and establish Korean branch campuses. Despite this indifference, in the long term, promoting outbound institutional mobility as well as attracting foreign institutions to Korea (inbound) should be prudently considered to increase the educational and research competitiveness of domestic universities, strengthen regional networks, and expand the influence of Korean education.

To sum up, the Korean government's objectives for internationalization strategies are twofold: to attract two hundred thousand international students by 2020, and to promote the global competitiveness of the domestic higher education sector so as to absorb outbound Korean students. In addition, the government has encouraged Korean universities to establish campuses overseas. By achieving these goals, the government aims to balance the size of the inbound and outbound mobility of students and institutions, and expects to improve its current deficit in international education.

6 More information can be found on the official website (http://www.igc.or.kr/en/main.do).

Financial Support for Higher Education Internationalization

The Korean government has implemented various financial support structures to promote the internationalization of higher education and to increase the competitiveness of Korea as a study-abroad destination. Government subsidies to universities are often tied to various measurements of levels of internationalization, including overall university rankings, the proportion of full-time foreign faculty, the number of international students, and the proportion of lectures taught in English. Thus, universities are also investing their own financial resources to provide more attractive scholarship programs and housing options for foreign faculty members and international students, because if they do, they will get more subsidies from the government.

The total government funding for Korean higher education in 2008 was US$4.181 billion, which accounts for 1.6 percent of the total central government budget and 11.7 percent of the total education budget. A substantial portion of the higher education budget is allocated to the Ministry of Education. However, there are other government ministries that are in charge of supporting the higher education sector, such as the Ministry of Strategy and Finance; the Ministry of Science, ICT, and Future Planning; and the Ministry of Trade, Industry, and Energy. They each operate their own financial support programs for universities, which in table 1.5 shows that the financial support for universities is greater than the central government's original higher education budget. This combined support for college and university, including research and development (R&D) support, in 2008 was US$5.479 billion, which accounts for approximately 2.1 percent of the central government budget.

The proportion of the budget allocated to supporting higher education (including R&D support) has been increasing consistently since 2008, reaching 3.1 percent in 2013. However, within this amount, the proportion of budget that supports internationalization was more than 3 percent from 2008 to 2011, but in 2012, it dropped to 1.8 percent due to a reduction in the size of the WCU Project. The WCU Project was introduced in 2008 with a budget of US$160.6 million, with the purpose of inviting globally renowned scholars to Korean universities. The government supported the WCU Project at select institutions with an annual budget of US$150–160 million from 2008 to 2011, but beginning in 2012 the annual budget was reduced to US$65 million. Thus, with the exception of the WCU Project, other subsidy programs for the internationalization of higher education have seen constant increases, rising from US$44 million in 2008 to US$118 million in 2013.

One of the largest projects in terms of budget allocation in 2013 was the

TABLE 1.5

Government support for higher education internationalization, 2008–13 (millions USD)

			2008	2009	2010	2011	2012	2013
GDP			1,104,492	1,151,708	1,265,308	1,332,681	1,377,457	1,428,295
Budget for central government	Total		257,200	284,500	292,800	309,100	325,400	342,000
	Education		35,600	38,200	38,300	41,200	45,500	49,900
	College and university education		4,181	4,637	5,044	4,977	6,221	7,681
Support for colleges and universities (including R&D support)	Total		5,479	6,536	6,633	8,376	9,420	10,506
	Internationalization	Subtotal	205	212	221	265	166	182
		Education	176	176	168	213	124	142
		R&D	29	36	53	53	42	40

Source: Higher education financial aid information system (from https://hiedupport.kedi.re.kr) and internal data from the Ministry of Education.

GKS program, in which a total of US$41 million was distributed to higher education institutions. This is composed of various government financial support programs for inbound students, such as Korean government scholarships, and for outbound Korean students. The government has allocated US$17 million for the Global Learning Program, which aims to enhance foreign language proficiency and work experience abroad for Korean undergraduates. US$2.4 million has been allocated to promote research collaborations among domestic and international faculty members, as well as US$1.9 million for the Brain Pool Program, which invites highly skilled researchers to Korea for a period of time.

Conclusion

The Korean government began to focus attention on its internationalization policy for higher education after the launch of the General Agreement on Trade in Services (GATS) and the WTO in 1995. The pressure to open up the education service market for higher education and the adult learning sector grew substantially, and it was inevitable that the Korean government would respond to such external changes. Therefore, one of the key characteristics of the internationalization of higher education in Korea is that it was external pressure that geared the government to respond to the rapidly changing global environment, and many of the policies were initiated by the Korean government. It attempted to expand cooperation with international organizations and major countries beginning in the mid-1990s and increased autonomy for individual universities to operate joint curricula and joint degree programs with foreign institutions. The government also put a great deal of effort into creating "global-friendly" educational environments, such as by reducing restrictions on the establishment of foreign branch campuses in Korea.

Another major characteristic of Korea's internationalization of higher education is that much of the policy approach was "inbound-oriented" in its strategy. With this approach, the Korean government tried to improve the deficit balance of the number of students studying abroad. It was anticipated to improve the competitiveness of Korean higher education by attracting internationally renowned scholars and foreign branch campuses. In order to achieve these goals, the government introduced the Study Korea Project, a comprehensive plan for internationalization policy in Korea. Moreover, an increase in the ratio of English-exclusive lectures in universities was believed to be able to absorb the study-abroad demand of domestic Korean students, and at the same time, it was expected that creating an English-friendly study environment would add competitiveness to Korea as a study-abroad destination for foreign students.

Because of government efforts, Korean higher education's internationalization level may seem to have advanced in a relatively short period of time. The total number of international students studying in Korea and the number of foreign faculty members working for Korean universities has increased substantially, with countries of origin also becoming more diversified. Although the number of Korean students choosing to study abroad (outbound mobility) still outnumbers those who come to Korea, the steep increase in the number of inbound students is easing the imbalanced inbound and outbound mobility ratio. Government and university efforts toward internationalization have also contributed to creating a more diversified learning environment. The number of GSIS and international colleges that teach almost all classes in English has increased greatly since the mid-2000s. Given the general assumption that many Korean students decide to study abroad to improve their English language proficiency, offering high quality English-exclusive courses and degree programs in Korea may be an effective way to respond to the demands of these students. Therefore, increasing the proportion of English-exclusive lectures for major subjects in Korean universities may be an effective tool for absorbing the study-abroad demand of domestic Korean students as well as for decreasing language barriers to foreign students who wish to study in Korea.

However, this inbound-oriented approach to the internationalization of higher education has certain limitations. One of the main reasons for the rapid increase in international student numbers in Korea can be largely explained by the influx of Chinese students, which ties the future of inbound international students in Korea to China's socioeconomic changes and trends. China's capacity to absorb domestic demand for higher education is rapidly increasing, meaning that fewer Chinese students may wish to study abroad in the future (Min 2013). Also, due to China's economic rise, more students prefer to study in Western countries rather than in Asia (Min et al. 2014). Therefore, the Korean government and universities should establish more concrete and customized strategies to attract students from a greater range of countries to achieve sustainable growth in higher education internationalization.

Another important trend in international student mobility in Korea is that the number of students in non-degree programs (language programs or short-term exchange programs) is increasing, whereas the number of students in degree programs has slightly declined since 2012. However, according to recent statistics provided by the Korea Immigration Service, the number of total international students in 2014 increased slightly (Cha 2015), which can be a positive sign for the future. International students in non-degree programs are equally important to universities and the government because their experiences in Korea may provide them with a more positive view of the country in general and may motivate them to study in Korea in long-term degree programs. However, since the Korean government aims to solve issues related to the decline in the number of domestic students, greater efforts must be made to attract international students studying for degree programs.

Ultimately, the most important goal of the internationalization of higher education in Korea is to ensure high quality and global competitiveness. Japan's internationalization strategy is also heavily based on increasing inbound mobility. However, the Japanese government's attention has shifted to improving internal standards for education and research competencies rather than simply increasing the number of international students or the proportion of English-exclusive lectures (Yonezawa 2011). China is also actively pushing to increase the global competency of its universities, but instead of setting uniform standards for all institutions, the Chinese government is considering the characteristics of each university and its location and applying selective support to achieve effective outcomes (Kim et al. 2013; Gu et al. 2012). The Chinese government is encouraging universities to develop unique and customized international programs based on each university's circumstances and needs (Gu et al. 2012).

In light of these local and international contexts, we believe that the Korean government must also enact more policy measures to improve the global competency of Korean universities rather than simply focusing on attracting more foreign students and scholars. The government should consider a comprehensive examination of the results of university evaluations and should perhaps provide differential internationalization support schemes for universities that are better equipped for further development. It should also provide consistent opportunities for domestic Korean students to have experiences in overseas institutions, research centers, and international organizations. Linking study experiences with work experiences abroad will allow Korean students to more effectively acquire the practical competencies needed for global society.

References

Cha, Dae-un. 2015. "Hangug chajneun yuhagsaeng dasi neul-eo" [International students in Korea increasing again]. *Yonhap News*, February 6. http://www.yonhapnews.co.kr/bulletin/2015/02/06/0200000000 AKR20150206060900372.html.

Gu, Ja-oek, Han-na Kim, Seung-chan Park, Young-jin Park, and Kyung-ja Lee. 2013. *Joonguk ui chunin gaehwek yeongu* [China's Thousand Talents program]. Seoul, Korea: Korea Institute for International Economic Policy, Korean Educational Development Institute.

Gu, Ja-oek, Young-jin Park, and Byung-hwan Ahn. 2012. *Joonguk ui waeguk daehak yuchi jungchek sarae yeongu* [A case study on Chinese government's policies to attract foreign universities]. Seoul: Korea Institute for International Economic Policy, Korean Educational Development Institute.

Ha, Yeon-seob, and Woo-sik Moon. 2012. *2 dangye Study in Korea chujin bang-an seolgye* [Research on policy design of the second phase of the "Study in Korea" project]. Seoul, Korea: Ministry of Education, Science and Technology [MEST].

Kim, Byung-cheol. 2012. *Joonguk ui haewae gogup inlyuk yuchi jeonlyak: Chunin gaehwek* [A strategy to attract high quality talents: Thousand Talents program]. *International Labor Brief* 10 (1): 66–74.

Kim, Mee-ran, Young-ran Hong, Eun-young Kim, and Byung-shik Ree. 2013. *Hankook godung gyoyuk kukjehwa jungchek jindan mit gaesun bangan yeongu* [A study on the policy on internationalization of Korean higher education and its implications]. RR 2013-12. Seoul, Korea: Korean Educational Development Institute.

Min, Gwy-sik. 2013. *Jaehan joongkugin yuhakseng hyunhwangwa hankook saengwhal chugung mit galdeong* [Current status of Chinese students in Korea: Adaptation to Korean life and conflict]. INChina Brief 246. Incheon, Korea: Incheon Development Institute.

Min, Gwy-sik, Soon-gi Chung, Bok-su Cho, Ji-young Kim, and Jin-young Kim. 2014. *Waekugin yoohakseng yuchi·jiwon hwakdaerul weehan jungchek yeongu* [A policy research on strategy to increase international students and support]. Seoul, Korea: National Institute for International Education.

Ministry of Education. 2014. *Daehak gyoook ui jil jaego mit haglyung ingu gupgam daebirul weehan gujogaehyuk choojin gaehwek* [The higher education structural reform plan for quality of education and rapid decline of the college student population]. Press release, January 28.

———. 2015a. *2015 nyun Gyoyookbu upmoo gaehwek* [Ministry of Education 2015 work plan]. Press Release, January 22.

————. 2015b. *Daehak gujogaehyuk pyungka gyulgwa balpyo* [Release of the university structural reform evaluation results]. Press release, August 31.

Ministry of Education, Science and Technology [MEST]. 2008. *Study Korea Project baljeon bang-an soolip* [Development plan for the Study Korea Project]. Press release, August 4.

————. 2011. *Daehak ui waegookin yoohaksaeng yuchi·gwanli yuklyang injungjae silsi* [Implementation of the International Education Quality Assurance System (IEQAS)]. Inauguration of the International Education Quality Assurance Committee. Press release, August 12.

————. 2012a. *Godeung gyoyuk kookjehwa choojin jeonlyak bogo* [A report on the propulsive strategy of internationalization of higher education in Korea]. Press release, August 30.

————. 2012b. *2020 nyun kaji oohsuhan waegookin yuhaksaeng 20 man-myung yuchi* [Attracting two hundred thousand high-quality international students by 2020]. Press release, October 29.

Organization for Economic Cooperation and Development (OECD). 2009. *Education at a Glance 2009*. Paris: OECD.

Presidential Committee on Education Innovation [PCEI]. 2006a. *Yukdae jungbu daetonglyung weewonhwe gyoyook gaehyuk bogoseo (III)* [A report on education reform by previous presidential committees (III)]. Seoul: PCEI.

————. 2006b. *Yukdae jungbu daetonglyung weewonhwe gyoyook gaehyuk bogoseo (IV)* [A report on education reform by previous presidential committees (IV)]. Seoul: PCEI.

————. 2006c. *Yukdae jungbu daetonglyung weewonhwe gyoyook gaehyuk bogoseo (V-1)* [A report on education reform by previous presidential committees (V-1)]. Seoul: PCEI.

————. 2006d. *Yukdae jungbu daetonglyung weewonhwe gyoyook gaehyuk bogoseo (V-2)* [A report on education reform by previous presidential committees (V-2)]. Seoul: PCEI.

Yonezawa, Akiyoshi. 2011. "The Internationalization of Japanese Higher Education: Policy Debates and Realities." In *Higher Education in the Asia-Pacific*, edited by Simon Marginson, Sarjit Kaur, and Erlenawati Sawir. Dordrecht: Springer.

2 Student Mobility in Korean Higher Education: Trends and Key Issues

Dae Bong Kwon

Mobility remains a dominant theme in most internationalization discussions. Growing higher education mobility worldwide indicates that it will continue to be a significant issue. This trend has been further precipitated by the rapid development of information technologies and the advent of the World Trade Organization (WTO), according to which education is now treated as a tradable commodity, and the exchange of students, academic staff, and research ideas has become the norm. This trend in the internationalization of higher education has been regarded as a way to strengthen the competitiveness of a higher educational institution by raising its reputation internationally.

Higher education in the Republic of Korea (hereafter Korea) has likewise been influenced by internationalization. As described by Baek and Kim in chapter 1, in the early 2000s, the government introduced a series of policy initiatives to internationalize the educational environment of Korean universities as a means of enhancing education quality and establishing a global knowledge network centered in Korea (Byun and Kim 2011). Due to a low birth rate and an aging population, retaining and importing high-quality human resources has become a major policy issue in many countries, including Korea (Bang 2013; KRIVET 2005; Ministry of Education 2014a; STEPI 2012). The Ministry of Education predicted that the number of students entering colleges will start to fall sharply in 2016 and will continue to fall until 2022 (NIIED 2014). This phenomenon has prompted Korean universities to turn to recruiting foreign students. The number of foreign students studying

Preliminary collection and analysis of relevant data for this chapter were conducted by Heh Youn Shin, graduate research assistant in the College of Education, Korea University.

in Korea has been increasing over the last decade; however, after finishing their studies, the majority of international students choose to return to their home countries rather than stay to work in Korea (STEPI 2012; NIIED 2014). It is indeed a great loss for the Korean government as well as the universities and companies that have supported these foreign students during their stay in Korea. Reasons for leaving Korea include the language barrier, relatively low wages compared to that of native Koreans, and difficulties in adjusting to Korean culture (GRI 2011; NIIED 2014). Therefore, the internationalization of higher education institution policies has been seen as pivotal to overcoming the diminishing human resources problem and enhancing the country's national prestige.

The purpose of this chapter is to review the current programs and policies implemented by universities and the government to internationalize higher education in Korea during recent years, and to attempt to answer three specific questions: What are the trends in both inbound and outbound student mobility? What types of programs promote internationalization in Korean universities? What are the main challenges associated with these reforms?

Trends in International Student Mobility in Korea

In the past decade, international student recruitment has become one of the central issues in the field of higher education. In the following section, recent trends in the number of foreign students studying in Korea and Korean students studying abroad are discussed.

Foreign Students in Korea

Only a few decades ago, there were a limited number of foreign students studying in Korea. Between 1980 and 2000, foreign students represented 0.1 to 0.2 percent of the total student body. However, their numbers increased rapidly in 2004, with a dramatic growth between 2005 and 2011 as a result of the Study Korea Project (see figure 2.1). Now foreign students account for about 2 percent of the total student body.

Foreign students studying in Korea can be classified into two groups: those who are enrolled in degree programs and those who pursue non-degree programs. As seen in table 2.1, in the years 2010–14 roughly two-thirds of foreign students were enrolled in degree programs. This is fairly typical, but during this period the proportion of foreign students in non-degree programs, which include exchange programs and language courses, has been slowly but steadily increasing.

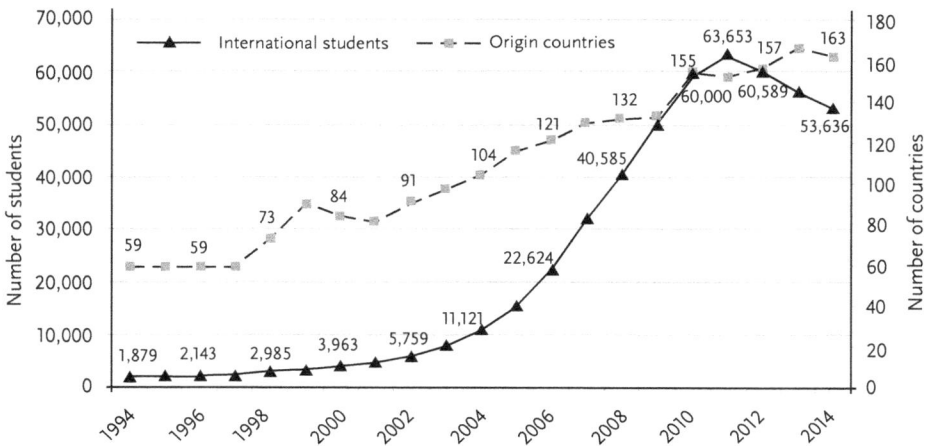

FIGURE 2.1 Foreign students studying in Korea and countries of origin, 1994–2014

Source: Korean Educational Statistics Service (http://kess.kedi.re.kr/eng).

Note: The number of international student represents foreign students enrolled in *degree* programs; it does not include students in non-degree programs such as language or exchange programs.

TABLE 2.1

Foreign students studying in Korea by degree vs. non-degree programs, 2010–14

Year	2010	2011	2012	2013	2014
Total number of students	83,842	89,537	86,878	85,923	84,891
Degree program	60,000	63,653	60,589	56,715	53,636
Non-degree program	23,842	25,884	26,289	29,208	31,255

Source: Korean Educational Statistics Service (KEDI) (http://kess.kedi.re.kr/index).

During this period of expansion, the countries of origin of foreign students have also become more diverse. In 1995, foreign students in Korea came from fifty-nine countries of origin, but in 2014 that increased to more than 160 countries. As detailed in table 2.2, in 1995, when the number of foreign students was comparatively small, these students came primarily from four countries that shared a relatively balanced distribution (United States 16.5 percent, Japan 17.7 percent, China 14.0 percent, and Taiwan 21.4 percent). However, the proportion of foreign students coming from China started to rapidly increase in the early 2000s, accounting for over three-quarters of all degree-seeking international students by 2010. Thus, the rapid growth of the foreign student population can be largely explained by the influx of Chinese students; as China developed, more Chinese students went to study abroad, not only in North America and Western Europe, their preferred destinations, but also in advanced Asian countries such as Japan and South Korea. The number of students originating from other countries, such as the United States, Japan, and Taiwan, has also increased consistently, but their proportion among the foreign student population has decreased. Meanwhile, the growth rate of Mongolian and Vietnamese students has exceeded that of foreign students as a whole due to a great number of scholarships being offered for talented students from developing countries as a part of Korea's official development assistance (ODA) in higher education.[1]

From 2010 to 2014, the inflow of Chinese students decreased, causing an overall decline in the number of foreign students beginning in 2012. One significant reason for the decrease in their numbers was the introduction of the International Education Quality Assurance System (IEQAS), implemented in 2012. Applying strict eligibility criteria, it restricted the admission and graduation of international students to those who scored grades of three and four, respectively, on the Test of Proficiency in Korean (TOPIK) (MEST 2011). At the same time, in step with China's economic growth, more Chinese students have headed to English-speaking countries as their study-abroad destination. In addition, over the last decade, the Korean government and universities have focused mainly on the expansion of the foreign student population, paying relatively little attention to improving the quality of educational services for them. This has resulted in negative experiences for foreign students and low satisfaction with education during their study in Korea (NIIED 2014). Furthermore, the dual use of English and Korean as the languages of instruction puts students from non-English-speaking countries at a disadvantage as they must learn both languages in addition to their subjects of study (NIIED 2014).

The quality of education provided by higher education institutions is one of the most critical factors in selecting a study-abroad destination.

[1] In 2010, Korea became the twenty-fourth member of the OECD's Development Assistance Committee (DAC), with unanimous approval by all committee members. The country is officially recognized as the only OECD country that has transformed itself from a recipient to an emerging donor, then to an advanced donor, and is now seen by developing countries, particularly those in Asia, as a source of knowledge and ideas drawn from an actual and still vivid experience of development. This gives Korea a clear comparative advantage in relating to and understanding developing countries and their needs, relative to older DAC members. Korea's ODA gained particular momentum during the the Lee Myung-bak administration (2008–12), under which the nation joined the DAC and successfully raised its ODA spending from 0.07 percent of its gross national income (GNI) in 2007 to 0.14 percent in 2012. As the newest member of the DAC in 2010 (Iceland and Czech Republic became the twenty-fifth and twenty-sixth members in 2013), Korea pledged to rapidly increase its ODA budget from 0.09 percent to 0.25 percent of its GNI by 2015 (Kwon 2015).

TABLE 2.2

Foreign students by country of origin, 1995–2014

	1995	2000	2005	2010	2014
Origin countries	59	84	116	155	163
Foreign students (percent)	1,983 (100.0)	3,963 (100.0)	15,577 (100.0)	60,000 (100.0)	53,636 (100.0)
China	278 (14.0)	1,378 (34.8)	10,107 (64.9)	45,944 (76.6)	34,482 (64.3)
Mongolia	18 (0.9)	54 (1.4)	305 (2.0)	2,196 (3.7)	2,236 (4.2)
Vietnam	11 (0.6)	62 (1.6)	559 (3.6)	1,667 (2.8)	2,148 (4.0)
United States	328 (16.5)	361 (9.1)	408 (2.6)	1,182 (2.0)	1,824 (3.4)
Japan	350 (17.7)	733 (18.5)	1,115 (7.2)	1,350 (2.3)	1,416 (2.6)
Taiwan	425 (21.4)	646 (16.3)	698 (4.5)	926 (1.5)	984 (1.8)
Others	573 (28.9)	729 (18.4)	2,385 (15.3)	6,735 (11.2)	10,546 (19.7)

Source: Korean Educational Statistics Service (http://kess.kedi.re.kr/eng).

Note: The number of foreign students represents those in *degree* programs; it does not include students in non-degree programs such as language or exchange programs.

According to a National Institute for International Education (NIIED) report (2014), priorities in choosing a study-abroad destination were (1) language, (2) educational level, (3) tuition, (4) study-abroad and immigration policies, and (5) other. For Chinese students, who comprise more than half of all foreign students in Korea, institutional and individual academic networks and level of education were the primary factors leading them to Korea (NIIED 2014). This fact emphasizes that Korea must devote increased attention to strengthening the quality of educational services to attract and retain foreign students in Korea.

Financial aid availability has been proven to be another important factor in a foreign student's choice of a higher education institution (Van der Meid 2003; NIIED 2014). For foreign students studying in Korea, between 30 and 100 percent of their tuition fees are paid by either the Korean government or the Korean universities themselves. The Ministry of Education provides various types of financial grants for foreign students, some of which cover full tuition and more, such as living expenses, round trip airfare, and medical insurance. For example, as part of the Global Korea Scholarship (GKS), the Foreign Exchange Students Support Program offers financial support for approximately five hundred students at Korean universities. Another distinguished scholarship is offered by the Korea International Cooperation Agency (KOICA) to graduate students from developing countries. The benefits of the KOICA scholarship include full tuition, a living allowance, airfare, health insurance, and textbook costs. A number of universities are participating as partner universities and offer graduate degrees to those from KOICA scholarship programs. Recently, the Ministry of Education proposed the Study Korea 2020 project, with an emphasis on increasing foreign students from developing countries through government scholarship programs.[2]

In addition, large companies frequently collaborate with universities to grant scholarships to foreign students studying in Korea. The Conditional Employment Contract Program is an industry-sponsored scholarship that guarantees foreign students employment upon graduation. Companies such as Samsung, SK Hynix, and LG Innotek have contracts with numerous university departments. Public institutions such as the Korea Creative Content Agency (KOCCA) and Korea Association for ICT Promotion (KAIT) can support these contracts established between industrial sponsors and individual universities (NIIED 2014). In addition, some companies operate their own scholarship foundations. For example, Samsung, through its Samsung Dream Scholarship Foundation, supports foreign students from developing countries who study in Samsung's partner universities.[3] According to its website, the Samsung Dream Scholarship Foundation covers living expenses for undergraduate students and offers tuition or academic support scholarships (living expenses) for graduate students.

Trends in Korean Students Studying Abroad

The number of outbound Korean students started to increase dramatically during the 1990s; figure 2.2 shows the increasing numbers of outbound degree-seeking Korean students. In 1998, there were 63,495 students studying in foreign universities, accounting for 2.2 percent of all Korean students enrolled in higher education. Although the growth rate has become moderate since 2010, the total number of outbound students is double that of 1998, comprising 3.3 percent of the total Korean student population in higher education.

As table 2.3 shows, traditionally the United States has been the preferred destination for Korean students studying abroad, accounting for 41 percent of outbound Korean students in both 2008 and 2014. Over the same period, the proportion of students heading to China increased from 12.1 percent to 17.3 percent. Those who chose to study in Japan decreased from 13.2 percent to 10.9 percent in the same time frame. The number of students

2 See the "Study in Korea" website, http://www.studyinkorea.go.kr.

3 Samsung's partner universities include Korea University, Seoul National University, Yonsei University, Kyunghee University, Sungkyunkwan University, Ehwa Womans University, and Handong University, to name a few.

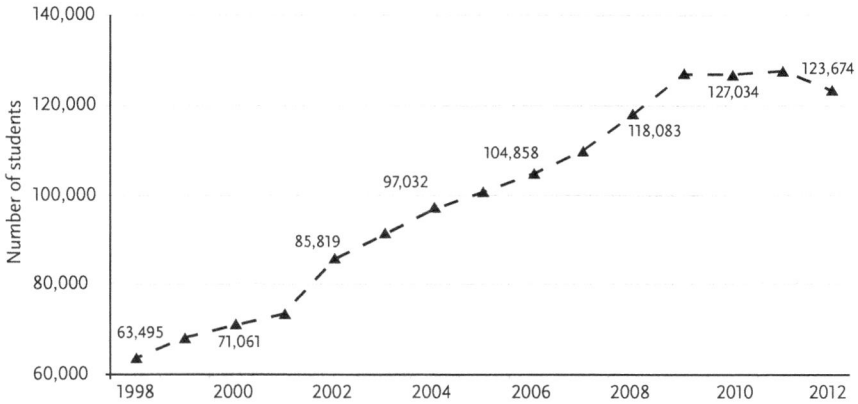

FIGURE 2.2 Korean outward mobile students, 1998–2012

Source: UNESCO Institute for Statistics (Retrieved on January 15, 2015, from http://data.uis.unesco.org).

Note: The data used for yearly outbound students have been extracted from UNESCO's Institute for Statistics. However, some countries may not have accurately reported the number of international students to UNESCO, which may result in underestimation of the total number of Korean students studying in foreign countries. The number of students represents Korean students abroad in *degree* programs; it does not include students in language programs or exchange students.

studying in the Philippines, where the official languages are English and Filipino, increased by approximately 3.5 percent between 2008 and 2014.

To absorb the high demand for study-abroad opportunities and to reduce the trade deficit in education services, the Kim Dae-jung administration (1998–2002) initiated various policies to open up the global higher education market and to attract foreign university branch campuses (Kim et al. 2013).

Inbound/Outbound Student Mobility Ratios

As stated earlier, although the number of degree-seeking foreign students in Korean institutions has increased dramatically, there are yet more outbound Korean students choosing to study abroad. Korea's inbound mobility ratio, which indicates the proportion of foreign students in domestic higher education institutions, was 1.77 percent in 2012 (see table 2.4). Compared to 0.11 percent in 2000, this is an increase of approximately sixteen times. The outbound ratio, the proportion of Korean students enrolled in higher education outside of Korea, was 3.68 percent in 2012. Thus, the overall inbound/outbound mobility ratio of Korean students was 0.5 in 2012, which indicates that there were almost half as many inbound students as there were outbound students. Since the number of inbound students has increased at

TABLE 2.3

Korean students studying abroad by country, 2008 and 2014

Year		United States	China	Japan	Australia	Philippines	Canada	UK	Germany	Others	Total
2008	Students	52,178	15,376	16,745	10,860	1,923	9,658	4,000	5,076	11,184	127,000
	Percent	41.1	12.1	13.2	8.6	1.5	7.6	3.1	4.0	8.8	100.0
2014	Students	57,985	24,339	15,304	10,847	7,073	6,691	4,160	3,938	10,223	140,560
	Percent	41.3	17.3	10.9	7.7	5.0	4.8	3.0	2.8	7.3	100.0

Source: Statistics from Ministry of Education (http://www.moe.go.kr/web/100088/ko/board/list.do?bbsId=350).

Note: The number of students represents Korean students abroad in *degree* programs; it does not include students in language programs or exchange students.

TABLE 2.4

Student mobility inbound/outbound ratio, 2000–12

		2000	2001	2002	2003	2004	2005	2006	2007	2008	2009	2010	2011	2012
Korea	Inbound (%)*	0.11	0.12	0.15	0.24	0.33	0.48	0.69	1.00	1.26	1.55	1.81	1.87	1.77
	Outbound (%)†	2.37	2.35	2.67	2.84	3.01	3.14	3.27	3.43	3.69	3.95	3.89	3.81	3.68
	Ratio‡	0.0	0.1	0.1	0.1	0.1	0.2	0.2	0.3	0.3	0.4	0.5	0.5	0.5
Japan		1.0	1.1	1.2	1.3	1.9	2.0	2.2	2.3	2.5	2.9	3.5	4.2	4.5
China		—	—	—	—	—	—	0.1	0.1	0.1	0.1	0.1	0.1	0.1
France		2.7	2.8	3.0	3.9	5.1	4.8	4.6	4.5	5.3	4.7	4.5	4.5	4.3
Germany		3.4	3.5	3.6	3.8	4.5	4.0	2.9	2.6	2.3	2.1	1.9	1.8	1.8
United Kingdom		10.0	8.1	7.6	8.0	12.5	13.8	14.2	13.9	15.7	15.6	15.8	14.7	15.3
United States		11.4	10.4	11.6	11.8	11.7	11.6	11.1	10.7	11.7	12.0	12.3	12.3	12.7

Source: UNESCO Institute for Statistics (http://data.uis.unesco.org).

Note: *Inbound mobility ratio is the number of students from abroad studying in a given country as a percentage of the total tertiary enrollment in that country; †Outbound mobility ratio is the number of students from a given country studying abroad as a percentage of the total tertiary enrolment in that country; ‡The inbound/outbound ratio is the number of foreign students per national student abroad.

a much faster rate than outbound students, the inbound/outbound ratio is consistently increasing.

Still, as shown in table 2.4, Korea's inbound/outbound student mobility ratio is substantially lower than those of other major OECD countries (except for China). Japan is a contrasting case. Japan's inbound/outbound student mobility ratio was 1.0 in 2000, which indicates that almost the same number of students were studying in Japan as were Japanese students studying abroad. However, by 2012, the ratio had increased to 4.5 as the number of inbound students continuously increased while the number of outbound students decreased. This has raised some concerns among experts and policymakers in Japan.

Institutional Changes in Korean Universities in the Context of Internationalization

As the internationalization of higher education has become a priority for universities, individual institutions have promoted various exercises to enhance their involvement in internationalization. Representatively, the following section focuses on the establishment of graduate schools of international studies, international colleges, and student exchange programs, followed by a short discussion of practical challenges.

Graduate Schools of International Studies in Korea

Discussion of the internationalization of higher education in Korea properly began in 1995, when the 5.31 Education Reform Report was published under the Kim Young-sam administration (1993–97). The Advisory Committee on Educational Reform then proposed establishing specialized graduate schools that could train professionals in the fields of international relations and regional studies, with the goal of internationalizing Korea's higher education sector. As a result, the Korean government initiated professional training projects for international manpower between 1996 and 2000 and provided US$76 million to nine universities.[4]

The chosen universities established graduate schools of international studies (GSIS) and fostered graduate programs in specialized areas. Consequently, the number of such graduate schools increased from two in 1996 to eleven in 1998. Since then, the numbers have remained more or less the same.

4 Kyunghee University, Korea University, Sogang University, Seoul National University, Yonsei University, Ewha Womans University, Chungang University, Hankuk University of Foreign Studies, Hanyang University (Lee et al. 2013).

Although the number of GSISs has remained relatively static since 1998, the number of students has increased continuously, particularly at the master's level (see figure 2.3). The number of enrolled students decreased slightly in the early 2000s, but when PhD programs were introduced in 2004, the numbers started to increase again. Although the number of PhD students was marginal, the possibility of attaining a doctoral degree may have stimulated students to pursue their studies further, leading to growth in the number of master's students.

Two of the key characteristics of a GSIS are that all courses are conducted in English and that students come from various backgrounds and nationalities (Kim et al. 2009). Most prior governmental and institutional policies about foreign students had focused on simply increasing student numbers, but the GSIS initiative also attempted to specialize the education that it offered and to control its quality. All courses related to international studies, including international trade, international business and management, international cooperation, regional studies, and international relations, were offered with the goal of providing students with the opportunity to obtain both academic and practical knowledge in each field. Moreover, most GSIS programs offer Korean Studies, which promotes Korea to foreign students as well as to the academic community worldwide (Kim et al. 2009). This is consistent with the Kim Young-sam government's policy of globalization: seeking to preserve central values and practices of Korea's indigenous culture in the midst of globalization (see Shin 2006).

International Colleges in Korea

International colleges are equivalent to GSISs in their academic design and purpose, but courses are offered at the undergraduate level instead. Most of the curriculum is reorganized for undergraduates, and all lectures for major courses are delivered in English. Ewha Womans University was one of the first institutions to adopt this model in 2001, when it established the Division of International Studies (DIS) after having successfully established a GSIS. Ewha's DIS attracted many high-achieving students in 2001 and 2002, triggering other institutions to establish similar international colleges. Data on the establishment of international colleges are depicted in table 2.5

As a result, Korea University established its international college in 2002, Hanyang University in 2004, Hankuk University of Foreign Studies and Hannam University in 2005, Kyung-Hee and Yonsei University in 2006, and so on. As of 2015, there are seventeen international colleges in Korea.

All nine international colleges established by 2009 were at private universities. The first public university to open an international college was

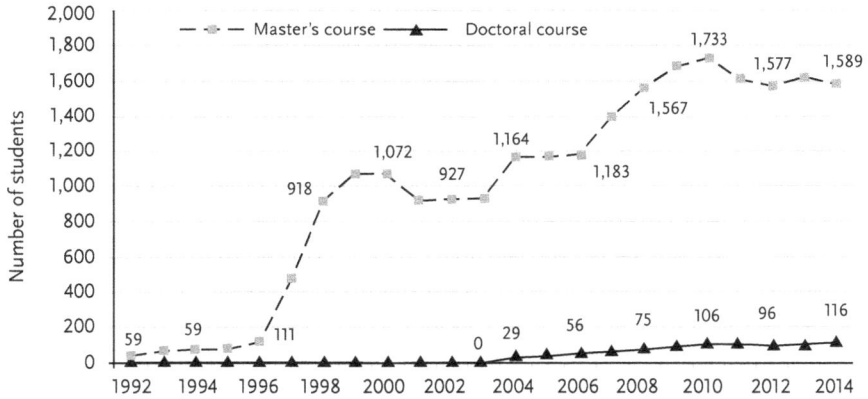

FIGURE 2.3 Students in graduate schools of international studies, 1992–2014
Source: Korean Educational Statistics Service (http://kess.kedi.re.kr/eng).

TABLE 2.5
International colleges in Korea, 2001–15

		2001	2003	2005	2007	2009	2011	2013	2015 Schools	2015 Student recruitment
4-year universities		162	169	173	175	177	183	188	189	340,586
International colleges		1	2	5	7	9	13	17	17	1,350
Type	Public	0	0	0	0	0	1	3	3	91
	Private	1	2	5	7	9	12	14	14	1,259
Region	Capital	1	2	4	6	6	8	9	9	943
	Province	0	0	1	1	3	5	8	8	407

Source: Data on establishment year and admission information was collected from each institution's website on January 19, 2015.

Pusan National University in 2011, and it was followed by Gongju National University in 2012 and Chonbuk National University in 2013. Until the mid-2000s, all international colleges were within universities located in the Seoul metropolitan area; the first regional international college was opened in 2008. As of 2015, the numbers of international colleges in the Seoul metropolitan area and regional areas are almost equal. Figure 2.4 illustrates the types and regional breakdowns of international colleges from 2001–15.

Other institutions also established schools, departments, and courses to strengthen their international education efforts. For example, Handong Global University offers specialized courses in which the lectures are delivered

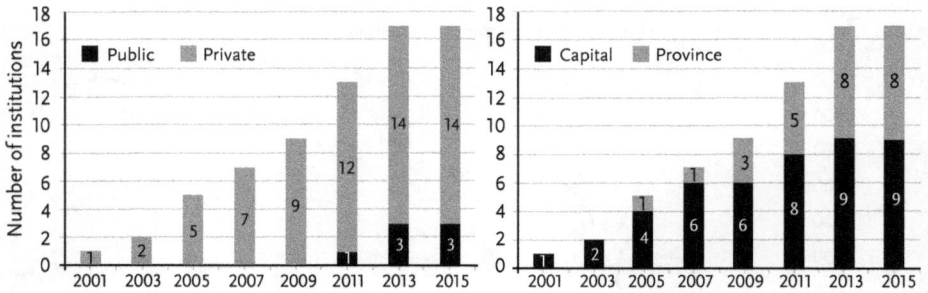

FIGURE 2.4 Korean international colleges by type and region, 2001–15

Source: Data on the establishment year and admission information was collected from each institution's website on January 19, 2015.

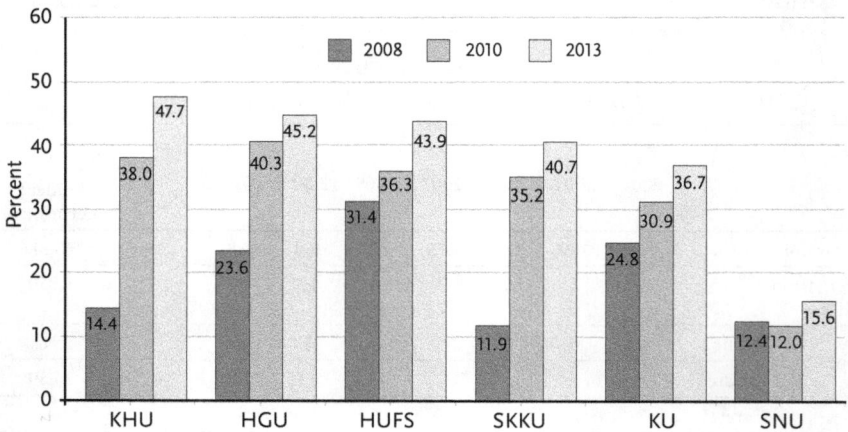

FIGURE 2.5 Ratio of English-exclusive lectures for classs in major subjects, select universities

Source: "Jung-Ang-Ilbo daehagpyeong-ga" [JoongAng Ilbo university rankings] (http://univ.joongang.co.kr).

Note: KHU= KyungHee University; HGU=Handong Global University; HUFS=Hankuk University of Foreign Studies; SKKU=Sungkyunkwan University; KU=Korea University; SNU=Seoul National University.

in English. Inha University's Asia Pacific School of Logistics launched in 2004; Sungkyunkwan University's Global Business Undergraduate Program in 2008, Global Economics department in 2009, and Global Leader department in 2012; and Sookmyung Women's University's School of Global Service in 2010 are different versions of the international college model, offering undergraduate courses in English and recruiting students with adequate foreign language proficiency. Such programs were created with the intention of promoting Korean students' global competencies as well as to provide learning platforms for international students who lack Korean language proficiency.

Major Subject Lectures in English

When evaluating a university's internationalization performance by international agencies such as Quacquarelli Symonds (QS) and *The Times*, typically the proportion of courses conducted in English is assessed along with the proportion of foreign students and foreign faculty members on campus. The Korean government has pushed universities to promote the international competencies and foreign language skills of Korean students and to attract foreign students to Korea as a desirable study destination.

As a result, the proportion of courses in English has increased in almost all universities since 2008. Figure 2.5 presents the recent trends in the proportion of English lectures at six exemplary universities that scored relatively high in the domestic *Joongang Daily* University Rankings in 2013. KyungHee University's English lecture ratio increased by approximately 33.3 percent between 2008 and 2013, while Sungkyunkwan University's increased by almost 28.8 percent during the same period. Conversely, Korea's top university, Seoul National University, had the lowest growth rate compared to other universities.

However, a number of previous studies have pointed out that a mere increase in the number of English-exclusive lectures has compromised the effectiveness of content delivery and thus the overall quality of such courses (Min 2013; Kim et al. 2013). In fact, some faculty members, especially in the fields of the humanities and social sciences, have resisted such efforts as a harmful product of neoliberalism.

Student Exchange Programs

With the ease of traveling and a widespread perception of the educational benefits of studying abroad, the number and types of student exchange programs have expanded impressively over the last decade.

Inbound Programs

Inbound exchange programs are mostly managed during academic semesters and designed as part of the formal academic curriculum. In most cases, "exchange" means a one-for-one exchange of students between partner universities. Depending on the partnership and agreement between the universities, the accepted foreign students attend the Korean institution for one semester or one academic year. If there happens to be only outbound students to the partner university and no inbound students, the exchange partnership may be suspended until at least one inbound student is recruited.

Visiting foreign students take courses based on the recommendation of the international office of the Korean (host) institution, and the grades and credits gained are transferred to their home universities. The basic understanding is that the credits are to be fully accepted by the home institutions. While most of the regular courses are open to exchange students, some courses are restricted to exchange students and others are especially designed to provide exchange students with an opportunity for greater interaction with Korean students. Yet, according to Shin (2011), the limited number of courses that are offered in English hinders foreign students from choosing Korean universities for exchange programs. Also, courses conducted in English tend to be at the introductory level. Even if students manage to take courses conducted in Korean, these might not be accredited in their home universities.

Given this situation, Korean universities have tried to attract more foreign students by providing more experiential learning opportunities through exchange programs, in conjunction with expanding the number of courses taught in English. As part of the curriculum, Korean language courses at different levels are offered. For example, Ewha Womans University, one of the more proactive universities in terms of running exchange student programs, offers Korean language courses at six different levels, from basic conversation to academic Korean, and free of charge for all exchange students.

Also, directed by their offices of international affairs, many universities organize international student festivals and international mini-Olympics where Korean and foreign students jointly participate and experience diverse cultures. In the same vein, mentorship programs or buddy programs pair Korean and exchange students together to assist in exchange students' adjustment to the cultural and educational environment at Korean universities. For example, the Korea University Buddy Assistants (KUBA) program at Korea University is well-known for its various activities and general satisfaction among participating students. Based on voluntary participation, the elected student committee organizes field trips, travel, cultural events on campus, etc.

Recently, Korean universities have become more competitive in their efforts to offer an "international summer school" or "international summer campus" as well. Normally, the duration period of such programs is about four to six weeks and represents an advanced form of exchange program that combines both academic study and experiential learning. A widespread selection of introductory courses is offered. Courses are taught by the faculty of the host institutions and also by specially invited professors from foreign universities.

To strengthen the competitiveness of the programs, several summer programs have recently begun to offer internship opportunities. Often the internship is structured within the program and the opportunities are provided by sponsoring companies. For example, in 2014, Yonsei University offered corporate internship placements in twenty-eight companies, including multinational corporations and government institutions, and research internship placements in twenty projects in different academic fields where students had the opportunity to work closely with professors. Students reported they were satisfied with these internships that enhanced their understanding about the field and work culture in Korea.

Overall, there have been increasing flows of foreign students into Korea and Korean universities through different types of study programs, often in competition with other local and foreign universities. The types of exchange programs mostly depend on the academic policies and capacities of individual universities. These inbound programs remain important to the future of the internationalization of Korean universities, given that the number of outbound domestic students far outweighs that of inbound international students.

Outbound Programs

As participation in international student exchange programs has become a common university experience worldwide, many Korean universities have established partnerships with foreign universities and have joined international education networks such as the International Student Exchange Program (ISEP), the Korean Association of Foreign Student Administrators (KAFSA), and the Asia-Pacific Association for International Education (APAIE). Through these networks, Korean students gain opportunities to attend partner universities for as long as one academic year. Basically, the study-abroad programs are designed to be academic oriented and the program characteristics are similar to those described in the previous section.

Aside from the formal exchange programs, individual universities also promote Korean students' participation in short-term exchange programs. Through joint research projects, students have the opportunity to take part in international conferences, seminars, symposia, and publication activities. However, these events tend to be irregularly organized. Depending on the capacity of individual universities, some offer consistent experiential learning opportunities for students. For example, the Global Leadership Development Center at Korea University runs an international internship program in partnership with the Washington Center (TWC) and Global

Society of Korea America (GSKA). These partner institutions are non-profit organizations that connect students to internships in diverse positions in both the public and private sectors. Sogang University, having established the German Research Center, offers internship opportunities at companies such as BMW, Siemens, Bosch, and Bayer in Germany. Similar programs are found at other universities as well, including provincial ones, with the aim of developing students' capacity for employment. In some cases, the internship results are approved for academic credits, depending on the characteristics of the internships and the internal policies of universities.

It is evident from these developments that individual universities and the Korean government are paying a great deal of attention to maximizing international exchange opportunities for students. Research-based universities have sought academic-oriented student exchange programs and joint research activities. In recent years, as higher education institutions have become more responsible for developing human resources possessing adequate skills and knowledge to join the world of work, there has been a continuous rise in the number and types of exchange programs oriented toward experiential learning.

Challenges in Collaborating with Foreign Universities

Although international exchange and collaboration with other universities have been emphasized, relatively little research has been devoted to identifying central obstacles or strategic guidelines to enable effective collaboration. In one of the few research projects of this kind, a study investigated the quality of joint and double degree programs between Korean and foreign universities at the request of the Ministry of Education, Science and Technology.

The study (Ha 2014) analyzed the challenges experienced by Korean universities. The results showed that, at the graduate level, securing the sustainability of the program was the most challenging issue in operating a joint degree program. Running a joint degree program was productive in increasing the research collaboration among professors of participating universities and strengthening the partnership. However, it did not affect the number of students applying to the program, whether Korean or international, despite the costs and effort necessary to facilitate the program. Next most challenging were administrative obstacles such as academic calendar differences, tuition fee structure agreements, and the securing of adequate funding and institutional support.

Conclusion

The higher education agenda in Korea, particularly over the past de-cade, has been characterized by a shifting emphasis on internationalization. Traditionally, the internationalization of higher education in Korea was perceived primarily as a possibility for domestic students to study abroad to earn an advanced degree from developed countries. However, with the Korean economy's dramatic progression over the past several decades, cou-pled with the forces of globalization, the internationalization of higher education is being newly interpreted in Korea. Education is perceived as a tradable commodity and, at the same time, an essential means of develop-ing human resources and enhancing national competitiveness. Accordingly, Korean universities have sought to internationalize their educational envi-ronments, attracting both domestic and foreign students.

Internationalization efforts are widespread in Korean universities, per-meating student activities, academic programs, and university services. Typical examples include student exchange programs, courses taught in English, joint degree programs, and foreign student recruitment. More re-cently, the internationalization of Korean higher education has entered a more advanced stage that goes beyond the aforementioned mobility of stu-dents and programs. The CAMPUS Asia program, a trilateral exchange pro-gram between students from China, Korea, and Japan, discussed in more detail in chapter 1, stands as an exemplary case of a systematic strategy to internationalize Korean higher education. It intends to strengthen higher education cooperation across Northeast Asia and build a stronger regional partnership among the participating countries. Also, the Incheon Global Campus is seeking ways to enhance effective collaboration between aca-demia and industry in an international context. These representative ex-amples are expected to contribute to the competitiveness of Korean higher education and the development of Korea into a regional educational hub.

However, there are critical issues to be considered in pursuing the inter-nationalization of higher education. The percentage of outbound Korean students, both degree-seeking and non-degree-seeking, shows no signs of decline. Accordingly, the possibilities of brain drain and the loss of human resources have been seen as a worrisome matter. As Shin and Choi show in chapter 5, Korea may need to rethink its current policy of brain circulation through study abroad. Also, in many respects, current internationalization endeavors still tend to emphasize quantity over quality. That is, they tend to target factors that are reflected in the internationalization index, such as increasing the "number" of partnerships with foreign universities, for-eign students and professors, and so on. However, the foremost issue to be addressed is the quality assurance of education and learning for both domestic and foreign students.

To ensure quality of education while facilitating internationalization, it is important for universities to reach a certain level of institutional autonomy. Currently, many universities depend on government policies and subsidies to promote internationalization. They lack concrete goals, mid- and long-term visions, clear strategies, and sufficient resources to continue internationalization efforts at the institutional level. It is hard to deny that a more effective orientation toward the internationalization of universities can be encouraged when governmental guidelines and support are provided. Yet the sustainability of these internationalization endeavors is ultimately determined by university autonomy. Otherwise, the exercises will last for only the short term affected by the government policy changes, and diversity in the internationalization efforts of each university will be lost. Eventually, this structure will result in a poor level of institutional quality, education, and student learning outcomes. Therefore, through improving university autonomy, the government and the universities should seek better ways to engage more effectively in the internationalization of higher education so that the achievements are represented by increasingly not the quantity but the quality of education.

As Kim, Cho, and Ko point out in the next chapter, while Korea's top-tier universities have made excellence a priority, the challenge for Korean universities will be to ensure quality across the entire higher education system.

References

Bang, Yonghwan. 2013. "Internationalization of Higher Education: A Case Study of Three Korean Private Universities." PhD diss., University of Southern California.

Byun, Kiyong, and Minjung Kim. 2011. "Shifting Patterns of the Government's Policies for the Internationalization of Korean Higher Education." *Journal of Studies in International Education* 15 (5): 467–86.

Gyeonggi Research Institute (GRI). 2011. *Gyeonggidoui oegugin yuhaksaeng yuchijeonlyak mit gwanlibangan yeongu: junggugin yuhaksaengeul jungsimeuro* [Chinese students in Korea and alternative agendas for improving the international students policy]. Suwon: GRI.

Ha, Yeonsub, Inwoo Park, Wonyong Lee, Yookyung Han, and Kahee Shin. 2014. *Guknaedaehakui oegukdaehakgwaui gyoyukgwajeong gongdongunyeong jil gwanri bangan maryeon* [The quality assurance of the joint degree programs of Korean and foreign universities]. Seoul: Ministry of Education.

Kim, Juhyun, Sujeong Nam, Dongkyu Shin, Mihyeon Lee, Hyeyeong Lim, Sinyeong Jeon, Yejie Cha, Mijie Choi, and Jiyeong Hong. 2009. *Hanguk eseo segye leul pumda: gugje daehagwone dojeonhala!* [GSIS confidential: The inside scoop on international studies]. Seoul, Korea: Edit-the-World.

Kim, Miran, Yeongran Hong, Eunyeong Kim, Byungsik Lee, and Nakyeong Yoon. 2013. *Hangug godeunggyoyug gugjehwa jeongchaeg jindan mit gaeseonbangan yeongu* [A study on the improvement of the Korean higher education internationalization policy]. Korean Education Development Institute (KEDI) RR 2013-12. Seoul: KEDI.

Korea Research Institute for Vocational Education and Training (KRIVET). 2005. *Oegugin yuhagsaeng yuchijeongchaegui jaegeomto: oegugin yuhagsaeng yuchihwagdaeleul wihan Study Korea peulojegteu jeongchaegeul jungsimeulo* [Reviewing the international students retention policy: based on the "Study Korea Project"]. Seoul: KRIVET.

Kwon, Yul. 2015. "The Recent Development of Korea's ODA Policy." *KIEP Opinions*, March 13. Seoul: Korea Institute for International Economics Policy.

Lee, Jungmi, Eunyeong Kim, Sohyeon Lim, Gilejae Lee, Dukho Jang, and Kyeonghee Han. 2013. *Daehagwon gyoyug unyeong siltae mit baljeonbangan yeongu* [A study on the condition of graduate education operation and improvement strategy]. RR 2013-11. Seoul: Korean Educational Development Institute.

Min, Guisik. 2013. "Jaehan jungguginyuhagsaeng hyeonhwanggwa hangugsaenghwal jeogeung mit galdeung" [Current status of Chinese students in Korea: Adaptation to Korean life and conflict]. *INChina Brief* 246, July 8. Incheon, Korea: Incheon Development Institute.

Ministry of Education, Science and Technology (MEST). 2011. "Daehaui oegugin yuhagsaeng yuchi kwanri yeokryang injeungje silsi Oegukin yuhagsaeng yuchi kwanri yeokryang wewonhoe baljok" [Implementation of the International Education Quality Assurance System (IEQAS). Inauguration of the International Education Quality Assurance Committee]. News release, August 12.

Ministry of Education. 2014. "Daehag kyoyug zil jego mit hakryung ingoo geubgam daebireul wehan daehak gujo gaehyeok chujin gyehyuk balpyo" [The higher education structural reform plan for quality of education and rapid decline of college student population]. News release, January 28.

National Institute for International Education (NIIED). 2014. *Oegugin yuhagsaeng yuchi mich jiwon hwagdaeleul wihan jeongchaegyeongu* [Expanding the maintenance and support of international students' policy research]. Seoul: NIIED.

Samsung Dream Scholarship Foundation. n.d. "Samsung Dream Scholarship Foundation." http://www.sdream.or.kr.

Shin, Gi-Wook. 2006. *Ethnic Nationalism in Korea*. Stanford, CA: Stanford University Press.

Shin, Tai Jin. 2011. *Hanguk daehakdeului haeoe haksulgyoryu hwalseonghwareul wihan gyohwanhaksaengjedoui munjejeom mit haengjeongjeok baljeonbangan* [The administrative tasks of student exchange program for activating overseas academic exchange in Korean universities]. *Korean Journal of Comparative Education* 21 (2): 155–85.

Science and Technology Policy Institute (STEPI). 2012. *Igonggye bunya oegukin seok mich baksa yuhaksaeng hyeonhwanggwa yuchibangan* [Research on ways to promote the recruitment of foreign graduate students of science and engineering]. Seoul: STEPI.

Van Der Meid, J. Scott. 2003. "Asian Americans: Factors Influencing the Decision to Study Abroad." *Frontiers: The Interdisciplinary Journal of Study Abroad* 9 (4): 71–110.

3 Building Research Capacity

FACULTY MOBILITY, INTERNATIONAL NETWORKS, AND
PERFORMANCE-BASED ASSESSMENT PRACTICES

Junki Kim, Hanah Cho, and Kilkon Ko

Globalization has stimulated not only student exchange, as laid out in by Kwon in chapter 2, but also the active exchange of knowledge and extensive global collaboration among scholars. Nevertheless, Korea's higher education competitiveness has been ranked around fortieth for the past five years (2009–13) out of all fifty-nine countries, according to an annual report on national competitiveness published by the International Institute for Management Development (IMD) (IMD World Competitiveness Center 2014, 12). This clearly shows that the competitiveness of Korean higher education lags behind its international counterparts.

Korea seems to be doing well in expanding the internationalization of higher education institutions (HEIs) by providing various scholarship opportunities and creating memoranda of understanding with foreign universities and research institutions. According to Ministry of Education statistics, the number of foreign scholars working in Korea has increased more than tenfold over the period 1994–2014. Nevertheless, this ballooning number is not without its pitfalls. The investments to date toward the internationalization of Korean HEIs have not been considered commensurate with the anticipated benefits (NIIED 2014). The Korean government, HEIs, and industries have invested large sums of money in recruiting talented foreign scholars, expecting greater or at least equivalent returns. However, since Korean HEIs do not conduct follow-up evaluations, it is difficult to gauge the effectiveness of such policies. In order to accomplish effective and meaningful internationalization, it will be necessary for Korean HEIs to reexamine the complex realities of internationalization and consider better alternatives to ensure a more informed or "intelligent internationalization" (Rumbley 2015).

Operating on the premise that the quality of HEIs is largely tied to the research capacity of their scholars, the Korean government has sought through various internationalization policies to attract talented foreign scholars, but with limited success. While foreign scholars have expanded in number, a corresponding improvement in quality in Korean HEIs has been doubted by many. The reason is the scope of Korea's internationalization policies has been limited to simply attracting a greater number of foreign faculty and researchers, rather than more importantly figuring out what to do with these potentially highly qualified human resources once they arrive in the country.

In this chapter we first describe the past and current efforts of Korean HEIs to attract foreign scholars. Next, we examine the internationalization of HEIs in relation to research capacity and networks. Finally, we conclude with some policy suggestions regarding how strong and effective research networks can nurture the internationalization of Korean HEIs.

Foreign Scholars in Korea

The number of foreign faculty members has increased steadily from 1994 as a result of the globalization policies of the Kim Young-sam administration (1993–97).

As shown in table 3.1, in 1994, full-time foreign faculty accounted for only 0.8 percent of the total full-time faculty (54,135) in Korea's HEIs. However, between 1994 and 2014 that number increased by almost fifteen-fold to 6,130. Moreover, the proportion of foreign faculty also jumped to 7.1 percent in 2013, surpassing Japan's 5 percent, despite that country's longer history of foreign faculty recruitment (McNeill 2011).

The increase in the number of foreign faculty slowed during the global financial crisis in 1997 (see figure 3.1). However, the rate started to speed up again in the early 2000s when the government proposed new policy initiatives to attract foreign faculty and strengthen research capacity, including the Brain Korea 21 (BK21) Project (1999–2012), the World Class University (WCU) project (2008–13), and the recently launched BK 21 Plus Project (2013–19).

Following Lee Myung-bak's 2008 inauguration, the recruitment of internationally renowned scholars and foreign professors was especially brought to the fore of government initiatives in order to reverse Korea's brain drain and foster internationally leading universities (Byun and Kim 2011). This initiative was carried out through the WCU project from 2008 to 2013. This project aimed to strengthen research capacity in key growth-generating fields and develop next-generation human resources by inviting internationally renowned scholars and researchers. The total budget of US$800 million

TABLE 3.1
Foreign faculty in Korea, 1994–2014

	1994	2000	2010	2011	2012	2013	2014
Number of foreign faculty	418	1,313	4,957	5,462	5,964	6,130	6,034
Number of total faculty	54,135	56,903	77,697	82,190	84,910	86,656	88,163
Percentage	0.8	2.3	6.4	6.6	7.0	7.1	6.8

Source: Korean Educational Statistics Service (KEDI) (http://kess.kedi.re.kr/index).

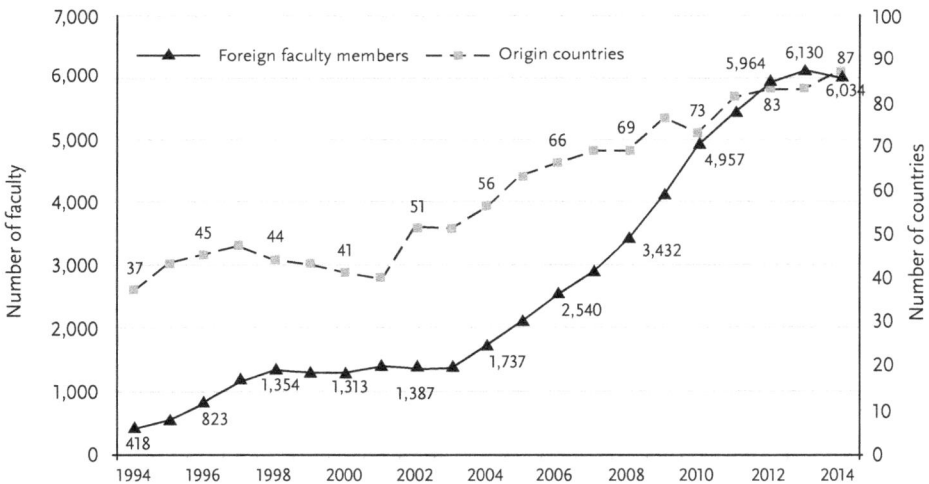

FIGURE 3.1   Foreign faculty members in Korea, 1994–2014
Source: Korean Educational Statistics Service (http://kess.kedi.re.kr/eng).

was allocated evenly between the humanities and social sciences, natural science, engineering, and other interdisciplinary areas. As detailed in table 3.2, the WCU project used a three-pronged strategy to achieve its aims: establish departments, recruit individual scholars, and invite world-class scholars.

As with students, the countries of origin of full-time faculty members also diversified. Before 2000, foreign faculty members originated from around forty different countries, but by 2014 this number had reached eighty-seven (see table 3.3). Most of these foreign faculty members came from the United States (42.8 percent), followed by Canada (14.3 percent) and China (8.8 percent).

TABLE 3.2

Status of WCU project operations, 2011

Strategy type	Description	Participating universities	Projects	Foreign faculty	Budget allocation (USD)
Type 1	Establish new departments through collaboration between recruited foreign and Korean faculty.	19	34	206	$1.07 billion
Type 2	Recruit foreign scholars to existing departments or research institutes to deliver lectures and conduct joint research.	18	44	72	$358 million
Type 3	Invite world-renowned scholars to deliver lectures and conduct joint research.	26	62	64	$121 million
Total		33	140	342	$1.55 billion

Sources: Kwon (2011); Cho (2014).

TABLE 3.3

Foreign faculty members by country, 1995–2014

	1995	2000	2005	2010	2014
Countries	43	41	63	73	87
Foreign faculty members (percent)	537 (100.0)	1,313 (100.0)	2,131 (100.0)	4,957 (100.0)	6,034 (100.0)
United States	294 (54.7)	597 (45.5)	848 (39.8)	2,052 (41.4)	2,585 (42.8)
Canada	21 (3.9)	233 (17.7)	405 (19.0)	834 (16.8)	864 (14.3)
China	22 (4.1)	87 (6.6)	173 (8.1)	448 (9.0)	533 (8.8)
Japan	57 (10.6)	161 (12.3)	243 (11.4)	381 (7.7)	375 (6.2)
United Kingdom	4 (0.7)	26 (2.0)	62 (2.9)	243 (4.9)	331 (5.5)
India	2 (0.4)	2 (0.2)	16 (0.8)	112 (2.3)	166 (2.8)
Others	137 (25.5)	207 (15.8)	384 (18.0)	887 (17.9)	1,180 (19.6)

Source: Korean Educational Statistics Service (http://kess.kedi.re.kr/eng).

Science Card as a Support System

Science Card is a distinctive visa issuance and residential permit system implemented to attract talented foreign scholars to Korean universities, particularly those in the fields of science and technology. As it is designed to be granted to those who intend to work in HEIs, prospective recipients must hold a master's degree with at least three years of work experience in R&D or a doctoral degree in a relevant field. The duration of the issued visa is five years and an unlimited number of entries and exits is allowed. Introduced in 2001, the Science Card was granted to only one person in that year. According to the official website (www.scard.go.kr) it was issued to more than a hundred people in each of the following years, and peaked in 2009 with 295 people receiving a Science Card. Since then, the number of visas issued has gradually decreased; ninety-nine were granted in 2012 and thirty-four in 2014.

Challenges in Attracting Foreign Scholars

The high cost of recruiting foreign researchers often stifles Korean universities from hiring them. On average, it costs about $71,000 per year to hire a foreign scholar, nearly twice the amount of hiring a Korean professor at a public university (McNeil 2011). Yet for foreign faculty coming from North America and Europe, that amounts to only about 60–70 percent of the average salary they would expect to receive in their home countries (NRF 2007). Providing additional financial support for foreign faculty in terms of living expenses, housing and moving, and children's education is a burden for Korean universities, except for a few top private institutions. This cost problem means it is not easy to motivate talented faculty to come to Korea unless they are relatively novice and single, or retired researchers. The situation is worse for universities in provincial regions. On top of the financial burden, many universities located outside of Seoul find it difficult to recruit foreign faculty due to their relatively small size and remote location.

Kim (2013) reported the results of a collaborative research project by the Ministry of Science, ICT and Future Planning (MSIP) and SRI International on the experiences of 459 foreign researchers in Korea. The results revealed that the most challenging factor in working and living in Korea was a primarily sociocultural matter. In particular, approximately 65 percent of the respondents reported language as a major concern. Accessibility to cultural facilities, social networks, medical services, and children's education also emerged as top challenging issues.

In addition, the respondents reported scarce opportunities for professional self-development in the relevant academic field and the restricted amount of research funding as unsatisfactory factors in working at Korean universities. Without sufficient financial and administrative support from universities, research production is stifled. Many universities tend not to release statistics on how long foreign faculty remain at their institutions, but in 2010 the Ministry of Education reported that foreign faculty stay about four months on average. This can be disappointing considering the financial expenses and effort invested in recruiting them. Recruiting full-time talented foreign faculty and retaining them in Korea will continue to be a challenge for Korean universities.

Research Performance of Korean Universities

We will refer to various types of data, mainly statistical resources from the Ministry of Education and Scopus, a large database for peer-reviewed literature and journals, to assess the research performance of Korean universities. We use Scopus co-citation analysis on the published articles to assess institutional strengths and demonstrate Korean HEI competencies within a global scientific landscape among different disciplines and competitors. Institutional research capabilities analysis uses the subject area performance based on the number of articles and citations, percentage of articles for each subject area, and multi-disciplinary research performance. The individual and team performance of each institution is measured by assessing the individual performance by the number of articles and citations, identifying the best performing researchers, and gathering data at an individual and institutional level. Institutional research capability analysis includes the subject area performance measured by the number of articles and citations, percentage of articles in each subject area, and multi-discipline research performance. The measure of individual and team performance is indicated by, first, individual performance by the number of articles and citations and, second, by identifying the best performing researchers and institutions and, third, by coworker data at an individual and an institutional level.

One of the aims of the internationalization of higher education in Korea is preventing "brain drain" and creating a global knowledge network (Byun and Kim 2011). With globalization, a significant degree of networking and collaboration become possible among universities and between universities and other sectors (Lewis, Marginson, and Snyder 2005). Knight (1997, 7) defines the competency approach to internationalization as putting emphasis on "the human element of the academic community—the students, faculty, and technical/administrative/support staff." Knight also states that greater collaboration among institutions in the academic as well as the private sector is necessary for students to perform well in the growing international economy. The key concept is integration. Integration must ensure "mutually beneficial relationships" (Knight 1997). Research and scholarly collaboration takes place through joint research projects, international conferences and seminars, exchange programs, and international research partnerships across sectors (Knight 1997).

This growing emphasis on research collaboration also indicates the need for constructing stronger networks within and outside the country. Table 3.4 below shows performance indicators by country. Academically advanced countries like the United States, Germany, and the UK have a higher percentage of international collaboration on average, with Germany and the UK having over 45 percent of their work done with scholars outside their respective countries.

International collaboration among countries has increased steadily. According to the SciVal benchmarking data presented in figure 3.2, international scholarly collaboration in the United States, Korea, Japan, and China reached 33.2 percent, 27.4 percent, 26.6 percent, and 18.3 percent, respectively, by December 2014. This trend of increasing international collaboration again emphasizes the need for creating a stable and strong research network in Korea, thereby ensuring that the quality of collaborative work among international scholars improves. It is necessary for Korean universities to utilize available resources in order to expand their scholarly network worldwide.

The quality of research publications in advanced countries is also improving. As seen in figure 3.3, in 2010 Korea published more than 16 percent

TABLE 3.4
Performance indicators by countries, 2010–14 (percent)

	International collaboration	Academic-corporate collaboration	Output in top percentiles	Publications in top journal percentiles
Korea	26.2	3.0	14.2	18.8
Japan	24.4	2.9	13.1	14.5
United States	29.5	2.8	20.0	26.9
Germany	45.7	3.1	20.5	21.5
United Kingdom	45.3	2.5	20.3	26.1
China	16.2	1.0	10.6	11.8

Source: SciVal (www.scival.com/overview).

Notes: "International collaboration" indexes publications coauthored with institutions in other countries; "academic-corporate collaboration" indexes publications with both academic and corporate affiliations; "output in top percentiles" measures publications in the top 10 percent most cited worldwide; and "publications in top journal percentiles" measures publications in the top 10 percent of journals by source normalized impact per paper (SNIP).

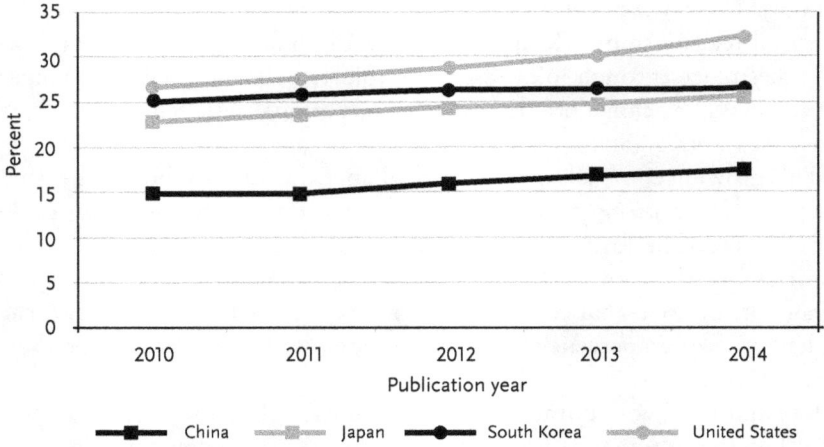

FIGURE 3.2 International academic collaboration in the United States, Korea, Japan, and China, 2010–14

Source: SciVal Benchmarking (http://www.scival.com).

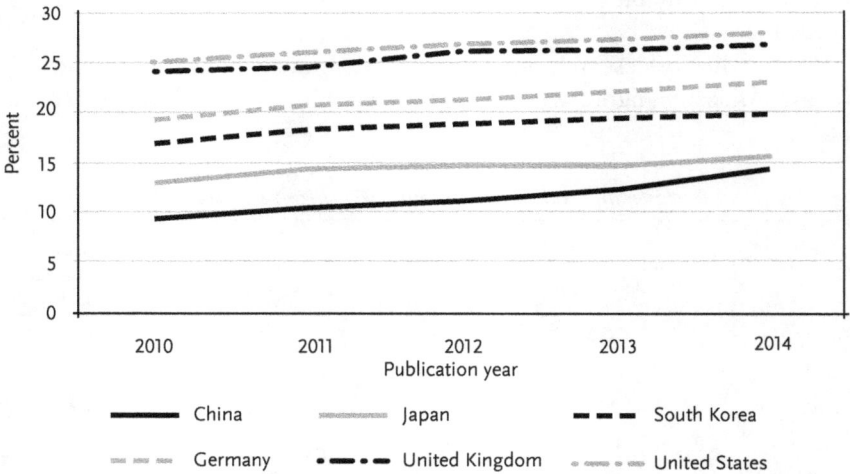

FIGURE 3.3 Publications in the top ten journals by select countries, 2010–14

Source: SciVal Benchmarking.

of its papers in the top ten journals, which is greater than that of Japan and China but falls behind the United States, the UK, and Germany. The percentage has been increasing every year, creating more opportunities for potential collaboration with other nations.

Collaboration impact indicates the average number of citations received by publications that have international and national coauthorship. Korea shows a higher international collaboration impact compared to Japan and China, but it is still lower than that of the United States, the United Kingdom, and Germany (see table 3.5). On the other hand, Korea's national collaboration impact is considerably lower than that of the other countries, suggesting that international collaboration has been more effective than national collaboration. The same holds true for the other nations as well—countries tend to generate more influential papers when they work with scholars in other countries. This again supports the importance of maintaining and improving the research networks that lead to a quality-focused internationalization of HEIs.

Overall, the current state of the internationalization of Korean HEIs shows that there is a growing emphasis on creating effective research collaboration among talented international scholars. Attracting capable foreign scholars and producing quality research collaboration can be initiated from networks associated with Korean HEIs. The internationalization of HEI policies, therefore, must consider strategies to build strong international networks within and outside the country.

Internationalization Strategies: Creating, Maintaining, and Expanding Effective International Higher Education Networks

Creating Networks by Attracting Talented International Human Resources with Customized Study Abroad Opportunities

In order to persuade international scholars to consider Korea as their optimal research location, it is essential that they be able to pursue their research interests in Korea. According to the data assessed by SciVal, the number of publications for Korea increased to 335,317 by December 2014 and the field-weighted citation impact reached 1.04, slightly greater than that of Japan (.96) and lower than that of the United States (1.44). As the numbers show, Korea possesses high potential and strong research competency; in particular, Korea demonstrates superior academic strengths in medicine, engineering, and materials science.

But despite these being Korea's top academic strengths, the majority of

TABLE 3.5

Collaboration impact of select countries, 2012

	International	National
Korea	7.4	4.0
Japan	6.8	4.1
United States	8.0	6.7
United Kingdom	8.4	5.8
Germany	8.2	5.6
China	6.6	3.4

Source: SciVal Benchmarking (http://www.scival.com).

TABLE 3.6

International students by region and study interest, 2013

Region	Lang. course	Lang. arts and social sci.	Eng.	Natural sciences	Art, music, phys ed.	Med.	Others	Total
Asia	15,414	34,816	8,487	4,032	3,672	490	8,377	75,288
Africa	294	768	328	103	8	8	58	1,567
Oceania	65	159	19	15	13	11	57	339
North America	588	1,670	156	301	144	180	949	3,988
South America	242	297	104	21	27	1	294	968
Europe	895	669	125	48	53	8	1,976	3,773
Total	17,498	38,361	9,219	4,520	3,917	698	11,710	85,923

Source: Ministry of Education, "2014 nyeondo gugnae oegug-in yuhagsaeng tong-gye" [2014 statistics of foreign students in Korea], www.moe.go.kr/web/100088/ko/board/download.do?boardSeq=124846.

Note: "Lang. course"= language courses; "Lang. arts and social sci."=language arts and social sciences; "Eng."=engineering; "Med."=medicine.

Korea's international students pursues study in the language arts and the social sciences, whereas the number of students in medicine and engineering is quite small, as seen in table 3.6. Approximately 65 percent of international students study Korean language and social sciences, compared to 11 percent who study engineering and 0.8 percent who study medicine.

This disparity between Korea's academic strengths and the subjects that foreign students want to study there highlights the need for more targeted internationalization policies. Korean HEIs must pursue a vigorous and more focused marketing strategy in medicine, engineering, and information technology, and attract larger numbers of young scholars. On the other hand, considering the high popularity of studying the Korean language, universities must refine their existing language classes by increasing the number of small-size classes and improving the quality of Korean language teaching. Understanding the different purposes of foreign students who want to study in Korea and reflecting their interests in internationalization policies will create effective higher education networks.

Initiate Networks by Expanding Government-University-Industry Collaborations

Another strategy to promote the internationalization of HEIs is to initiate international higher education networks through collaborative efforts between the government, university, and industry. Knowledge production is becoming a "hybrid network," with increasing collaboration and communication between the government-university-industry "triple Helix" (Heimeriks, Horlesberger, and Van den Besselaar 2003). Emphasizing collaboration between government, industry, and university is not something new in Korea. Creating research networks between government-university-industry for the internationalization of HEIs is evident in the Global Hub College (GHC) business run by the Ministry of Education. GHC supports Korean industries in foreign countries by providing university-level job education for the foreign students working for those companies (Ministry of Education, Science and Technology 2011). US$3 million is annually invested in the GHC program, and the government provides incentives to the top three institutions.

Maintaining Networks by Preserving Relationships with Talented Scholars

Consistent communication and collaborative research efforts lie at the heart of international higher education networks (NIIED 2014). Once admitted to Korean HEIs, international students and faculty undergo tremendous difficulties adjusting to life in Korea. In order to maintain networks with international researchers even after they leave Korea, it is important to build positive relationships. The most effective way to retain highly educated international scholars is to provide jobs in Korea. However, applying for a job in Korea is extremely difficult for international researchers and the employment rate of international students in Korea has been extremely low. Approximately ten thousand foreign students graduate from the Korean HEIs every year, but less than one hundred of them get a job in Korea, according to a report from the Ministry of Education's National Institute for International Education in 2014. In 2009, from the data for forty-five universities in Korea, on average 21.2 foreign students graduated, but only 1.1 received a job in Korea (NIIED 2014). Additionally, according to a survey conducted by the Science and Technology Policy Institute (STEPI) in 2012, of 1,003 Korean companies, only 11.8 percent employed foreign students and only 10.4 percent responded positively about hiring more international students in the future.

There are several reasons why foreign student employment rate is low in Korea. From a STEPI survey on the reasons for not hiring international students, 29.2 percent of Korean companies responded that they were doubtful of the necessity of employing foreign workers. The second-most-important reason concerned the difficulty of managing foreign employees (16.6 percent) and the third was the language barrier (16.3 percent), followed by lack of expertise (12.4 percent) and wage burdens (11.9 percent) (STEPI 2012). According to a survey of Korean companies, of international students who had studied in Korea for more than two years, 50 percent of those hired by Korean companies resigned before their performance could be evaluated (NIIED 2014). There is a widespread perception that international workers are inferior to native Korean employees in marketing and general work-related areas, and due to cultural differences, Korean employers feel that foreign workers tend to avoid difficult work (NIIED 2014). Moreover, foreign workers think they deserve wages equal to other employees in Korea, whereas in reality there is a substantial difference between the wages of Korean and international employees. Moreover, Korean companies often dispatch foreign workers to their native countries. This results in serious complaints because the workers' wages also decrease according to the average wage of that country.

The Foreign Human Resources Management System (FHRMS), run by NIIED, is one of the current job search programs for international students. The FHRMS provides a database of foreign students and scholars studying in Korea, including their nationalities, majors, ages, affiliations, and final education status. International students can upload their résumés and statuses to the website, and companies can search for appropriate international students and even receive recommendations about promising candidates. Currently, there are 1,082 foreign students in universities looking for jobs, 206 researchers in research institutes, 268 foreigners in industries, and 137 in other areas (NIIED 2015). Foreign scholars can use the FHRMS to learn about work opportunities and apply for jobs in Korea and universities, HEIS, and companies can reach out to available foreign students and researchers.

Besides having difficulties finding jobs, the most popular complaint from international students studying in Korea is the lack of Korean classes in schools (NIIED 2014; KRIVET 2005). Although universities open classes in English for foreign students, in order to get a job and stay in Korea for several years, foreign students require basic language skills. However, there are a limited number of Korean classes open to international students in a semester, and students find it difficult to schedule other classes to fit around their Korean language class (KRIVET 2005). Moreover, constant performance evaluation is also necessary regarding whether students regularly attend classes and whether they have satisfied all the conditions they agreed to before coming to Korea, in order to check their status while in Korea. Networks of international students and scholars can be maintained only if HEIs track their performance and willingly provide counseling upon request.

Furthermore, universities personnel in charge of international students are inadequate, and faculty and international students are dissatisfied with the quality of school programs (NIIED 2014; GRI 2011). Aside from administrative support, international students and faculty need people who can give advice on everyday problems. However, after admitting international students, institutions seem ignorant of their daily struggles.

It is difficult for foreign students and researchers to study in an unfamiliar country. Even if the government, universities, and industries succeed in creating large international higher education networks, they will perish if not maintained. Therefore, to prevent highly educated international scholars from leaving Korea and becoming disconnected, the government as well as HEIs and industries must cooperate to help them find stable jobs and secure wages and must provide a harmonious work environment for both international and Korean workers.

Expanding Networks by Reaching out for Potential Collaboration

Conducting follow-up evaluations is pivotal to expanding international higher education networks. Foreign students' confidence in the government-sponsored study abroad program in Korea has increased as students who have received scholarships have returned to their native countries and become policymakers there (NIIED 2014). While creating and maintaining international higher education networks is essential, at the same time, we must consistently and aggressively expand these networks by connecting those who have studied in Korea with existing as well as potential study abroad students and researchers in other regions. The international students and researchers who have experience studying in Korea are valuable resources for expanding research networks as they can create links between scholars in their native countries and Korean scholars. In fact, it was found that study-abroad alumni act as very effective magnets back at their home institutions (KRIVET 2005). Currently, the Korean government does not keep track of the specific destinations of international researchers once their study in Korea is over, because it is extremely difficult and almost impossible to follow their employment status upon graduation (NIIED 2014). Altbach and Knight (2007) pointed out the necessity of evaluating the quality and validity of internationalization programs but wondered whose responsibility it would be to evaluate network arrangements. Evaluation of international students is a complex process, especially when multiple stakeholders are involved, such as the government, university, industry, and students themselves. Nevertheless, there must be a generally agreed-upon form of evaluation to estimate the effects of the international researchers on Korean HEIs and to keep track of their progress while in Korea. Most of the time, the government as well as the HEIs are passive about reaching out to their alumni, sending administrative emails without expecting any reply (NIIED 2014). Despite the difficulties involved in collecting information about alumni, the government must encourage HEIs to conduct follow-up evaluations, as this is critical to expanding international HEI networks. Providing the work experiences of alumni and former researchers will broaden job opportunities for current international students as well as attract potential study abroad students and researchers.

Another effective way to expand international higher education networks is to create academic and research memoranda with other institutions. Aside from government-led efforts to develop collaboration between Korean and foreign universities, individual universities try to intensify their research capacity by establishing research networks with universities in other countries. For example, Universitas 21 is an international network of twenty-one leading research-intensive universities in thirteen countries. The goal of this network is to promote collaboration and cooperation between the member institutions on an advanced scale that is qualitatively different from traditional bilateral alliances.

To sum up, Korean HEIs must conduct rigorous follow-up evaluations and expand relationships with international students and researchers. Although it is difficult to keep track of international students, the government and HEIs should take a more active stance in maintaining relationships with their alumni and using them to attract potential study-abroad students and researchers and expand international higher education networks. Ultimately, after admitting international scholars, institutions must constantly interact with them, keep track of their performance, and create more collaborative research opportunities with them.

The Future of the Internationalization of Korean HEIs

As Korea strives to continue to develop a highly educated workforce despite its aging population, to promote national competency, and build collaborative relationships in the international community, the internationalization of HEIs is of great interest to the country. This chapter has approached the development of the internationalization of Korean HEIs from the network perspective. Quality improvement of the internationalization of HEIs can be achieved by creating, maintaining, and expanding international higher education networks between international scholars and between the government, industries, and universities. Creating networks is the first step of internationalization, mainly by attracting international researchers to Korea. This can be accomplished through customized internationalization policies that reflect scholars' research interests and active promotion of Korea's academic strengths such as engineering, medicine, and information technology. In addition, various scholarships and collaboration opportunities between the government, universities, and industries to support international scholars studying in Korea can also create effective international higher education networks. Nevertheless, the internationalization of higher education must not be restricted to creating a large international network. Greater emphasis must be placed on maintaining and expanding existing networks in order to achieve the effective internationalization of HEIs in Korea. To maintain international higher education networks, the government, universities, and industries should continuously interact with international scholars during their stay in Korea and also help them to find jobs upon graduation or near the end of their contracts. To expand international networks, HEIs must conduct thoroughly organized follow-up evaluations to assess the performance of researchers while they are in Korea and their impact on the development of Korean HEIs.

The ultimate aim of the internationalization of HEIs in Korea is to enrich the available human resources and nurture collaborative academic networks around the world. Therefore, Korean higher education institutions should shift from quantity-oriented internationalization strategies to more quality-oriented approaches. To that end, Korean HEIs should strive to build stronger research networks with foreign scholars and their institutions and promote quality research collaboration so as to transform Korea into a prosperous research hub.

References

Altbach, Philip G., and Jane Knight. 2007. "The Internationalization of Higher Education: Motivations and Realities." *Journal of Studies in International Education* 11 (3–4): 290–305. doi:10.1177/1028315307303542.

Byun, Kiyong, and Minjung Kim. 2011. "Shifting Patterns of the Government's Policies for the Internationalization of Korean Higher Education." *Journal of Studies in International Education* 15 (5): 467–86. doi:10.1177/1028315310375307.

Cho, W. H. 2014. "A Study on the Evaluation of the World Class University Program Selection." Phd diss., Chungnam National University. In Korean.

Gyeonggi Research Institute (GRI) 2011. 국내 중국인유학생 실태와 유학생 정책 개선방안 [Chinese students in Korea and alternative agendas for improving the international students policy].

Heimeriks, Gaston, Marianne Horlesberger, and Peter Van den Besselaar. 2003. "Mapping Communication and Collaboration in Heterogeneous Research Networks." *Scientometrics* 58 (2): 391–413.

Institute for Management Development (IMD) World Competitiveness Center. 2014. *IMD World Talent Report*. Lausanne, Switzerland: IMD.

Kim, J. Y. 2013. "A Study on Policy for Attracting and Utilizing Overseas Talents." Korea Institute of Science & Technology Evaluation and Planning. In Korean.

Knight, Jane. 1997. "Internationalisation of Higher Education; A Conceptual Framework." In *Internationalisation of Higher Education in Asia Pacific Countries*, edited by Jane Knight and Hans de Wit. Amsterdam, the Netherlands: European Association for International Education, in cooperation with IDP Education Australia and the Programme on Institutional Management in Higher Education of the Organisation for Economic Cooperation and Development.

Korea Research Institute for Vocational Education and Training (KRIVET). 2005. 외국인 유학생 유치정책의 재검토 – 외국인 유학생 유치확대를 위한 "Study Korea 프로젝트" 정책을 중심으로 [*Reviewing the international students retention policy: based on the "Study Korea" project*].

Kwon, K. S. 2011. *Performance and Emerging Issues of WCU Project*. Korean Education Development Institute. In Korean.

Lewis, Tanya, Simon Marginson, and Ilana Snyder. 2005. "The Network University? Technology, Culture and Organisational Complexity in Contemporary Higher Education." *Higher Education Quarterly* 59 (1): 56–75. doi:10.1111/j.1468-2273.2005.00281.

McNeil, David. 2011. "South Korea Brings in Foreign Professors by the

Thousands, but Is It Ready for Them?" *The Chronicle of Higher Education*, February 27. http://chronicle.com/article/South-Korea-Brings-in-Foreign/126508/.

Ministry of Education, Science and Technology. 2011. "2011년 해외산업체 연계 외국인 유학생 교육선도 전문대학 육성사업 기본계획" [Basic plan for promoting a specialized college for foreign students approved by industries abroad].

National Institute for International Education (NIIED). 2014. "외국인 유학생 유치·지원을 위한 정책연구" [Expanding the maintenance and support of international students policy research].

———. 2015. "Foreign Human Resources System." http://www.hurik.go.kr/hurik/Statistics/SC34.jsp. Accessed February 3, 2015.

National Research Foundation of Korea (NRF). 2007. "Enhancement of Research Competitiveness and International Network through Invitation of Talented Foreign Faculty." In Korean. Unpublished internal document.

Science and Technology Policy Institute (STEPI). 2012. 이공계 분야 외국인 석박사 유학생 현황과 유치방안 [Research on ways to promote the recruitment of foreign graduate students of science and engineering].

Rumbley, Laura E. 2015. "'Intelligent Internationalization': A 21st Century Imperative." *International Higher Education* (80): 16–17.

4 Korean Higher Education

INTERNATIONALIZATION, BUT NOT DIVERSITY

Rennie J. Moon and Gi-Wook Shin

In this chapter, we discuss a paradox of internationalization in Korean higher education. That is, we ask why, despite the official emphasis on internationalization and recruiting foreigners, culturally the internal sociology of South Korean universities remains highly local in practice in terms of embracing diversity. We show that there is a noticeable gap between efforts to recruit foreign students and efforts to implement inclusive practices as reflected in university curricula and in the intercultural relations between local and foreign students. Based on our findings, we argue that fostering a culture of respect for diversity should be a major aspect of higher education internationalization in Korea. In particular, we discuss how recently adopted discourses of inclusion in Western countries can serve as appropriate and fruitful policy discourses for a Korean higher education system that seeks to internationalize (and, more broadly, for Korean society). We conclude by recommending basic reforms for promoting inclusive practices in Korean universities.

Internationalization of Higher Education and Diversity

The growing movement of student and faculty across societies naturally creates more culturally diverse campuses, often cited as a desirable result of and a key motive for pursuing internationalization, particularly in Western countries. In the United States and Europe, such changes have in turn led to significant discursive and programmatic efforts to create a culture of respect for diversity and inclusion, although with much intraregional and internal variation in situations and strategies. Over the past few decades, for example, the European policy rhetoric, despite its critics, has consistently articulated the value of "interculturality," "diversity," and respect for cultural differences as a broader discourse for European higher education (Ramos 2014; Lähdesmaki and Wagener 2015). Some well-known examples are the statement on the Contribution of Higher Education to Intercultural Dialogue (Bergan and van't Land 2010), the White Paper on Intercultural Dialogue (Council of Europe 2008), and the declaration of the European Year of Intercultural Dialogue in 2008. In the United States, diversity as a major discourse emerged initially as a reaction to a narrow concern with maintaining affirmative action in university admissions, focusing on increasing numbers and admitting more racial minorities. Over time, however, universities broadened their focus from what scholars have conceptualized as "structural diversity" or numerical representation of students, to behavioral and organizational concerns of "educational diversity," "interactional diversity," and fostering "an inclusive campus climate" (Jayakumar 2008; Clarke and Antonio 2012). The United States as an immigrant country has a much longer history/tradition in intercultural studies than Europe (Wachter 2003) and thus implementation at the organizational and individual levels is seen as more advanced in the United States (de Wit 2011). For instance, most American universities today have an office that manages diversity issues on campus (Gose 2006). Foreign students account for as much as a third of the student body of some American universities,[1] sometimes even outnumbering the total number of traditionally underrepresented domestic minority students.[2] This dramatic growth in foreign students at American universities, especially over the past decade (a 70 percent increase since 2003) (Institute of International Education 2015), has sometimes resulted in rising tensions between foreign and local students. For American universities with traditionally low numbers of minority students, such challenges are relatively new and similar to those facing Asian universities. Yet despite the problems, American universities valorize diversity and due to efforts, improvements are being made at some universities.[3]

However, in contrast to this institutional affirmation of diversity in

[1] "Most International Students, National Universities," *US News & World Report*, http://colleges.usnews.rankingsandreviews.com/best-colleges/rankings/national-universities/most-international/page+3.

[2] For example, at the University of Iowa the number of Chinese students outnumbers the combined African-American and Latino student populations. See "Culture Clash in Iowa: The Town Where Bubble Tea Shops Outnumber Starbucks," *CNN*, http://edition.cnn.com/interactive/2015/07/us/culture-clash-american-story/.

[3] See "Culture Clash in Iowa: The Town Where Bubble Tea Shops Outnumber Starbucks," *CNN*, http://edition.cnn.com/interactive/2015/07/us/culture-clash-american-story/.

higher education in Western countries, this is not the case in Korea and most other Asian nations. One major reason is that Asian countries primarily attract foreign students as a means to particular ends, such as enhancing university prestige, creating "education hubs," filling gaps in declining college student populations, and improving international higher education rankings (Cheng, Cheung, and Yeun 2011). Many Asian universities maintain lower standards of admission for foreign students than for local students in an effort to raise their international rankings by means of the key performance indicator of expanded foreign student enrollment (Palmer and Cho 2012). This instrumental logic also applies to the major internationalization reforms in Asian countries in past decades, such as expanding English-medium courses and establishing exchange programs with foreign universities. As a result, we see that Asian universities actively promote "structural diversity," but unlike their U.S. and European counterparts, are much less preoccupied with the more substantive educational and organizational-related concerns that accompany greater diversity, as exemplified by recent clashes between foreigners and their host country institutions in Singapore[4] (Lewis 2014), China,[5] and South Korea (Kim 2005) because of differences in political views, identities, and notions of academic freedom. Unfortunately, for many universities across Asia, considering the intrinsic educational value of a culturally diverse student and faculty body or addressing problems with divisive campus climates is an afterthought at best.

Korean Higher Education: Internationalization, but not Diversity?

South Korea, too, follows this general pattern. It has rapidly and aggressively internationalized its higher education system with a particular focus on three areas: increasing courses taught in English, promoting exchange programs with foreign (both Western and non-Western) universities, and attracting foreign students and faculty. Study Korea, a project begun in 2004, for instance, aimed to attract one hundred thousand foreign students by 2012. In 2006, the government launched the Strategy for the Internationalization of Higher Education, which eased regulations for running dual- or joint-degree programs and exchange programs between Korean and foreign universities. Brain Korea 21, aimed to develop ten

4 John Morgan, "Singapore-style Academic Freedom," *Inside Higher Ed*, http://bit.ly/1SZxtou.

5 Isaac Stone Fish, "No Academic Freedom for China," *The Daily Beast*, November 22, 2011, http://www.thedailybeast.com/articles/2011/11/21/no-academic-freedom-for-china.html.

world-class research-oriented universities by 2012, sought to place Korea in the world's top ten countries in terms of the number of research articles published in international journals indexed by the Science Citation Index (sci). World Class Universities (wcu), a project launched in 2008, invited large numbers of prominent foreign scholars to conduct collaborative research with Korean faculty in key growth-generating science, technology, engineering, and mathematics (stem) fields (e.g., nanotechnology, interdisciplinary studies), investing roughly US$740 million in the project over five years. As a result of these efforts, the number of foreign students in Korean universities reached 84,891 in 2014 and the number of foreign faculty has increased steadily over the last two decades from just 418 (or 0.8 percent of total faculty) in 1994 to 6,034 (or 6.8 percent of total faculty) in 2014 (Korean Educational Statistics Service 2015). Invited faculty, research, and graduate scholarships funded by Brain Korea 21 and wcu resulted in modest gains in research output in the sciences, and the global rankings of a few of the top Korean universities have improved over the years. Therefore, similar to other Asian cases, although Korean universities have engaged in internationalization, promoting diversity (beyond increasing foreign student and faculty numbers) has not been a part of this agenda.

In the case of Korean higher education, there is a noticeable gap between efforts to recruit foreign students and efforts to implement inclusive practices. For example, at the level of university curricula, courses tend to focus on the nation as a bounded unit rather than recognize its subnational cultural groups and identities, suggesting that the view of Korea as an ethnically and racially homogenous entity is still very much a dominant theme in the higher education curriculum and, by extension, in Korean society. Also, in contrast to the sizeable presence of courses focusing on groups such as women, the disabled, and the aged in Korean society, courses focusing on racial and ethnic groups in Korea society are conspicuously (and interestingly) absent, further implying that Koreans have difficulty acknowledging difference, especially in the form of racial and ethnic diversity. Instead, Korean universities offer a few umbrella courses on "multiculturalism" (which, ironically, is a discourse that tends to support policies of assimilation), raising suspicion as to whether college students ever receive any in-depth exposure to the histories, realities, and contributions of diverse groups in Korean society. Furthermore, the majority of courses addressing cultural differences focus on international (not internal) diversity, demonstrating that diversity in Korea is viewed as something "out there" in the world that is still very unfamiliar and perhaps undesirable (Moon 2016).

Such views are also reflected at the micro level, in the everyday interactions between foreign and local students. Both Korean and foreign students report very low levels of cross-cultural interaction with their foreign peers with basic factors such as language and cultural differences acting as major barriers to interaction. Furthermore, foreign students often perceive and experience a strong sense of cultural chauvinism and ethnocentrism in their daily encounters with Korean peers and faculty, often stating, for example, that they felt a sense of solidarity among Koreans that was "too extreme" or that "Koreans seem to like to live among themselves in their own ways" (Moon 2016). Perhaps this is not surprising, given that much research shows that a lack of knowledge about diversity is responsible for conflict, misunderstanding, and low levels of interpersonal interaction (Pasque et al. 2013). Interestingly, similar to the way Korea engages with internationalization in an instrumental way at the national level, Korean students describe or explain the nature of their interactions with foreign students by employing instrumental language such as whether or not interacting with foreigners fulfills certain "needs" or brings "benefits" to the Korean nation, suggesting that Korean students tend to hold a pragmatic view of foreigners rather than embrace them as full members or regard diversity as intrinsically valuable (Moon 2016). This has much to do with the fact that most foreign students originate from China and underdeveloped countries, gain easier admission to Korean universities than Korean students, and often attend on generous scholarships from the Korean government (as part of official development assistance [ODA] programs). Thus, in the same way that Koreans view migrant workers as filling undesirable jobs and thus serving an instrumental function for the Korean economy, Korean students perceive foreign students as being substandard students who are nonetheless admitted to Korean universities for specific functional, national goals and purposes (e.g., to improve the reputation of Korea's universities as internationalized, to demonstrate Korea's image as an advanced donor country, etc.).

Foreign faculty, too, rather than being valued as full, contributing members of their academic communities, are often perceived as temporary skilled labor. They are generally excluded from academic management roles and the administrative business of the universities in which they are employed (Kim 2011). Thus, Korean universities seek to employ foreign professors, not so they can realize the full potential of their abilities and talents and contribute ideas, but for largely instrumental reasons. The number of foreign faculty, their ability to publish in international journals and teach courses in English, all help to raise domestic and international rankings as key measures of internationalization. Some foreign faculty accustomed to the democratic atmosphere of American universities leave the Korean system because they feel devalued in their departments and communities.[6] Also, similar to foreign students, there is a tendency among Koreans to perceive foreign faculty as "second-tier" scholars who failed to secure employment in their countries of origin, thus reinforcing the logic that foreign scholars, despite their low qualifications, are employed by Korean universities to fulfill certain functional roles.

Korea's approach to the internationalization of higher education can thus be seen as a case of "appropriation of globalization," where aspects of globalization are selectively adopted and implemented for instrumental reasons but without substantially altering local values and culture (Shin 2006). The Korean government and universities have closely worked together to proactively recruit foreigners for instrumental purposes, but core Korean values of ethnic nationalism remain firmly entrenched to produce a kind of "ethnocentric" internationalization (Kim 2011). At best, universities assist foreign students and attend to their adjustment needs[7] but neglect to foster a tolerant, inclusive university culture where foreigners are considered full, valued members of Korean universities and society.[8]

What about Multiculturalism?

Some may argue that Korea's promotion of multiculturalism is an indicator of improvement in the direction of recognizing and valuing greater diversity in Korean society. However, while the Korean version of multiculturalism may seem well-meaning and politically correct on the surface, the policies that are implemented in the name of multiculturalism are highly selective and assimilationist and therefore contradict the positive rhetoric and basic principles of multiculturalism. Whereas multiculturalism in Western countries usually applies to a broad spectrum of ethnic minorities and immigrant groups, the Korean version of multiculturalism is highly specific and was designed to support only one group in particular—families in which one of the parents was foreign. Koreans coined a new term for these people, "multicultural families," to avoid negative connotations associated

---

6 Personal communication with a foreign professor working in Korea.

7 Tellingly, the main programs offered at Korean universities that bring together Korean and foreign students are called "community service" mentoring or tutoring programs where Korean students receive academic credit or a small scholarship in return for "volunteering" in linguistic, academic, and university/cultural adjustment courses for foreign students (Kim 2012).

8 In this regard, foreign students are similar to migrant labor who are brought to Korea to fill the labor shortage of 3D (dirty, dangerous, and demeaning) industries and largely excluded from most multicultural programs of Korea.

with international marriages between American military servicemen and Korean women and their "mixed-blood" children. The Korean government had four goals in mind for these support policies: to help "marriage immigrants" settle successfully and find employment at an early stage, to provide financial assistance for migrants, to aid multicultural families in raising healthy children in order to increase future global human resources, and to raise awareness of multiculturalism in Korean society (Shin 2012). The Multicultural Families Support Act was adopted in 2008, building on the 2005 policies in a systematic way that would present multicultural families with welfare benefits such as medical care, schooling, opportunities for cultural and leisure activities, and access to social networks (Moon 2010). As early as April 2006, the government had granted legal status to people of mixed-race backgrounds and to their families as an effort to address problems of prejudice and discrimination (Shin 2012). Universities were "required to admit a certain number of 'mixed-race' students, for example, and special programs were proposed with a view to providing educational assistance, legal and financial aid, and employment counseling to poor families" (Shin 2012, 382). In addition, the law barring "mixed race" Koreans from serving in the military was revised (Lim 2009).

Although unskilled foreign migrant workers account for a much larger share of immigrants in Korea, they are not considered beneficiaries of such programs and measures. Many critics have argued that the Korean government confines its multicultural scope to international marriage households because the government accepts international marriage as a legitimate means of solving the labor shortage while maintaining a relatively homogeneous country (Kim 2009). In fact, many of the government-organized multicultural policies have been more favorable toward international brides than toward migrant workers, since the former are seen as contributing to the reproduction of the Korean nation, while the latter's contributions are economic and thus temporary.

In addition to being selective, the Korean version of multiculturalism also tends to be highly assimilationist. Most policies and programs, under the name of "multiculturalism," largely aim to assimilate immigrants into Korean society and culture rather than recognize and accept the cultures, identities, and rights of immigrants and minorities, explaining why the backbone of multicultural programs consists mostly of Korean language and cultural learning programs. Although some civic organizations run Vietnamese language programs for the Korean husbands of Vietnamese female marriage migrants, such cultural programs are exceptional.

In the same way, although multiculturalism has been officially adopted as a goal of Korean public education, multicultural education is still interpreted as helping immigrant children adapt or assimilate to the Korean school environment (Hong 2010). At the college level too, an analysis of undergraduate course catalogs used in 2012/13 at three major Korean universities shows that Korean universities offer very few courses on multiculturalism (Moon 2016). A closer look at such courses also reveals that they tend to be consistent with the dominant public discourse on multiculturalism and multicultural education as being largely assimilationist, stressing ideas of harmony and adaptation to Korean culture and values with almost no attention to particular ethnic and racial groups or their unique histories, potential contributions, and value to Korean society. The course offerings in Korean universities can be contrasted with Western (mostly American) universities that commonly offer and require students to take ethnic studies and other courses exploring multicultural issues in the domestic context (Humphreys 2000).

Even the few courses on multiculturalism in the Korean college curriculum focus on how to teach "multicultural education" in primary and secondary schools. Such courses are relatively new, having been added to the curriculum of the nation's teacher colleges only a few years ago. The addition was a response to rising concerns with the poorer academic performance and high dropout rates in primary schools of children born from marriages between Korean men and foreign (mostly Southeast Asian) brides. These courses primarily focus on how pre-service teachers can help such children better adapt to Korean schools and "address the needs of the multicultural student population in K-12 educational settings" (Seoul National University 2012, 561). This is in contrast with teacher education courses on multicultural education in the West, which emphasize how to empower the mixed ethnic and racial identities of diverse students.

Korea's multicultural policies have, despite their rhetoric, been recognized as being in accordance with what Castles and Miller (1998) would classify as the *assimilationist model*, defined as a set of policies that seek to incorporate immigrants into society through a one-sided process of adaptation through which these immigrants are expected to give up their distinctive linguistic, cultural, and social characteristics and become indistinguishable from the majority population. In other words, Korea's multicultural policies, though they may have good intentions, demand that immigrants join Korean society at the price of cultural assimilation, rather than facilitate the coexistence of diverse cultures and values.

An Alternative Discourse: Diversity?

Given the misguided rhetoric of "internationalization" and "multiculturalism" in Korea and the persistence of nationalist, assimilationist policies in higher education and other social sectors, we argue that Korea should consider an alternative policy paradigm, one that distances itself from the currently widespread public/policy discourse around multiculturalism and where policies actually reflect and support cultural pluralism in Korean society. Here, we consider the more recent discursive reformulation toward the concept of "diversity" in Western countries (especially in the EU and in global discourse) which significantly departs from the idea of migrants as vulnerable groups in need of welfare support and services or as targets of social integration. Rather, it redefines diversity as a broad, all-inclusive concept that supports positive, active, reciprocal engagement between individuals/groups as well as considers migrants as a creative resource for innovation and development.

While multiculturalism and diversity are admittedly overlapping concepts, recent scholarship has tended to distinguish between the two. Diversity is a more neutral, broader, and more inclusive term that encompasses and treats all differences equally (rather than stressing issues of race, ethnicity, and identity as in multiculturalism).[9] It also places greater value on positive intercultural mixing and interaction, learning intercultural skills, communication, and institutional capacity to deal with cultural conflict (rather than focusing on the integration of migrants) (Meer and Modood 2012). Lastly, it is considered a factor that promotes innovation and development (rather than asserting the value of preserving cultures) (Khovanova-Rubicondo and Pinelli 2012).

In the United States, diversity is widely institutionalized across sectors. For example, it is a key criterion in college admissions and faculty recruitment. Although "affirmative action" has disappeared in many parts of the country, diversity has come to play a key role in American university policies. Most American colleges have a "diversity office" to promote diversity among students, faculty, and staff. The same can be said of leading American corporations, many of which have institutionalized "diversity management" to capitalize on the range of individual differences and talents to increase organizational effectiveness. Of course, basic knowledge and skills are prerequisites, but Americans seem to firmly believe that having a

9 "Cultural Diversity," *UNESCO*, http://www.unesco.org/new/en/social-and-human-sciences/themes/international-migration/glossary/cultural-diversity.

variety of backgrounds and experiences can help hatch new ideas and innovative technologies (Florida 2005; Page 2008; Hiebert, Rath, and Vertovec 2015).

In Europe, the discourse of diversity has been an attempt to respond to widespread critiques and negative connotations of multiculturalism as a failed social policy. Over the past decade, in many Western countries of immigration, multiculturalism's overemphasis on the maintenance of culture has been thought to contribute to social breakdown, separatism and ghettoization, ethnic tension, and the growth of extremism and terrorism (Vertovec 2010). Rather than overemphasizing and maintaining differences, more recent discourses of diversity and interculturalism are about maximizing interaction, addressing cultural conflict, and valuing diversity for innovation and development. In other words, such discourses go beyond simply recognizing and providing resources to support the continuity of traditions and identities among immigrant groups or putting in place compensatory measures to promote tolerance and respect, particularly among the dominant group toward minorities. Instead, they emphasize the importance and necessity of interaction and mutual benefits (Meer and Modood 2012).

Defined in this way, and despite its potential flaws, diversity may be a helpful concept to introduce in the Korean context. Since multiculturalism discourse in Korean society is strongly associated with foreign brides or marriage migrants and their origins in underdeveloped countries, diversity as a broader, all-inclusive concept could potentially diffuse the focus away from this particular target group by casting all groups equally along with majority groups. In a related vein, commentators have raised concerns that multiculturalism in Korea is a rhetoric that ultimately portrays foreign brides as helpless, passive victims and has led to both negative minority self-perceptions as well as negative stereotyping (Kim 2012). Since notions of diversity emphasize forms of positive, active, reciprocal engagement between individuals and groups, such a discourse could lessen this perception of multiculturalism as providing special treatment for needy, victimized individuals. Instead, diversity as a policy paradigm would emphasize more positive connotations of empowerment and agency on the part of both majority and minority groups.

Historically, migration discourses have focused on the social integration of migrants, but the recent diversity paradigm places greater importance on the relational dynamics of exchanges and interactions between migrants and their host society members. This is the normative basis on which recent policy concepts such as "interculturality" and EU initiatives such as "intercultural cities," intercultural education, and others have been recently carried out (Wood 2010). Similarly, research on diversity in American higher education has underscored the importance of improving "interactional diversity" as a major goal (Hurtado, Alvarado, and Guillermo-Wann 2015). This intercultural element of diversity is also useful for the Korean context since there is a strong tendency in Korea to conflate multiculturalism with migrants' one-sided cultural adaptation. That is, multiculturalism is largely interpreted as migrants making an effort to adapt (or Koreans helping migrants to adapt) to Korean society and culture. This is the same for foreign students in Korean universities, who are seen as individuals in need of assistance to adapt to the Korean university environment rather than as a source for intercultural enrichment. Rather than ignoring diversity (as with guest-worker approaches) or denying diversity (as with assimilationist approaches), a diversity paradigm could encourage Koreans to engage with diversity at the micro level and also address issues of cultural conflict or tension openly through public debate, with the involvement of all stakeholders.

Diversity as a creative resource for innovation and development also has useful applications for the Korean case. A voluminous body of literature across a wide range of fields, sectors, and industries has documented and continues to refine the mechanisms through which diversity stimulates innovation and various indicators of social, cultural, and economic development (Florida 2005; Hiebert, Rath, and Vertovec 2015). For instance, Scott Page, professor of complex systems, political science, and economics at the University of Michigan, shows in his book *The Difference* how "the power of diversity creates better groups, firms, schools, and societies." In his view, collections of people with diverse perspectives and heuristics outperform collections of people who rely on homogeneous ones, and the key to optimizing efficiency in a group is diversity. In this work, Page pays particular attention to the importance of "identity diversity," that is, differences in race, ethnicity, gender, social status, and the like. Policy documents and statements have drawn on such arguments and evidence to advocate for diversity as a source of creativity and talent that powers innovation (Wood and Landry 2008; Collins and Friesen 2011).

Such a discourse would be timely given that the Korean economy has reached a critical stage where the demand for recruiting foreign talent and finding new engines of economic growth (especially in non-manufacturing sectors that require innovation) in order to remain globally competitive are both very high (Shin and Choi 2015). To this end, the previous administration of Lee Myung-bak promoted a "knowledge-based economy" while the current Park Geun-hye government is pursuing a "creative economy," emphasizing the development of the advanced business services sector and complementing Korea's historical strengths in electronics hardware with software expertise. The competition for talent in high-tech industries is intense, however, and Korea as a mono-ethnic, xenophobic country has made it difficult to attract and retain top-tier talent. Not surprisingly, the Global Talent Competitiveness Index released last year by INSEAD, France's world-renowned graduate business school, places South Korea twenty-eighth in the overall rankings of 103 surveyed countries and sixty-sixth in the "Attract" pillar of the index, which measures the degree of openness to minorities and immigrants. One of the biggest challenges facing foreign residents in Korea is a lack of understanding of their religious and cultural beliefs. Indian engineers working in South Korea complain of the poor acceptance of Indians by the local population, and of an especially poor understanding of their religion and culture (Shin and Choi 2015). Foreign professors teaching at Korean universities live as "foreigners," never to be accepted into the "inner" circles.[10] It is unlikely that these talented people would like to work longterm for universities and enterprises that are unable to embrace differences in skin color and culture. Under these circumstances, even if some foreign professionals happen to be hired, they may not be able to realize the full potential of their abilities, let alone bring about innovation. In this context, a diversity-for-innovation framework, one that views foreigners not as temporary residents but as assets and potential sources of innovation, would be both timely and beneficial.

Also, this idea builds and improves on a past discourse that has focused largely on unskilled labor and its instrumental function to fill undesirable jobs in the Korean economy and thus maximize Korea's national interests. This kind of thinking is also reflected in the higher education sector, where foreign students are often thought of instrumentally as filling the gap in the declining college-age population or helping Korean universities raise their international rankings through expanded foreign student enrollment. In contrast, a diversity-for-innovation framework suggests a more positive-sum relationship in which natives and foreigners are both valued and should be coactive and interdependent to bring about shared, mutually beneficial economic goals.

Higher Education Reforms to Promote Diversity

Korean universities can draw from a wide range of evolving policies, programs, and models from Western countries to support cultural diversity in

10 Personal communication with Korean professors and foreign professors based in Korea.

higher education at various levels (educational, interpersonal, institutional, etc.). In the United States, the vast majority of institutions have supported diversity initiatives through their own institutional resources, motivated by educational, intellectual, and moral imperatives (Musil et al. 1999). For example, the chief diversity officer, who provides senior leadership for strategic planning and implementation of mission-driven institutional diversity efforts, has become an increasingly professionalized administrative position in colleges and universities across the United States (Williams and Wade-Golden 2013). For instance, at the University of Washington, the chief diversity officer is the vice president and vice provost for minority affairs and diversity.[11] American universities also proactively assess and improve the campus climate for diversity (Hart and Fellabaum 2008; Worthington 2008), which includes community members' attitudes, perceptions, behaviors, and expectations around issues of race, ethnicity, and diversity (Hurtado et al. 1999). There have also been widespread attempts to improve the representation and inclusion of diversity in the curriculum (Carr 2007) as well as develop intergroup dialogues as part of curricular and cocurricular student engagement efforts (Gurin, Nagda, and Zúñiga 2013; Toporek and Worthington 2014). Furthermore, American higher education institutions have worked to integrate broad campus-wide diversity initiatives into institutional strategic planning (Harvey 2014; Smith 2009).

In Europe, diversity in higher education is articulated and supported as part of broader social policies at both the pan-European and country levels (Bergan and Restoueix 2009; Bergan and van't Land 2010). For example, the recent "Intercultural Cities" pilot project initiative by the Council of Europe and the Europe Commission encourages and provides guidelines to member countries about how "to design and implement policies that foster community cohesion and turn cultural diversity into a factor of development rather than a threat."[12] Such policies and projects undertaken by individual countries are then compiled and made available to policymakers by EU-sponsored programs such as Sharing Diversity.[13]

Local governments and universities in Korea could adapt and implement similar policies to improve college campus climates. Foreign students and faculty, in particular, as a significant source of ethnic and racial diversity,

11 "Chief Diversity Officer," *University of Washington*, http://www.washington.edu/diversity/cdo/.

12 "Key Resources: Cultural Diversity," *Compendium: Cultural Policies and Trends in Europe*, http://www.culturalpolicies.net/web/cultural-diversity-resources.php.

13 "Sharing Diversity: National Approaches to Intercultural Dialogue in Europe," *Intercultural Dialogue*, http://www.interculturaldialogue.eu/web/index.php.

should be valued for their presence and potential contributions. Much research demonstrates the positive effects of diversity on various academic and social outcomes (ability to form out-group friendship networks, increased cultural awareness, acquiring global citizenship skills, improving the campus climate, innovation, etc.) (Shook and Fazio 2008; Longerbeam 2010). To achieve such outcomes and based on such research evidence, Korean colleges and universities can begin to implement concrete institutional efforts such as establishing a diversity office or creating a chief diversity officer administrative position, creating diversity and intergroup dialogue courses and requirements that are structured to help students explore different social identity groups (such as national origin, sexual orientation, culture, race, gender, religion, class), providing workshops and professional development for faculty on critical pedagogy, and maximizing intercultural contact through bi-cultural roommate arrangements, multicultural residence hall assignments, and the promotion of intercultural content and goals in extracurricular activities (Stearns, Buchmann, and Bonneau 2009; Yeung, Spanierman, and Landrum-Brown 2013). Universities are ideal settings for students from different backgrounds to meet, generate new ideas, and interact with one another; often the university provides the first opportunity for many young adults to interact closely with members of different cultural groups. Facilitating this and their long-term effects for innovation and development should be a major goal of the internationalization of higher education in Korea.

Conclusion

Like many advanced Western nations, Korea pursues global standards and "politically correct" agendas such as internationalization, transparency, technological innovation, and development. However, Koreans appear to pursue them primarily with instrumental, economic motives in mind, tending to overlook the updating of social and cultural values, or "software," that should accompany such agendas. For instance, in the Western world, valuing the diversity of communities and cultures on moral and ethical grounds is commonly thought of as quintessential in these pursuits. To Koreans, however, diversity seems to be considered unimportant or even irrelevant, demonstrating that Korea, while politically and economically prosperous, still lags behind the world's most advanced countries in social and cultural terms. In higher education, internationalization is promoted and idealized and foreign students are actively recruited to Korean campuses, but again for instrumental reasons without consideration for the moral, intellectual, and educational imperatives associated with accommodating greater diversity. In stark contrast to higher education institutions in the West, the value of diversity in Korean universities is neglected at virtually all other levels—in the curriculum, in students' interactions, in university administration and governance, and in the campus climate. In reality, the curriculum remains thoroughly nationalist, Korean students keep to themselves and retain racist attitudes, inclusive decision making in Korean university governance is almost unheard of, and it would be difficult to characterize Korean campus climates as being positive in terms of intercultural relations. This has much to do with the fact that the Korean government and universities appropriate internationalization from often contradictory nationalist and assimilationist logics.

In Korea, it seems doubtful that the current discourse of multiculturalism will ameliorate this situation. Multiculturalism in the Korean context is essentially assimilationism in rhetorical disguise, racist and nationalist at the policy level, and poorly conceptualized and misunderstood as a concept by the Korean media, policymakers, and the general public (Kim 2012; Yoon 2014). We argue that a better discursive framing around "diversity"—conceptualized as an all-inclusive term emphasizing cross-cultural interaction and interdependency to achieve shared goals of innovation and development—would be timely, relevant, and more appropriate for Korea's situation. This framing would move away from certain negative and deeply ingrained connotations of multiculturalism, such as the sympathetic view of migrant brides and their families as victimized objects in need of welfare assistance. Rather, it would encourage a more agentic, symbiotic vision for both natives and immigrants. Diversity as an engine for innovation and national development is also a timely and appropriate discourse because it resonates with the current Park government's promotion of a "creative economy" and also because it evokes and takes advantage of what Koreans care about most deeply—national interests and standing in the global community.

Lastly, promoting diversity is important because it offers a practical framework for creating the types of educational and institutional programs and policies that have thus far been wholly neglected by Korean universities. Korean universities often proclaim that their mission is to produce "global citizens," but they should first realize that this requires more than simply recruiting foreigners and offering more courses in English. Much more urgent is the creation of a campus environment and culture that values and respects cultural diversity.

References

Bergan, Sjur, and Jean-Philippe Restoueix, eds. 2009. *Intercultural Dialogue on Campus*. Higher education series no. 11. Strasbourg: Council of Europe.

Bergan, Sjur, and Hilligje van't Land, eds. 2010. *Speaking Across Borders: The Role of Higher Education in Furthering Intercultural Dialogue*. Higher education series no. 16. Strasbourg: Council of Europe.

Carr, Jean Ferguson. 2007. "Diversity and Disciplinary Practices." In *Diversity Across the Curriculum: A Guide for Faculty in Higher Education*, edited by Jerome Branche, John W. Mullennix, and Ellen R. Cohn, 30–37. Bolton, MA: Anker Pub. Co.

Castles, Stephen, and Mark J. Miller. 1998. *The Age of Migration: International Population Movements in the Modern World*, 2nd ed. London, England: Macmillan Press.

Cheng, Yin Cheong, Alan C. K. Cheung, and Timothy W. W. Yeun. 2011. "Development of a Regional Education Hub: The Case of Hong Kong." *International Journal of Educational Management* 25: 474–93.

Clarke, Chris G., and Anthony Lising Antonio. 2012. "Rethinking Research on the Impact of Racial Diversity in Higher Education." *Review of Higher Education* 36 (1): 25–50.

Collins, Francis Leo, and Wardlow Friesen. 2011. "Making the Most of Diversity? The Intercultural City Project and a Rescaled Version of Diversity in Auckland, New Zealand." *Urban Studies* 48 (14): 3067–85.

Council of Europe. 2008. *White Paper on Intercultural Dialogue: Living Together in Dignity*. Council of Europe.

de Wit, Hans. 2011. "Global Citizenship and Study Abroad: A European Comparative Perspective." In *Trends, Issues and Challenges in Internationalisation of Higher Education*. Amsterdam: Centre for Applied Research on Economics and Management, 77–91.

Florida, Richard L. 2005. *Cities and the Creative Class*. New York, NY: Routledge.

Gose, Ben. 2006. "The Rise of the Chief Diversity Officer." *The Chronicle of Higher Education* 53 (6): B1.

Gurin, Patricia, Biren A. Nagda, and Ximena Zúñiga. 2013. *Dialogue across Difference: Practice, Theory, and Research on Intergroup Dialogues*. New York, NY: Russell Sage Foundation.

Harvey, William B. 2014. "Chief Diversity Officers and the Wonderful World of Academe." *Journal of Diversity in Higher Education* 7 (2): 92.

Hart, Jeni, and Jennifer Fellabaum. 2008. "Analyzing Campus Climate Studies: Seeking to Define and Understand." *Journal of Diversity in Higher Education* 1.4: 222.

Hiebert, Daniel, Jan Rath, and Steven Vertovec. 2015. "Urban Markets and Diversity: Towards a Research Agenda." *Ethnic and Racial Studies* 38 (1): 5–21.

Hong, Won-Pyo. 2010. "Multicultural Education in Korea: Its Development, Remaining Issues, and Global Implications." *Asia Pacific Education Review* 11 (3): 387–95.

Humphreys, Debra. 2000. "National Survey Finds Diversity Requirements Common Around the Country." *Diversity Digest.* Accessed November 10, 2010. http://www.diversityweb.org/digest/Foo/survey.html.

Hurtado, Sylvia, Jeffre Milem, Alma Clayton-Pedersen, and Walter Allen. 1999. *Enacting Diverse Learning Environments: Improving the Campus Climate for Racial/Ethnic Diversity.* ASHE/ERIC Higher Education Reports Series.

Hurtado, Sylvia, Adriana Ruiz Alvarado, and Chelsea Guillermo-Wann. 2015. "Thinking about Race: The Salience of Racial Identity at Two-and Four-Year Colleges and the Climate for Diversity." *Journal of Higher Education* 86 (1): 127–55.

Institute of International Education. 2015. *Fast Facts Open Doors 2015.* http://www.iie.org/Research-and-Publications/Open-Doors.

Jayakumar, Uma M. 2008. "Can Higher Education Meet the Needs of an Increasingly Diverse and Global Society? Campus Diversity and Cross-Cultural Workforce Competencies." *Harvard Educational Review* 78 (4): 615–51.

Khovanova-Rubicondo, Kseniya, and Dino Pinelli. 2012. "Evidence of the Economic and Social Advantages of Intercultural Cities Approach: Meta-analytic Assessment." *Council of Europe/Intercultural Cities.* http://www.coe.int/t/dg4/cultureheritage/culture/Cities/Default_en.asp.

Kim, Andrew Eungi. 2009. "Demography, Migration and Multiculturalism in South Korea." *The Asia-Pacific Journal* 6 (February 1). Accessed October 20, 2010. http://www.japanfocus.org/-andrew_eungi-kim/3035.

Kim, Sookyung. 2012. "Racism in the Global Era: Analysis of Korean Media Discourse Around Migrants, 1990–2009." *Discourse & Society* 23 (6): 657–78.

Kim, Terri. 2005. "Internationalisation of Higher Education in South Korea: Reality, Rhetoric, and Disparity in Academic Culture and Identities." *Australian Journal of Education* 49 (1): 89–103.

———. 2011. "Globalization and Higher Education in South Korea: Towards Ethnocentric Internationalization or Global Commercialization of Higher Education?" In *Handbook on Globalization and Higher Education*, edited by Roger King, Simon Marginson, and Rajani Naidoo. Cheltenham, UK: Edward Elgar Publishing.

Korean Educational Statistics Service. 2015. http://kess.kedi.re.kr/eng/index.

Lähdesmäki, Tuuli, and Albin Wagener. 2015. "Discourses on Governing Diversity in Europe: Critical Analysis of the White Paper on Intercultural Dialogue." *International Journal of Intercultural Relations* 44: 13–28.

Lewis, Harry. 2014. "Can the Great American Universities Take Root in Asia?" *International Higher Education* (74): 10–11.

Lim, Timothy. 2009. "Who is Korean? Migration, Immigration, and the Challenge of Multiculturalism in Homogeneous Societies." *The Asia-Pacific Journal* 30 (July 27). Accessed October 20, 2010. http://japanfocus. org/-timothy-lim/3192.

Longerbeam, Susan D. 2010. "Developing Openness to Diversity in Living-Learning Program Participants." *Journal of Diversity in Higher Education* 3 (4): 201.

Musil, Caryn McTighe, Mildred García, Cynthia A. Hudgins, Michael T. Nettles, William E. Sedlacek, and Daryl G. Smith. 1999. *To Form a More Perfect Union: Campus Diversity Initiatives.* Washington, DC: Association of American Colleges and Universities.

Meer, Nasar, and Tariq Modood. 2012. "How Does Interculturalism Contrast with Multiculturalism?" *Journal of Intercultural Studies* 33 (2): 175–96.

Moon, Kyoung-Hee. 2010. "The Challenge Of Becoming A 'Multiethnic Korea' In The 21st Century." *East Asia Forum*, March 18. Accessed October 20, 2010. http://goo.gl/6xOghL.

Moon, Rennie J. 2016. "Globalization Without Cultural Diversity? Higher Education in Korea." *Comparative Education* 52(1): 91–108.

Page, Scott E. 2008. *The Difference: How the Power of Diversity Creates Better Groups, Firms, Schools, and Societies.* Princeton: Princeton University Press.

Palmer, John D., and Young Ha Cho. 2012. "South Korean Higher Education Internationalization Policies: Perceptions and Experiences." *Asia Pacific Education Review* 13: 387–401.

Pasque, Penny A., Mark A. Chesler, Jessica Charbeneau, and Corissa Carlson. 2013. "Pedagogical Approaches to Student Racial Conflict in the Classroom." *Journal of Diversity in Higher Education* 6 (1): 1.

Ramos, Maria da Conceição Pereira. 2014. "Mobility, Internationalisation, Higher Education: European Challenges." In *Handbook of Research on Trends in European Higher Education Convergence*, edited by Alina Mihaela Dima, 44. Hershey, PA: Information Science Reference.

Seoul National University. 2012. *Sŏultaehakkyo Kyogwajŏng: Kwamokkaeyo*

(Haksagwajŏng)/ Descriptions for Undergraduate Courses. Seoul National University: Seoul.

Shin, Gi-Wook. 2006. *Ethnic Nationalism in Korea: Genealogy, Politics and Legacy.* Stanford, CA: Stanford University Press.

———. 2012. "Racist Korea?: Diverse but Not Tolerant of Diversity." In *Race and Racism in Modern East Asia: Western and Eastern Constructions*, edited by Rotem Kowner and Walter Demel, 369–90. Leiden: Brill.

Shin, Gi-Wook, and Joon Nak Choi. 2015. *Global Talent: Foreign Labor as Social Capital in Korea.* Stanford, CA: Stanford University Press.

Shook, Natalie J., and Russell H. Fazio. 2008. "Interracial Roommate Relationships: An Experimental Field Test of the Contact Hypothesis." *Psychological Science* 19 (7): 717–23.

Smith, Daryl G. 2009. *Diversity's Promise for Higher Education: Making it Work.* Baltimore, MD: John's Hopkins University Press.

Stearns, Elizabeth, Claudia Buchmann, and Kara Bonneau. 2009. "Interracial Friendships in the Transition to College: Do Birds of a Feather Flock Together once They Leave the Nest?" *Sociology of Education* 82 (2): 173–95.

Toporek, Rebecca L., and Roger L. Worthington. 2014. "Integrating Service Learning and Difficult Dialogues Pedagogy to Advance Social Justice Training." *The Counseling Psychologist* 42 (7): 919–45.

Vertovec, Steven. 2010. "Towards Post-Multiculturalism? Changing Communities, Conditions and Contexts of Diversity." *International Social Science Journal* 61 (199): 83–95.

Wächter, Bernd. 2003. "An Introduction: Internationalisation at Home in Context." *Journal of Studies in International Education* 7 (1): 5–11.

Williams, Damon A., and Katrina C. Wade-Golden. 2013. *The Chief Diversity Officer: Strategy, Structure, and Change Management.* Sterling, VA: Stylus Publishers.

Wood, Phil. 2010. *Intercultural Cities: Towards a Model for Intercultural Integration: Insights from the Intercultural Cities Programme*, Joint Action of the Council of Europe and the European Commission. Strasbourg: Council of Europe Publishing.

Wood, Phil, and Charles Landry. 2008. *The Intercultural City: Planning for Diversity Advantage.* Sterling, VA: Earthscan.

Worthington, Roger L. 2008. "Measurement and Assessment in Campus Climate Research: A Scientific Imperative." *Journal of Diversity in Higher Education* 1 (4): 201.

Yeung, Jeffrey G., Lisa B. Spanierman, and Joycelyn Landrum-Brown. 2013. "'Being White in a Multicultural Society': Critical Whiteness Pedagogy in a Dialogue Course." *Journal of Diversity in Higher Education* 6 (1): 17.

Yoon, In-Jin. 2014. "From a Migrant Integration of Distinction to a Multiculturalism of Inclusion." In *Global and Asian Perspectives on International Migration*, edited by Graziano Battistella, 101–17. Switzerland: Springer International Publishing.

5 From Brain Drain to Brain Linkage

KOREAN STUDENTS ABROAD AS TRANSNATIONAL BRIDGES

Gi-Wook Shin and Joon Nak Choi

Study abroad has a crucial impact on human capital formation. Human capital, or "productive wealth embodied in labor, skills, and knowledge," increases the productivity of economic activities much like physical capital investments such as tools or factories.[1] Sending students abroad can increase a country's human capital, when students return home after being educated overseas. This process has provided Korea with crucial human capital and helped fill the nation's need for top talent. Yet many of the best students who study overseas do not return home, and Korean students are no exception. The Brain Drain Index, calculated by the International Institute of Management Development (IMD), suggests that Korea has experienced "brain drain" more severely than most other advanced economies. From 2005 to 2013, Korea has fluctuated between 3.40 and 5.91 on an index where 0 indicates severe brain drain and 10 indicates no brain drain at all. Korea scored worse than Japan, which ranged between 4.87 and 6.75, but better than China, which scored between 2.93 and 3.66. In comparison, the United States ranged between 6.64 and 7.88 during the same time period. Overall, Korea experiences less brain drain than developing countries like China but more than other advanced countries like Japan and the United States.[2]

In recent years, a lively debate about brain drain as opposed to brain circulation has been taking place among Korean policymakers, the media, and

---

1 "Glossary of Statistical Terms," *OECD*, http://stats.oecd.org/glossary.
2 Data from the Institute for Management Development (2005–13).

This chapter is adapted from Shin and Choi (2015), chapter 3.

the public. Some observers have expressed concerns about the brain drain that results from students remaining overseas permanently after graduation. The negative impact of this phenomenon reaches across many different economic sectors, but is perhaps most damaging in research, development, and other endeavors in the creative economy. According to a study by the Korea Trade-Investment Promotion Agency (KOTRA),

> the leakage of high-quality labor weakens our research and development capabilities, which translates to weakened competitiveness for Korean firms and the nation as a whole, and may create an extreme scenario where we must rely on foreign labor and technology.[3]

Furthermore, the *chogi yuhak* trend of overseas study for secondary or even primary education has exacerbated concerns about brain drain. Over the past decade, Koreans have begun to send their children overseas at a younger age to avoid a secondary school system in Korea that is very stressful for the students and the parents alike. The *chogi yuhak* practice originated among middle- and upper-class families who sent their children abroad to elite private institutions in the United States and Europe, even though they could have attended top universities in Korea. In recent years, however, the practice has spread to a wider range of socioeconomic backgrounds, and *chogi yuhak* students have spread out across a broader range of institutions and countries. The number of *chogi yuhak* students remains a small proportion of all Koreans studying abroad but reached over twenty thousand in 2008, declining somewhat after the global recession. If *chogi yuhak* students tend to originate from elite backgrounds, and if they are more likely to remain overseas after graduation, *chogi yuhak* would exacerbate brain drain in a particularly harmful way.

Other observers, however, have questioned the seriousness of brain drain as a problem, as what appears to be brain drain at first glance may actually be brain circulation. This phenomenon describes Koreans who remain overseas after graduation and accumulate work experience, but eventually return to Korea after having gained useful specialized skills. Such brain circulation can provide substantial benefits. For instance, Saxenian (2006) examined the life journeys of Taiwanese, Indians, and Israelis who attended U.S. graduate schools and chose to remain in the United States to work in Silicon Valley after receiving degrees. Her study found that such individuals played

3 Kim Youngjin, as cited in an ETNews.com article by Guen Il Yoon (http://www. etnews.com/20150102000040). The original quote reads: "고급 인력 이탈은 연구개발 능력 저하로 이어지고 연구 약화는 곧 기업과 국가의 경쟁력 약화를 의미해 앞으로 해외 인력과 기술에 의존해야 하는 극단적인 상황이 벌어질 수 있다".

a critical role in establishing high-technology industry clusters in Hsinchu, Bangalore, and Haifa. While Saxenian does not cite the Korean case, her story is applicable to Koreans as well, especially given Korea's attempts to create an ecosystem for entrepreneurship resembling Silicon Valley.

In this chapter, we engage this conversation, not only by investigating the question of brain drain versus brain circulation, but also by exploring if and how even brain drain itself can contribute to Korea. Following the current lines of debate, we first investigate the question of brain drain versus brain circulation, focusing on the factors that influence whether students choose to remain abroad or to return home. However, we go beyond the current debate by considering the possibility that even clear cases of brain drain can create benefits for Korea. No matter how well Korea recruits students abroad to come back home, some students will undoubtedly never return, and these have been considered cases of brain drain. However, we contend that such students could nevertheless generate other important benefits by connecting their adoptive homelands to Korea, although they might not make a human capital contribution to the country. That is, even brain drain can create connections between Korea and the rest of the world—in other words, *social capital*—that provide benefits equaling or even exceeding those of human capital in an increasingly globalized world. We examine such a potential through an analysis of Korean students studying at top colleges in North America, at both the undergraduate and graduate levels.

Study Abroad for Koreans

Study abroad, brain drain, and brain circulation have great relevance to Korea today. Yet they are far from new to the country. Indeed, Koreans have been studying abroad for most of the past two millennia. Many of the brightest minds of the Silla, Koryŏ, and Chosŏn dynasties studied Buddhist and Confucian classics in China. Korea supposedly experienced brain drain when some of these students chose to remain in China. One such individual was the Buddhist monk Wŏnch'ŭk. Born in Silla, he became one of the two star pupils of Xuanzang—the inspiration for the famed novel *Journey to the West*. Wŏnch'ŭk himself gained wide renown in the Tang dynasty and never returned home. Simultaneously, dynastic Korea benefited from notable examples of brain circulation. Perhaps the most famous example is Jang Bogo. Born in Silla, Jang traveled from there to Tang China and eventually became a junior general in the Wuning district (today's Jiangsu Province) where he built ties with ethnic Silla communities in China. After returning to Silla, these transnational ties enabled Jang to dominate maritime trade between Silla, Heian Japan, and Tang China for decades.

As Korea entered the modern world, young Koreans looked away from China and toward Japan for modern education. Many of the leaders of the Kapsin coup in 1894 were students of Fukuzawa Yukichi at his newly established Keio Institute (later Keio University). This pattern continued and intensified throughout the colonial era, as many Korean families sent their sons to study at elite Japanese schools. One notable example was Shin Kyŏkho, who left Korea to study at a high school affiliated with Waseda University. In 1948, Shin founded the Lotte Group, and later reestablished a presence in Korea after Japan and Korea normalized relations. Today, he splits his time between Korea and Japan, and Lotte is one of the most notable corporations with a truly binational identity, along with Royal Dutch Shell.

Since Korea's liberation after World War II, the United States has emerged as Koreans' preferred destination of study abroad, and the number of Korean students going there has steadily increased over the years. Of the 123,370 Korean students overseas for an undergraduate degree as of 2011, 36,234 (29.4 percent of the total) were studying in the United States. Of these students, 19.2 percent majored in the sciences and engineering. An additional 18,223 (14.8 percent) and 12,629 (10.2 percent) were, respectively, studying in Australia and Canada. The United States is a still more attractive destination for Korean graduate students, educating 23,386 (57.3 percent) of 40,799 total. Of these students, 30.4 percent pursued degrees in the sciences or engineering (Hong and Cho 2012). As figure 5.1 shows, the number of Korean students in the United States increased rapidly through 2008, before leveling off during recessionary conditions.

The main reason Koreans prefer to study in the United States is essentially the same as why their ancestors previously went to China and Japan—they still expect to receive a better education there, despite the rapid improvement of Korean universities (see chapters 2 and 3 in this volume). As Ramirez and Furuta show in chapter 9, the United States has had a long history of recruiting foreign students. A recent survey (Hong and Cho 2012) found that 87.9 percent of surveyed Korean students in the United States believed that they were receiving a better education in the United States. Indeed, 57.4 percent of them listed the superiority of a U.S. education as the primary reason they were studying abroad. Largely for this reason, the number of Korean students in the United States nearly doubled in the decade following 1999–2000.

Human Capital and Brain Circulation

For the purpose of social and economic development in Korea and

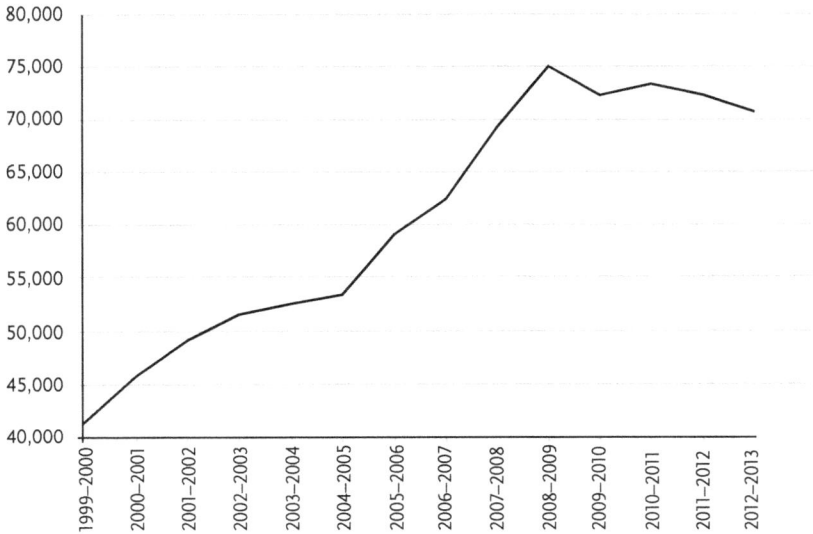

FIGURE 5.1 Korean students in the United States, 1999–2013

Source: Institute of International Education, "International Students: Leading Places of Origin," Open Doors Report on International Educational Exchange (http://www.iie.org/opendoors).

elsewhere, study abroad is most often associated with human capital. Human capital represents a key ingredient for national development, facilitating productive economic activities much like physical capital investments. Gary Becker (2008) explains:

> To most people, capital means a bank account, a hundred shares of IBM stock, assembly lines, or steel plants in the Chicago area. These are all forms of capital in the sense that they are assets that yield income and other useful outputs over long periods of time. But such tangible forms of capital are not the only type of capital. Schooling, a computer training course, expenditures on medical care, and lectures on the virtues of punctuality and honesty are also capital. That is because they raise earnings, improve health, or add to a person's good habits over much of his lifetime. Therefore, economists regard expenditures on education, training, medical care, and so on as investments in human capital. They are called human capital because people cannot be separated from their knowledge, skills, health, or values in the way they can be separated from their financial and physical assets.

Human capital complements physical and financial capital, as the most advanced technology and the best capitalized projects have little chance of success in the absence of workers with the proper skills. For this reason, the "long-term economic growth of an advanced country . . . is with certainty highly correlated with the skill level of its residents" (Kirkegaard 2007, 1–2).

For the purpose of increasing Korea's human capital, the question of whether study abroad results in brain drain or brain circulation has great relevance. As noted above, over 160,000 Koreans were studying overseas as of 2011. If these students were to remain overseas, they would deprive the Korean economy of skilled workers. While the Korean economy has a surplus of university graduates as a whole, several critical sectors are experiencing severe labor shortages. For instance, the Samsung Economic Research Institute (SERI) recently estimated that Korea will face a shortfall of a half million qualified software engineers over the next five years. A Samsung executive recently lamented, "No matter how hard we try, we cannot find enough software engineers in Korea to meet our needs."[4] More broadly, the Korean economy has been experiencing a severe shortage in "global talent"—individuals with key technical or professional skills conferring valuable advantages for firms competing in global markets.[5] For instance, the French business school INSEAD recently ranked Korea 28 out of 103 countries in the 2013 Global Talent Competitiveness Index, a disappointing performance considering the country's economic strength. Such evidence suggests that Korea produces an abundant supply of college graduates yet faces shortages of global talent in key sectors such as software engineering. These shortages will only become worse over the next few years, as the Korean labor pool will soon begin to shrink at an accelerating rate, reflecting one of the most rapid demographic changes ever recorded. Under these circumstances, whether or not Korean students who have remained overseas return home someday will have a substantial impact on the future performance of the Korean economy.

To investigate whether study abroad leads toward brain drain or brain circulation, we analyze the data obtained from an online survey of eighty-nine Korean students at American universities and in-depth interviews with twenty-four selected from the sample.[6] Respondents tended to be very well educated, highlighting the human capital potential that they possess. About a third of respondents had undergraduate degrees from the top thirty U.S. universities, with most of the others having received undergraduate degrees from top Korean universities. Furthermore, even those graduate student respondents without undergraduate degrees from the top thirty universities

4 *Chosun Ilbo*, "Going All the Way to Bangladesh to Find Software Engineers." August 2, 2013.

5 See Shin and Choi (2015) for details.

6 The survey was conducted in spring 2011, and the interviews in spring 2012.

were currently attending high-ranked universities in North America. Indeed, we received the highest number of responses from current undergraduate and graduate students at Stanford, Cornell, and the University of Chicago, and also got many responses from Brown, Yale, Emory, and the University of California, Los Angeles. About 40 percent of respondents majored in engineering as undergraduates; about 20 percent of respondents either obtained or were pursuing master's or PhD degrees. Although our sample of Korean students was not necessarily representative of the total population, our findings should nevertheless illuminate such students' value as human and social capital.

Our respondents viewed a possible return to Korea moderately favorably, averaging 3.31 on a 5-point Likert scale. This is consistent with prior research. Examining U.S. government data, Kirkegaard (2007) found that a sizable proportion of Korean students in the United States return home, although some choose to remain in the United States. Surveying Korean students in the United States, Hong and Cho (2012) found that 56.7 percent of these students intended to return to Korea for their first jobs and that an additional 12.7 percent intended to return at some point after their first jobs. As discussed in detail elsewhere (in Shin and Choi 2015), our analysis shows that a combination of several factors—time spent in Korea, embeddedness in Korean society, and a Korean social identity—account for these students' moderately high interest in returning to Korea.

Our analysis also reveals several counterintuitive relationships between the desire to remain abroad and the desire to return home. On one hand, some interviewees expressed a reluctance to go home because they considered it easy to return to Korea at any time, but difficult to return overseas. As a graduate student in neuroscience emphasized, "There are many cases where Koreans working here are recruited back to Korea, but there is no opposite flow." On the other hand, other interviewees expressed a desire to return home, but to work overseas first. One graduate student in engineering emphasized that "if I worked here for two years [before returning to Korea], I would get credit for two years' worth of work experience [on the Korean job market]. But if I worked here longer and raised my salary more, I not only get credit for more work experience, but I would also get additional bargaining points" (see Shin and Choi 2015 for details). These findings are consistent with a survey of graduate students in the United States reporting that among students not intending to return immediately to Korea, 66.7 percent referred to U.S. jobs as superior opportunities for career development and 28.6 percent cited the ability to command a higher salary in Korea after working overseas first (Hong and Cho 2012). Upon their return, they can make a crucial human capital contribution to Korea, facilitating brain circulation.

Social Capital and "Brain Drain"

Regardless of how successful the government and businesses become at recruiting Korean students to return home, some will choose to remain overseas for various reasons. Almost 70 percent of science and engineering Korean PhD holders in the United States from 2006 to 2009 reported that they would prefer to stay and work in the United States. Furthermore, the growing prevalence of *chogi yuhak* will make it only more difficult for Korea to count on the return of individuals studying abroad, as *chogi yuhak* students who become accustomed to their host countries early on are less likely to want to return home after their studies. By staying overseas, such students will not be contributing human capital to Korea, and concerns about brain drain have only intensified over the years. Yet the current discourse has focused mainly on human capital, in large part overlooking the potential for brain drain to generate social capital, and as such there has been a lack of strategic policies that would generate, support, and promote social capital. In contrast, the new approach that we advocate here highlights the building of transnational bridges connecting Korea to key foreign markets rather than only accumulating human capital inside a nation's geographic boundaries. In other words, brain drain can become "brain linkage" through transnational bridging between home and host societies.

Social capital refers to connections between individuals, which can increase economic productivity much like human capital (Coleman 1988). Social connections enable the sharing of information, improving access to market information and innovations. Furthermore, people linked by social connections have less fear of being backstabbed, enabling them to cooperate at a deeper level (Bourdieu 1977; Powell 1990; Putnam 1995). For these reasons, social capital is widely considered a strategic resource for firms and countries alike, on par with physical capital, financial capital, and human capital as a driver of corporate profits and economic growth.

Here, we focus on one type of social capital in particular, which we call transnational bridges. Putnam (1995) distinguishes between two types of social capital, bonding and bridging. *Bonding social capital* refers to the dense ties linking members of the same group. Social network analysts have long proposed that the social ties linking socially homogeneous individuals facilitate trust and emotional bonding among the group's members, generating solidarity against outside threats (Coleman 1988; Portes and Sensenbrenner 1993; Putnam 1995, 2000). In contrast, *bridging social capital* is created by

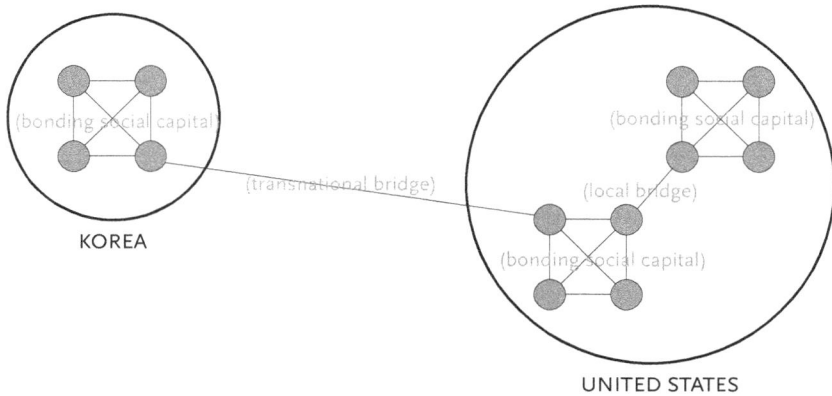

FIGURE 5.2   Bonding social capital, local bridges, and nonlocal bridges
Source: Authors.

ties with outsiders. "Bridges" linking otherwise disconnected groups are important as they facilitate trust, spread information, and circulate innovations (Granovetter 1995; Burt 1992, 2004). Some bridges connect actors in the same geographic area, creating linkages among different groups all located there. Research on Silicon Valley and other "industry clusters" (e.g., Saxenian 1994) has found that such local bridges improve productivity and facilitate innovations.[7] However, recent studies have found that bridges are even more useful when they link groups separated by geographic distances (Bathelt, Malmberg, and Maskell 2004; Maskell, Bathelt, and Malmberg 2005; Bunker-Whittington, Owen-Smith, and Powell 2009). When bridges connect actors in different geographic areas, they link not only social but also geographic distance. Such bridges are relatively rare because most people predominantly know people in the same geographic area and know relatively fewer people elsewhere in their own country, let alone in other countries (Saxenian 1994; Dahl and Sorenson 2008; Tharenou and Caulfield 2010). Figure 5.2 illustrates the difference between bonding social capital, local bridges, and nonlocal bridges. Nonlocal bridges embody transnationalism, a state where actors are simultaneously embedded in different sociogeographic locations across the world (Schiller, Basch, and Blanc 1995). To highlight this aspect of nonlocal bridges, we henceforth label them "transnational bridges." Figure 5.2 shows an illustrative example, differentiating bonding social capital (within groups in each country) and locally bridging

7 See Cortright (2006) for a review.

social capital (between groups in each country) from transnational bridges between countries.

Although all forms of social capital provide substantial benefits, transnational bridges are particularly useful. Like local bridges, transnational bridges span gaps in network structure, linking previously disconnected groups. However, transnational bridges also span geographic and cultural distance. Bridging geographic distance is valuable because geographically colocated individuals share similar types of knowledge. Even if they are socially disconnected, such individuals are exposed to the same environment and are likely to have similar knowledge and information. Thus, they benefit less from sharing their knowledge relative to individuals in geographically distant locations, who each possess more knowledge novel to one another (Bunker-Whittington, Owen-Smith, and Powell 2009). However, to fully benefit from sharing novel knowledge, individuals must not only have communication channels but also be able to understand one another. Cultural and institutional differences between two societies can hinder mutual understanding (Shenkar 2001). Transnational bridges mitigate cultural distance because they transmit, in addition to raw information, the background information about local contexts needed to understand such information (Bathelt, Malmberg, and Maskell 2004; Maskell, Bathelt, and Malmberg 2005). For instance, ethnic Korean residents in many foreign countries have been shown to significantly increase the trade between Korea and these foreign countries, indicating that they are playing a bridging role (Choi 2003). Although transnational bridges are more difficult to establish, they can provide the valuable opportunity to share information and cooperate across vast distances. Students studying abroad offer a good potential pool of such transnational bridges.

To identify Korean students who wish to remain in the United States but would like to maintain their ties with Korea and Koreans, we conducted a correspondence analysis of the eighty-nine surveyed Korean students, including all relevant characteristics of these respondents (i.e., variables). Correspondence analysis is an analytical technique that divides individuals according to their empirical characteristics. We applied this technique to the surveyed students to generate groups of students that possess substantial internal homogeneity, but differ from one another. Although casual observers may consider Koreans studying abroad to be fairly homogeneous, our analysis reveals that they differ from one another in two important dimensions specified below. Furthermore, these differences appear to have great bearing upon our other focal area of interest—why some Korean students want to

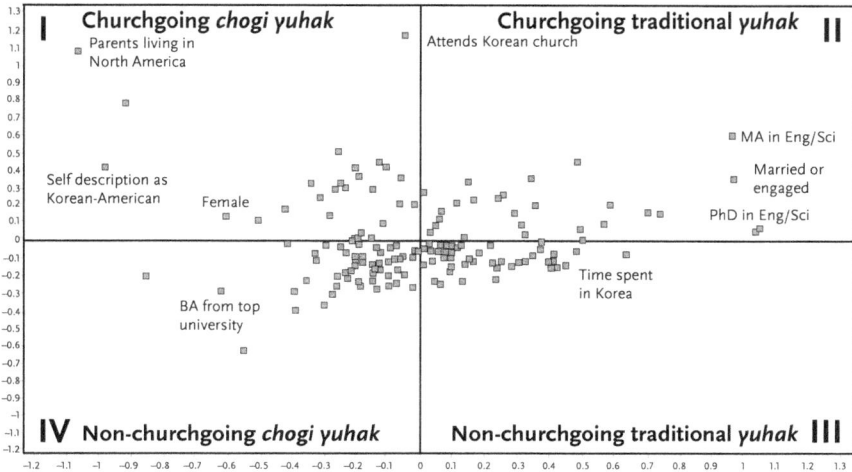

FIGURE 5.3 Correspondence analysis of Korean students in North America
Source: Shin and Choi (2015).

return home or stay abroad more than others (see Shin and Choi 2015 for further details).

As figure 5.3 shows, our correspondence analysis produces empirical dimensions that closely match two intuitive ways to explain the variation among Korean students. The most important dimension differentiating Korean students from one another, shown on the x axis, corresponds to *chogi yuhak* versus traditional *yuhak*. On one hand, individuals located to the right of figure 5.3 are older, married, or engaged; spent greater time in Korea; and have either obtained or are currently pursuing MAs or PhDs. Such individuals fit the profile of traditional *yuhak* students who received an undergraduate education in Korea before seeking advanced degrees in the United States. This group predominantly consists of males studying science or engineering. On the other hand, individuals located to the left are younger, single, have spent less time in Korea, and tend to be female. Furthermore, such individuals are more likely to attend universities in the United States or Canada for undergraduate programs and have a parent living in North America, and may even have acquired an identity as Korean American in addition to their strong affinity with Korea, reflecting the shifting and fluid nature of national identity (see chapter 8). Such individuals fit the profile of *chogi yuhak*, students who head overseas before graduating from college or even high school, sometimes accompanied by one or more parents. In short, the traditional *yuhak* versus *chogi yuhak* student status is one important dimension to separate Korean students overseas from one another.

Another and perhaps less obvious but more interesting dimension, shown on the y axis, corresponds to a respondent's church attendance. Korea has the largest Christian population by percentage (29 percent) of all the countries in Asia, and many Korean students coming to study in North American are from Christian families. Observers have long noted that Koreans avidly attend Korean churches while studying in North America, especially Protestants who combine religious worship with activities to promote Korean culture and identity. Members of Korean churches often assert that "attending a Korean church is a declaration not only of one's religious affiliation, but of one's ethnicity and commitment to that particular ethnic community as well" (Lee 1998, as quoted in Oh, n.d.). Individuals located near the top of figure 5.3 tend to go to a Korean church more often than individuals located near the bottom. The likelihood of Korean church attendance is strongly associated with the presence of parents living in North America, but no other variable is correlated with it. In other words, the frequency of Korean church attendance differentiates Korean students from one another, unrelated to any other variable except that frequent churchgoers tend to have more family members living in North America.

These two dimensions divide sampled Korean students into four groups corresponding to the quadrants shown in figure 5.3. Group I represents *chogi yuhak* churchgoers, group II represents traditional *yuhak* churchgoers, group III represents traditional *yuhak* non-churchgoers, and group IV represents *chogi yuhak* non-churchgoers. To be sure, these groups share many important features with one another, including Korean-language fluency, opinions of Korea, self-described Korean identity, and marital preferences. They also present little variation in average interest in working with Koreans (ranging from 3.38 to 3.46 on a 5-point scale) or working for Korean firms (ranging from 2.85 to 3.12). However, the groups reveal differing levels of interest in returning to Korea—group III shows the strongest interest (3.88/5.00), followed by groups II and IV (3.13 and 3.21/5.00, respectively) and finally group I (2.75/5.00), which shows at best a lukewarm interest in returning home. This pattern suggests that *chogi yuhak* status and Korean church attendance have independent and additive effects diminishing students' likelihood of returning home. We elaborate on this observation with details below.

The Effects of Chogi Yuhak on Returning to Korea

Not surprisingly, *chogi yuhak* students have less interest in returning home. The two groups of *chogi yuhak* students (groups I and IV) are mainly undergraduates having spent an average of 7.88 and 6.94 years, respectively, in Korea after age seven, while the two groups of traditional *yuhak* students (groups II and III) are mostly older graduate students who, respectively, spent an average of 16.93 and 16.12 years there. We count the years following age seven because socialization outside the family environment intensifies after a child enrolls in primary school. On the other hand, the *chogi yuhak* groups have spent far more time in North America (9.00 and 5.67 years, respectively, for groups I and IV) than the traditional *yuhak* groups (both averaging less than three years). Largely for this reason, some *chogi yuhak* students have developed Korean American identities (63 and 21 percent of groups I and IV, respectively) in addition to their native one (81 and 88 percent, respectively), while no respondent in groups II and III reported such an additional identity. Group I (*chogi yuhak* churchgoers) is also unique in having an average of one parent living in North America, while other groups typically have both parents staying in Korea. Considering that groups I and IV are less familiar with Korean culture and society, have a greater familiarity with North America, have acquired emerging Korean American identities, and often have parents living in North America (for group I), it is not surprising that such students have less interest in returning to Korea.

The Effects of Korean Church Attendance on Returning to Korea

Frequent attendees of Korean churches also have less interest in returning home. Among *chogi yuhak* students, churchgoers (group I) expressed much less interest in returning home (2.75/5.00) than non-churchgoers (group IV) (3.21/5.00). Likewise, among traditional *yuhak* students, churchgoers (group II) revealed a weaker interest in returning home (3.13/5.00) than non-churchgoers (3.88/5.00). The negative relationship between Korean church attendance and interest in returning to Korea is surprising given that Korean churches are believed to function as a stronghold of Korean community, culture, and identity. According to the conventional wisdom, frequent churchgoers would be expected to retain more of a Korean identity and be more interested in returning home.

What explains this counterintuitive finding? Prior research on ethnic enclaves (Portes 1995; Portes and Rumbaut 2001) provides some clues. Several geographic locations in North America (e.g., Koreatown in Los Angeles, Flushing in New York City, and Bloor Street in Toronto) host high concentrations of Korean immigrants. Like other ethnic enclaves—or localized concentrations of immigrants from a given foreign country—Koreatown and other Korean enclaves provide the comforts of home in a distant land. For instance, Koreatown in Los Angeles, the largest Korean enclave in North America, is dotted with Korean-language signs advertising coffee shops, stores, *noraebang*, and other services more typical of Seoul than a typical North American city. Spoken Korean language is so pervasive that it is commonly said that a Korean immigrant can live there quite comfortably without ever having to learn English. Providing key services in a familiar environment, Korean enclaves should not only reinforce Korean students' native identities but simultaneously root them to their host countries.

Korean churches seem to play much the same role. Besides their religious functions, as a meeting place for ethnic Koreans, often in a predominantly non-Korean neighborhood, Korean churches are sites for intense social interaction that reinforce Korean language, identity, and social cohesion (Kwon, Ebaugh, and Hagen 1997). It follows that Korean churches provide their members with a strong sense of belongingness and social support, functioning much like ethnic enclaves, but distributed all over North America. In 2013, there were 4,233 Korean churches in the United States alone, one church for every 403 Koreans living in the States.

Our interviews with students who are frequent Korean churchgoers highlight the importance of churches as key places to meet and socialize with other Koreans. Some students attend Korean churches to expand their social circles. They emphasized that, besides "spiritual reasons," social motivations provided a strong secondary rationale for finding a specifically Korean church. One student specifically related the lengthy process that she undertook to find the church that offered the most comfortable social environment. Church attendance offers Korean students an opportunity to maintain close ties with Korea and their Korean identities while building networks with their new environment and even coming to identify with their host society.

Churchgoing Chogi Yuhak Students as Transnational Bridges

Our discussions above clearly suggest that among Korean students in the United States, *chogi yuhak* students who regularly attend Korean churches (group I) are the least likely to return home but at the same time may have the highest potential to function as transnational bridges, becoming Korean transnationals embedded within American society. Korean churches may represent sites for "selective acculturation," which occurs when immigrants maintain their home cultures while becoming full members of the host society. Selective acculturation, however, requires that immigrants connect with the host society at their own time and choosing, protected by a safe enclave or other agglomeration of coethnics. Korean churches can provide such safe havens, enabling Korean students to retain their native identities and maintain their connections to Korea and Koreans while gradually embedding themselves in American or Canadian society.

Our survey data support this proposition. On average, group I respondents have a lower interest in returning home than other groups (2.75/5.00) but a moderately high interest in working with Koreans (3.38/5.00) and some interest in working for Korean firms (3.00/5.00), just like other groups. While most (81 percent) continue to identify as Korean, many (63 percent) also identify as Korean American. The proportion identifying as Korean American is far higher for this group than otherwise comparable *chogi yuhak* students who do not regularly attend church (21 percent). This suggests that the selective acculturation occurring in Korean churches actually accelerates the emergence of a Korean American identity. Group I members attend Korean churches an average of 8.59 sessions per month—about twice a week.

During interviews, *chogi yuhak* students said that belonging to a Korean church helped them selectively acculturate to the United States by allowing them to retain a sense of being Korean and remaining tied to Korea, while simultaneously building connections to a larger society outside this protected enclave. These students have a strong potential to bridge the United States and Canada with Korea because they have retained Korean identities and ties to Korea while building connections with their surrounding environments. Such individuals benefit from selective acculturation. In contrast, traditional *yuhak* students attending Korean churches do not experience such benefits. Indeed, Korean church attendance appears to retard their ability to acculturate to North America and build social ties outside the Korean community. Such individuals have limited potential to bridge Korea with North America, largely because they are not embedded within their host societies.

Overall, churchgoing *chogi yuhak* students have been given the opportunity to acculturate to the United States on their own terms, maintaining close ties with Korea and their Korean identities while building networks with their new environment and even coming to identify with their host society. In particular, students who have one parent living with them in North America while the other still lives in Korea have an extra motivation to bridge their two "homes." Simultaneously, such students have the same level of interest in working for Korean firms or otherwise working with Koreans as other groups of Korean students studying abroad. Consequently, churchgoing *chogi yuhak* students have a particularly good chance at functioning as transnational bridges between Korea and North America.

From Brain Drain to Brain Linkage

With globalization, growing numbers of young people are leaving their countries for advanced studies overseas. Upon their return with advanced degrees, they can provide an important pool of human capital to their home countries. However, some students may choose to stay in the host countries after graduation, or undertake "voluntary migration," thus raising the question of brain drain. In the conventional view, returning students can be an important source of human capital to their own society and economy. The challenge is to reduce career migration, especially by increasing the number and quality of opportunities back home. However, from the new perspective, which attends to the value of social capital and transnational bridges, countries can also benefit by leaving their students overseas. By facilitating transmigration, countries can become better connected with the rest of the world, gaining transnational bridges, but this is not an easy task (see Saxenian 2006). Reducing career migration and encouraging transmigration are particularly important for a country like Korea, which has long educated many of its brightest individuals overseas.

Our study reveals that Korean students' interest in returning home, working with Koreans, or working for Korean firms is conditioned largely by two factors—whether they are *chogi yuhak* versus traditional *yuhak* and their degree of participation in a Korean church. Sojourn length and age differentiate older graduate students who attended college in Korea from younger *chogi yuhak* students. Older graduate students unsurprisingly express more willingness to repatriate than their younger *chogi yuhak* counterparts. *Chogi yuhak* students often acquire a Korean-American identity, which diminishes their interest in returning. One fascinating and unexpected finding is that frequent attendees of Korean churches also have less interest in returning home, surprising given that Korean churches have been viewed as a stronghold of Korean community, culture, and identity. We interpret this counterintuitive finding as indicating that Korean churches function much like ethnic enclaves that provide key services in a familiar environment, not only reinforcing students' Korean identities but also rooting Korean students in their host countries. As a result, they would feel quite comfortable in staying at the host countries after education. This finding also suggests that students located in ethnic enclaves such as Koreatown in Los Angeles might also show less interest in returning home, which merits further research.

Current debates on Korea's brain drain focus on students who return home, overlooking how students who remain in their host countries after graduation might function as social capital. In the conventional view, students who remain abroad have little to contribute to Korean society and may be considered examples of brain drain. Accordingly, most efforts have focused on inducing them to return home, which is hailed as brain circulation. However, the new approach that we advocate here suggests that such students also represent valuable assets who could bridge Korea and their host countries, a phenomenon that we call "brain linkage." Accordingly, we ought to pay more attention to Korean students who may remain in their host countries after graduating but who are nevertheless able and willing to work with Koreans and perhaps work for Korean firms. Indeed, we identify churchgoing *chogi yuhak* students in the United States as individuals who are simultaneously embedded within their host society and their home society (Korea). These individuals have the most potential to bridge the United States with Korea, providing social capital benefits to Korea if not providing a human capital contribution. A challenge for Korea is to transform brain drain into brain linkage by providing relevant individuals with rich identity-related social and cultural experiences. If they can maintain close ties with Korea, they may be considerably more likely to play a bridging role. The value of such transnational bridging will only grow with increasing economic globalization in the coming years.

References

Becker, Gary. 2008. "Human Capital." In *The Concise Encyclopedia of Economics*. http://www.econlib.org/library/Enc/HumanCapital.html.

Bathelt, Harald, Anders Malmberg, and Peter Maskell. 2004. "Clusters and Knowledge: Local Buzz, Global Pipelines and the Process of Knowledge Creation." *Progress in Human Geography* 28: 31–56.

Bourdieu, Pierre. 1977. *Outline of a Theory of Practice*. New York: Cambridge University Press.

Bunker-Whittington, Kjersten, Jason Owen-Smith, and Walter W. Powell. 2009. "Networks Propinquity, and Innovation in Knowledge-Intensive Industries." *Administrative Science Quarterly* 54: 90–122.

Burt, Ronald. 1992. *Structural Holes: The Social Structure of Competition*. Cambridge, MA: Harvard University Press.

———. 2004. "Structural Holes and Good Ideas." *American Journal of Sociology* 110 (2): 349–399.

Choi, Inbom. 2003. "Korean Diaspora in the Making: Its Current Status and Impact on the Korean Economy." In *The Korean Diaspora in the World Economy*, edited by C. Fred Bergstein and Inbom Choi, 9-29. Washington, DC: Institute for International Economics.

Coleman, James. 1988. "Social Capital in the Creation of Human Capital." *American Journal of Sociology* 94: S95–S120.

Cortright, Joseph. 2006. *Making Sense of Clusters: Regional Competitiveness and Economic Development*. Washington, DC: Brookings Institution.

Dahl, Michael S., and Olav Sorenson. 2008. "The Social Attachment to Place." Working paper.

Granovetter, Mark S. 1995. *Getting a Job: A Study of Contacts and Careers*, 2nd ed. Chicago: University of Chicago Press.

Hong, Sungmin, and Gawon Cho. 2012. "Entry and Exit Patterns of Sciences and Engineering Human Resources in 2012." Unpublished paper.

Kirkegaard, Jacob Funk. 2007. *The Accelerating Decline in America's High-Skilled Workforce: Implications for Immigration Policy*. Washington, DC: Peter G. Peterson Institute for International Economics.

Kwon, Victoria Hyonchu, Helen Rose Ebaugh, and Jacqueline Hagen. 1997. "The Structure and Functions of Cell Group Ministry in a Korean Christian Church." *Journal for the Scientific Study of Religion* 36 (2): 247–56.

Lee, S.J. 1998. "Dispelling the Myth." *Z&d: Korean American* (ZandD.com). December.

Maskell, Peter, Harald Bathelt, and Anders Malmberg. 2005. "Building Global Knowledge Pipelines: The Role of Temporary Clusters." DRUID Working Paper 05-20, Danish Research Unit for Industrial Dynamics, Copenhagen.

Oh, Lisa S. n.d. "On Being Korean American and the Role of Church in Many Korean People's [sic]." *UrbanMinistry.org*, http://www.urbanministry.org/wiki/being-korean-american-and-role-church-many-korean-peoples.

Portes, Alejandro. 1995. *The Economic Sociology of Immigration*. New York: Russell Sage Foundation.

Portes, Alejandro, and Rubén G. Rumbaut. 2001. *Legacies: The Story of the Immigrant Second Generation*. Berkeley, CA: Univ of California Press.

Portes, Alejandro, and Julia Sensenbrenner. 1993. "Embeddedness and Immigration: Notes on the Social Determinants of Economic Action." *American Journal of Sociology* 98: 1320–50.

Powell, Walter W. 1990. "Neither Market nor Hierarchy: Network Forms of Organization." In *Research in Organizational Behavior*, edited by Barry M. Staw and Larry L. Cummings, 12: 295–336. Greenwich, CT: Jai Press.

Putnam, Robert. 1995. "Bowling Alone: America's Declining Social Capital." *Journal of Democracy* 6 (1): 65–78.

———. 2000. *Bowling Alone: The Collapse and Revival of American Community*. New York: Simon and Schuster.

Saxenian, AnnaLee. 1994. *Regional Advantage: Culture and Competition in Silicon Valley and Route 128*. Cambridge, MA: Harvard University Press.

_____. 2006. *The New Argonauts: Regional Advantage in a Global Economy.* Cambridge, MA: Harvard University Press.

Schiller, Nina Glick, Linda Basch, and Cristina Szanton Blanc. 1995. "From Immigrant to Transmigrant: Theorizing Transnational Migration." *Anthropological Quarterly* 68 (1): 48–63.

Shenkar, Oded. 2001. "Cultural Distance Revisited: Towards a More Rigorous Conceptualization and Measurement of Cultural Difference." *Journal of International Business Studies* 32 (3): 519–35.

Shin, Gi-Wook, and Joon Nak Choi. 2015. *Global Talent: Skilled Labor as Social Capital in Korea.* Stanford: Stanford University Press.

Tharenou, Phyllis, and Natasha Caulfield. 2010. "Will I Stay or Will I Go? Explaining Repatriation by Self-Initiated Expatriates." *Academy of Management Journal* 53 (5): 1009–28.

6 The Internationalization of Higher Education

JAPANESE PERSPECTIVES

Motohisa Kaneko

In contrast to the exponential growth of the international mobility of students since the end of the last century (OECD 2014), Japanese development in this respect has been rather modest. What are the factors behind this stagnancy? Why should it be rectified and what are the obstacles that must be overcome? These are the questions that I intend to address in this chapter.

Stagnating Internationalization

It is important at the outset of this analysis to note where Japan stands globally regarding the internationalization of higher education, particularly with respect to student mobility.

Levels of Inbound and Outbound Mobility

Although the expansion of international mobility is a universal trend, industrialized countries show contrasting patterns of inbound and outbound mobility. *OECD Education at a Glance* (2015) provides two indicators: (1) percentage of national tertiary students enrolled abroad and (2) number of international students per national student abroad. I call (1) "outbound relative size" and (2) "inbound/outbound ratio." These indicators for selected counties are shown in figure 6.1.

It illustrates that, for the United States, the United Kingdom, and Australia, the inbound/outbound ratios are high, while the outbound shares are low. These countries clearly constitute the hubs of international student mobility. They attract students from all over the world, not only because of the high academic reputation of their universities, but also because of the use of the English language, deemed a universal medium in the globalized world. It is also important that in some of these countries higher education institutions (HEIs) are encouraged to accommodate foreign students as a source of revenue (UNESCO 2013).

Meanwhile, in the cases of Germany and France, inbound/outbound ratios are low while outbound shares are relatively high. This reflects to a large extent the development of a regional framework of student exchange under the name of the ERASMUS project, which was created and nurtured by strong political initiatives. Between the two groups, Japan stands out with low levels of both indices for inbound and outbound flows. Obviously, Japan lacks the advantages that the United States and other major English-speaking countries enjoy in terms of attracting a large number of students. Moreover, Japan lacks access to an effective regional framework comparable to ERASMUS.

Nonetheless, it should be noted that, over time, Japan has seen a gradual expansion in both inbound and outbound student mobility. In particular, the influx of students into Japan has been growing substantially since the 1990s (figure 6.2). This is partly due to a government policy to increase the number of foreign students through expanded scholarships and other means. Also, until recently, there had been a large excess in demand for higher education in China, a portion of which was directed to Japan. Lately, this growth has slowed.

More alarming, however, is the trend in outbound mobility from Japan. While the number of students leaving Japan to study abroad increased substantially in the 1990s, it started to stagnate around the turn of the century, then started to decline toward the 2010s. The size of the outbound flow is now half of that of the inbound flow.[1]

Even though a part of the decline of outbound flow is attributable to the decline of the size of the college-aged population, it seems very likely that the motivation for going overseas to study has lost its momentum. Social critiques maintain that Japanese youth, being accommodated in a comfortable society, have become increasingly "inward-looking." If this is the case, Japanese youth may be uninterested in the outside world in the coming years.

---

[1] Similar trends of stagnation in recent years can be found with Taiwan and Korea. In Korea, the number of students going overseas to study had grown rapidly from 216,000 in 2008 to 262,000 in 2011. But it fell to 219,000 by 2014 (Kim Yonju, "Kankokujin ryugakusei 3 nen renzoku de gensho," *Chosun Ilbo*, Japanese version, December 8, 2014).

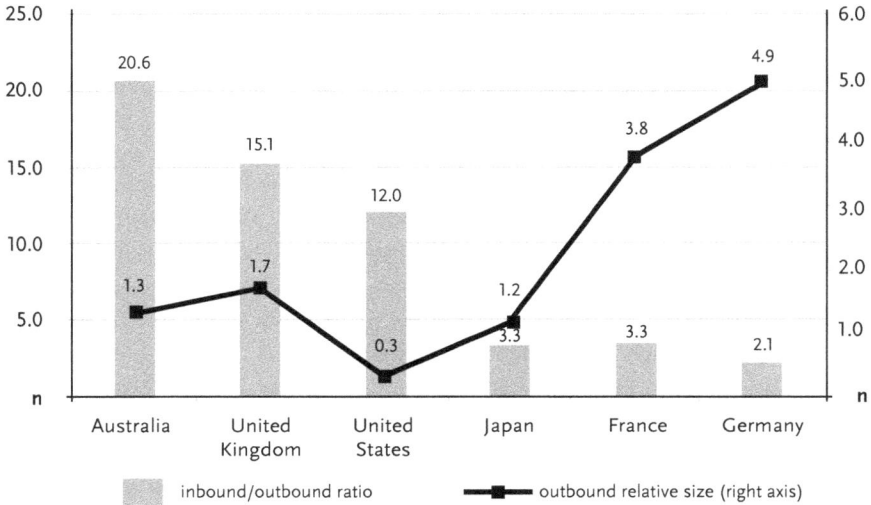

FIGURE 6.1 Global student mobility, select countries, 2012
Source: OECD Education at a Glance 2015, table C4.5.

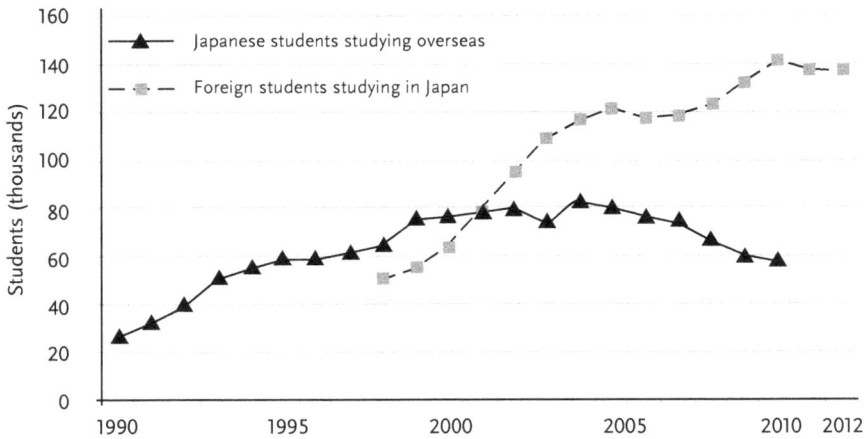

FIGURE 6.2 Changes in inbound and outbound student mobility in Japan, 1990–2012
Source: Japan Student Services Organization (JASSO) and School Basic Survey, Japan, various years.

Motivations for Studying Abroad

I would argue that the motivation to study abroad should be seen in a dynamic context. It helps at this point to reflect on why the international mobility of students expanded substantially beginning in the 1990s. While the expansion can be attributed to various factors, including government policies and institutional efforts, there is no doubt that the demand for the opportunity to study abroad has increased substantially. One can hypothesize that there are three major types of motivation to study abroad:

I. *Catch-up:* The classic motivation to study abroad. If a knowledge or skill is unavailable in a home country, some students will go to foreign institutions where such knowledge is available. In many cases, students are financed by sponsors such as the government of the home or the host country. This is a typical type of study abroad at an elite stage of higher education development.

II. *Economic Interest*: The second type of studying abroad involves the anticipation of immediate economic returns. In some countries, the experience of studying abroad promises advantages in securing better employment opportunities. Some students go to a foreign country to study, then seek employment in the host country. As developing nations grow economically, this type of demand rapidly intensifies. This is the major force in the massification of studies abroad.

III. *Educational Enrichment*: Increasingly, many HEIs in industrialized countries encourage students to go overseas as a part of their educational programs, with the assumption that such an experience will enrich personal and academic growth. This creates demand for educational enrichment through student exchange programs.

Even though it is difficult to account for the recent expansion of student mobility simply by distinguishing between different types of motivation, it seems likely that each of these three types of motivation is playing some role. Students in the least developed countries still hope to obtain knowledge available only in some developed countries. There are increasing numbers of students from middle-income countries seeking the opportunity to study abroad, frequently financed by their own families, to secure advantages in the labor market or through employment in the host country. Finally, short-term studies in foreign institutions, as a part of an educational program, seem to be growing rapidly in wealthier countries.

Shifts in Demand and the Transitional Trap

If we examine the motivations to study abroad from the perspective of a single country's economic development, we can posit that the relative significance of the three types of motivation would shift, as shown in figure 6.3.

The catch-up demand (type I) should be the earliest to expand. At the early stages of economic development, domestic institutions of higher education are unable to provide sufficient opportunities for advanced academic and professional training. Consequently, students have to go overseas to pursue these opportunities. But, as a society develops, domestic institutions accumulate academic capacities. Then demand for catch-up study abroad declines.

As the economy develops further, type II demands arising from economic incentives would grow. This is not necessarily because of the increases in expected benefits from studying abroad, but rather because the capacities to invest in studying abroad grow. With economic development, the middle-income class that can afford to pay the costs of studying abroad increases in size, thus augmenting demand. Over time, however, this demand may also stagnate as immediate economic returns diminish as the differences in living standards diminish. At later stages of development, type III demands arising from the expected benefit of enriched educational experiences would start to rise. This may not take place solely through market forces, because the benefit is neither tangible nor immediate. Either the government or the HEIS themselves must take the initiative in recognizing this benefit.

It is important to note that, in the transition from the dominance of type

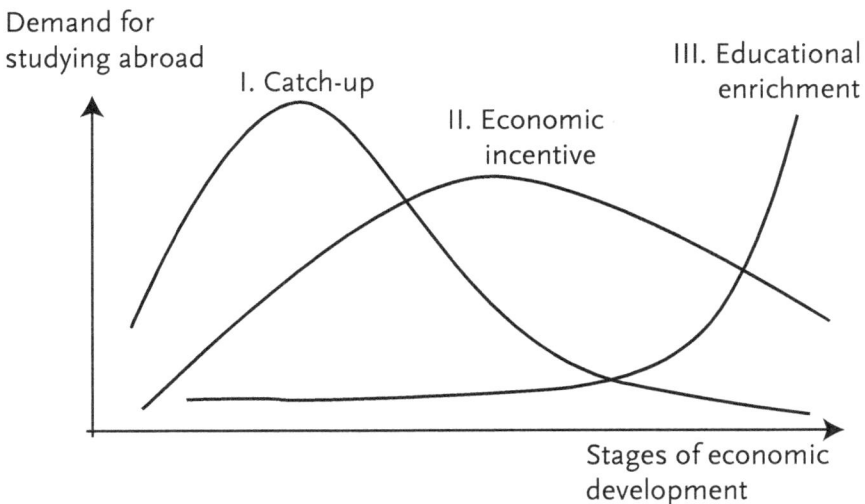

FIGURE 6.3 Shift in the demand for studying abroad
Source: Author.

I and type II demands to type III demand, the total demand for studying abroad may not increase, and might even decrease. I tentatively call this a *transitional trap*. Even though it is difficult to prove that the recent stagnation of outbound mobility of students from Japan has been caused by this trap, one can argue at least that the patterns of motivation can play significant roles over time.

Motivation Gap and Latent Needs

The transitional trap described above arises from the fall of type II demand and insufficient growth of type III demand. From this perspective, it is important to understand where type II stands and what type III can potentially be.

Motivation Gap

It would seem trivial to observe that, in this increasingly globalized world, universities should be internationalized. In fact, the media speak about the advances of globalization every day. Political discourses are rampant with calls to nurture a younger generation with a higher command of foreign languages, particularly the English language. Politicians argue that the new generation will be vital in asserting national interests in the economic and political arenas of a more competitive world.

However, analyses of college graduates reveal that this is not necessarily true (Kaneko 2014b). Japanese business firms do not value language abilities as a critical attribute in recruiting college graduates. At work, the ability to speak a foreign language is not so essential as it is frequently assumed to be in the popular narrative of the globalization of work. Our survey of about twenty-four thousand college graduates revealed that only about 3 percent use English regularly at work. Even including those who use English occasionally, the proportion does not exceed 15 percent, as shown in figure 6.4.

The same survey also showed that only 3 percent of Japanese college graduates have experience working outside of Japan. The rate is somewhat higher among those working in large corporations, which tend to be involved in a greater number of global activities. Still, the proportion reaches only 3.9 percent for those working in corporations employing ten thousand or more (Kaneko 2014b). Moreover, most young people feel that average wages and living standards in Japan compare favorably to those of other counties. It was found that the wage levels of workers who used a foreign language frequently at work are significantly higher than those of their counterparts, but the difference is less than 10 percent.

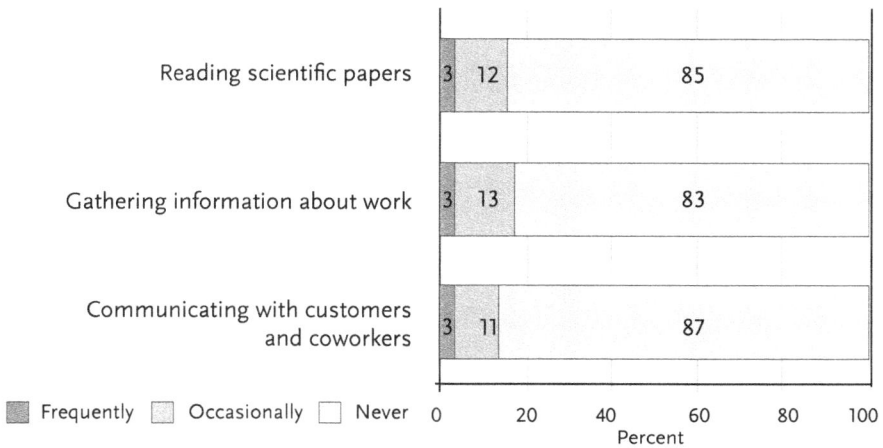

FIGURE 6.4 Frequency of using English at work, by purpose

Source: Calculated by the author based on Center for Research on University Management and Policy (CRUMP), 1979 College Graduates Survey (n=23,939) (http://ump.p.u-tokyo.ac.jp/crump/cat77/cat83/).

Skewed Distribution of Demand for Studying Abroad

It is also suggestive to analyze the distribution of demand for studying abroad. Figure 6.5 shows the proportion of students who studied abroad by selectivity of institution and field of study.

A striking observation that emerges from the figure is that there are significant differences in the frequency of experiences of studying abroad by selectivity of institution. In the humanities and social sciences (HSS), as many as 18 percent of students at less selective institutions have some experience of studying abroad, as compared to only 9 percent of those in highly selective institutions. A similar pattern can be found with the students in natural sciences and engineering (NSE). Another important observation is that the incidences of experience of studying abroad vary by the field of academic specialization. It is high among students in HSS, but lower in NSE and health-related disciplines (HRDs); only 6 percent of HRD students had studied abroad.

These observations reflect to an extent the differences in curricular requirements for students. Particularly for students in HRDs, completing laboratory work requirements makes it difficult for the students to be away from their home institutions. Nonetheless, differences in requirements alone cannot explain the differences between the HSS and NSE fields.

The differences indicate that incentives for studying abroad vary from one type of student to another. Students at selective institutions, or those in the HRDs, enjoy advantages in securing employment opportunities. In

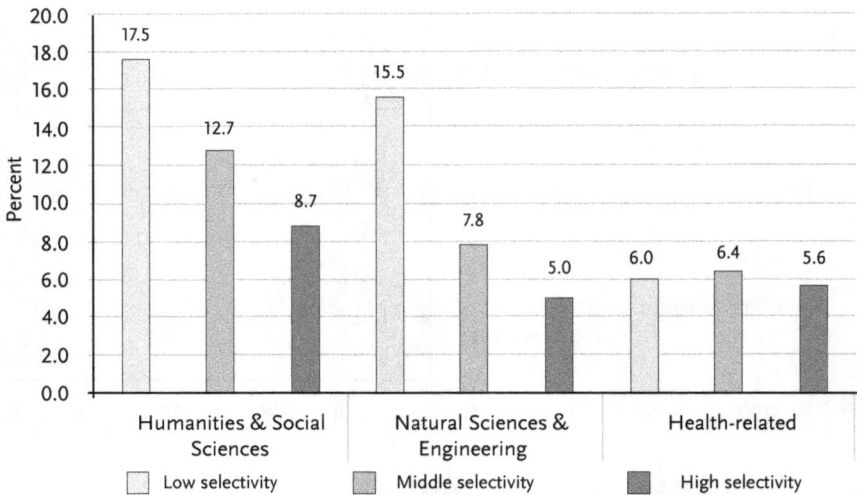

FIGURE 6.5 Students who studied abroad by selectivity of institution and field of study
Source: Calculated by the author from the Center for Research on University Management and Policy (CRUMP), 2006–07 College Student Survey (n= 45,159) (http://ump.p.u-tokyo.ac.jp/crump/cat77/cat82/).

contrast, those in the HSS and NSE fields at less selective institutions are forced into less advantageous positions. It is those students who need to have some distinction in the labor market, and the experience of studying abroad can be one means of offsetting this disadvantage.

This does not imply that studying abroad is unimportant for students; rather, it demonstrates the need to promote study abroad among students at more selective institutions and in the hard sciences. Even so, it is important to recognize that, in reality, the decision to study abroad is often motivated by factors omitted from the popular narrative of internationalization.

One might even argue, cynically, that government calls for the internationalization of higher education result in the exploitation of the general public—students are enticed to spend extra resources to study abroad, despite the fact that, for most, the actual economic benefit from this investment may be limited. Meanwhile, large corporations can reap the benefits without paying for the costs.

At the very least, it should be noted that the narrative of internationalization propagated on the ground of immediate economic return is not in and of itself sufficient ground to shift the values of the next generation and of the universities educating this generation.

Latent Need for Internationalization

We are faced, then, with a fundamental question: Why should Japanese universities be internationalized? What are the benefits of internationalization? In fact, I think that there is sufficient evidence to argue that Japanese universities should be compelled to internationalize if they wish to advance academically and become more relevant to social needs.

One aspect is research. Until recently, Japanese research productivity had been growing steadily, particularly in the postwar period. Publications in international journals had increased substantially, catching up with the publication rates of leading European nations by the turn of the century. In the past decade, however, research productivity has been stagnating. With respect to publication indices, Japan has now been overtaken not only by European countries but also by China. It is clear that the deficiency arose from a comparative lack of scientific papers written (NISTEP 2011). Growth increases in European countries came about through cooperation within Europe as well as with American institutions. China's rise can be largely accounted for by increased cooperation with the United States. Japan has so far failed to exploit these opportunities. It is imperative that Japan take part in these international research networks. This implies a need for change in research organizations and graduate education.

The case for internationalizing undergraduate education is less obvious, but I believe it is even more significant. It has to do with the changing nature of Japanese youth and the universalization of higher education. With the postwar economic growth, higher education in Japan grew enormously. Now the participation rate in four-year universities and colleges has reached 50 percent. With half of Japanese youth now advancing to four-year postsecondary institutions, Japan has entered the universal stage of higher education. Nevertheless, it has become increasingly clear that Japan's higher education system has significant problems with respect to quality of education and student learning outcomes.

One obvious reason for this is the change among students in motivation to learn. Japan has long been characterized by fierce competition among youth to advance to higher levels of education and institutions of higher prestige. These aspirations reflected the modernization of Japanese society as a whole. The majority of the population aspired to the higher standard of living of the middle class, and school education was the most direct route to this goal. Aspirations of social ascent motivated study.

As the better part of the population obtained this relatively high standard of living, the old pattern of aspiration began to be thwarted. Meanwhile, children experienced protected childhoods. Their environments have become increasingly monotonous. As Japan's industrial structure underwent radical transformation, traditional career paths disappeared. Children have fewer opportunities to be exposed to the real process of work. One of the consequences of such a process is that Japanese youth face difficulties in establishing identities and career prospects.

In a survey of college students (Kaneko 2014a), as many as 40 percent responded that they do not have a clear idea of what they will do after graduation. They hope to arrive at some idea through their experiences in college. Nonetheless, academic training in college does not necessarily help students to mature. Figure 6.6 presents results from a 2009 survey on how recruitment officers at business firms rate the characteristics of recent college graduates.

It is interesting to observe that their evaluation of the generic competencies of college graduates, such as interpersonal skills, logical thinking, and reading and writing abilities, are not necessarily low, as pointed out elsewhere. It is with respect to maturity that personnel officers find recent college graduates to be most deficient.

It can be argued that studying abroad can be an effective means for maturation. Studying abroad can force students to adjust to very different environments and cultures; crises encountered in the process can result in

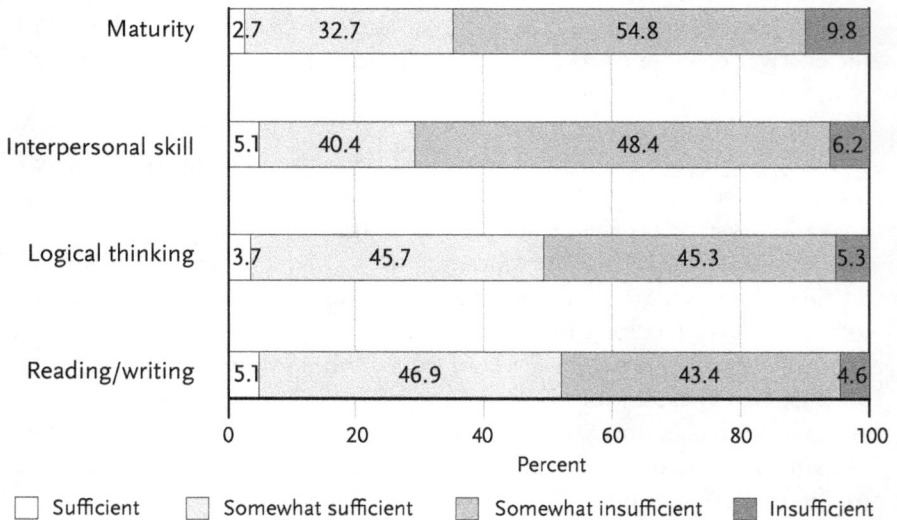

FIGURE 6.6 Employer perceptions of new college graduates

Source: Calculated by the author from Center for Research on University Management and Policy (CRUMP), 2009 Survey of Personnel Officers (N=8,157) (http://ump.p.u-tokyo.ac.jp/crump/cat77/cat83/).

students reflecting on and reevaluating themselves and their past experiences; and studying abroad can demand that students work with people who have backgrounds radically different from their own.

So far, though, this is a hypothetical contention. Even if there were cases where an individual derived benefits from such an experience, they would be deeply related to personal factors and therefore difficult to be conveyed to others. However, there is circumstantial evidence that indicates that such effects do in fact occur (Kaneko 2013a, 2014a). Studying abroad is positively correlated with such positive behavior as time devoted to independent study, self-evaluation of competences, and reflection on future career prospects. Nonetheless, these correlations by themselves fall far short of convincing the general public of the importance of study abroad.

Translation of Latent Need into Shared Objective

The discussion above indicates that, on the one hand, the actual benefit of study abroad may not be as substantial as is assumed by the popular narrative of internationalization. On the other hand, these "actual" benefits are not necessarily recognized. It is because of this gap between immediate returns and the potential benefit of study abroad that Japanese higher education is, at least for the time being, caught in the transitional trap.

In order to solve the impasse, the assumed latent need of the merits of international experiences has to be reframed as a shared objective robust enough to shift the belief and behavior of the general public. That process will ultimately require deliberate shifts in social policy and changes to the structure and underlying assumptions of higher education institutions. In order to overcome the transitional trap, government initiatives must play a significant role. This will present challenges to HEIS.

Government Initiatives

Responding to perceived needs, the Japanese government has launched various initiatives to promote the internationalization of higher education in the past decade. These government initiatives fall into three categories, namely, competitive grants, the creation of platforms for student exchange, and financial support for students to study abroad. Major ongoing programs are summarized in table 6.1.

Competitive Institutional Grants

The first area of initiatives is composed of competitive grants to HEIS for reforms aimed at the expansion of international cooperation and the exchange of faculty members and students. Since the 1990s, the Ministry of Education, Science, Culture and Sports (MEXT) has shifted government subsidies of higher education to competitive grants to institutions to induce changes in certain preferred directions. The first major grant program of this kind was the Center for Excellence program, which named international cooperation as one of its integral components. Since then, there have been a number of competitive grants, many of which have included an international component. In 2009, the Global 30 project was launched with the intention of fortifying the international activities of selected leading institutions. Through open bidding and selection, thirteen institutions were selected to be given funds over five years.

A major initiative undertaken in FY 2014 was the Leading Doctoral Programs, which are aimed at augmenting the academic capacities of graduate programs so that they are competitive at international standards. In the bidding process, it was specified that a proposal should include some component that enhances the exposure of students to academic activities in foreign institutions.

The Super Global University grant is directly aimed at the internationalization of HEIs. The grant is given to institutions based on an evaluation of plans to enhance international exchanges. The selection criteria include organizational reforms to support international activities, employment of foreign faculty members, an increase in students going abroad, and an increase in students coming from foreign institutions. In its initial year of 2014, seventy-two institutions were selected for this program.

The Capacity Building for Internationalization grant is provided to institutions to build and strengthen administrative sections and facilities to support the international exchange of researchers and students. In FY 2014, ninety-three institutions were selected to receive the grant.

Formation of Platforms for Student Exchanges

The second area of government initiatives is the construction of platforms to facilitate student exchange and credit transfer with foreign institutions. Joint degrees and double degrees have been issued by some Japanese institutions in cooperation with foreign institutions, but the criteria for granting such degrees have not been clearly defined, leading to confusion about the validity of these degrees. In order to accommodate and encourage institutions to build student exchange programs, the MEXT revised the National University Standards to stipulate requirements for the issuing of joint degrees.

Earlier I mentioned that Japan's lack of a regional framework

TABLE 6.1

Major government initiatives for the internationalization of higher education

Type	Initiative title	Description
Competitive grants to institutions*	Leading Doctoral Programs	• Grants to create doctoral programs geared to international competitiveness • Emphasis on international exchanges • 51 programs, 18.5 billion yen
	Super Global University	• Grants to universities to expand international exchanges of students • 72 institutions, 9.7 billion yen
	Capacity Building for Internationalization	• Grants to help build institutional capacity for international exchanges of researchers and students • 93 institutions, 3.9 billion yen
Formation of platforms for student exchange	Standards for Joint Degrees with Foreign Institutions	• Revision of National University Standards
	CAMPUS-Asia (Collective Action for Mobility Program of University Students)	• Platforms for exchanging students and transferring academic units • Covers China, Korea and Japan
Financial support for students	National Scholarship for Foreign Students	• Government-sponsored scholarship program • More than nine thousand students
	Loan/Grant Program for Studying abroad	• Loan/grant program for undergraduate and graduate students • Operated by the Japan Student Services Organization

Source: Compiled by author.

Note: *Competitive grants are those defined in the National Budget, FY 2015.

comparable to ERASMUS in Europe is one of the nation's distinct disadvantages in expanding student exchanges. Although there have been a few regional frameworks to facilitate student exchange and unit transfer, they have been unable to accommodate high levels of student mobility. In 2010, however, the Japanese government, in cooperation with the Chinese and Korean governments, launched the Collective Action for the Mobility Program of University Students in Asia (CAMPUS Asia) initiative. This is meant to be a regional platform for student exchange.

Financial Aid for Students

Japan has a long history in inviting foreign students to study in Japanese institutions. Since its establishment in 1956, the Government Scholarship Grant program has expanded. Currently, the scholarship is granted to almost ten thousand foreign students annually and is the largest government grant program in Asia. Lately, as the focus of government policy has expanded to include outbound mobility, some additional initiatives have been created. One is a loan and grant program for Japanese students at both graduate and undergraduate levels. A scholarship program financed by contributions from business firms was established in 2014. These scholarship programs are operated by the Japan Student Assistance Organization.

Institutional Initiatives

There is no doubt that at the outset of modernization Japanese universities were international in nature. Many teachers were foreigners, and lectures were delivered in English or other European languages. Since then, Japanese universities have grown increasingly domestic as academic standards have risen over time. While international exchange in particular has been considered at the core of academic activities, it has been limited to research.

A new wave of internationalization initiatives, including in undergraduate education, emerged in the 1990s. A new generation of universities and programs were established with internationalization as a core ideal. A typical example is Ritsumeikan Asia-Pacific University, established in 2000; foreign students make up half of its student body, with the remaining half being Japanese. Another case is Akita International University, which opened in 2004. Even though it was established by Akita Prefecture, its mission is to prepare students for international activities. All students are required to study in a foreign institution for at least one academic year.

The competitive grant programs launched with the Global 30 program have had significant effects. Universities sought to receive the grants not only for the funds that they would provide, but also for the distinction of having been chosen in a national selection process. In order to be awarded a grant, universities had to devise plans for various sorts of internal reforms. One of the changes considered in the process was that of the academic calendar. The University of Tokyo proposed to change the beginning of its academic year from April to September, to synchronize with the majority of foreign institutions. This proposal failed to materialize due to difficulties in implementation, but it consequently led to a quarter system that allowed students to attend summer programs overseas. A few institutions followed suit.

The Super Global University grant will undoubtedly have a major impact on Japanese universities as well. Potential recipients of the grant include not only research universities but also private institutions that enroll a large number of students. This implies that the focus of internationalization will be extended to the mass-sector of higher education. These developments indicate that efforts toward internationalization are entering into a new stage in which the scope of reforms must be expanded and intensified. It is about not only sending students out but also receiving students from foreign institutions. The number of both inbound and outbound students should be considerable in order to have a significant effect on the student body as a whole. Another issue is the quality of study-abroad experiences. Instead of sending students to short-term summer programs mainly for learning languages, it will be necessary to organize more intense study programs that are systematically knit into the curriculum of the home institution. In this sense, internationalization can no longer be a marginal activity for an institution of higher learning. As the scope of reforms becomes more pervasive, it will bring about a series of important changes within institutions.

Obstacles and Challenges

In order to advance to a new stage of internationalization, Japanese universities will face serious obstacles and challenges, which can be divided into three areas, organization, resources, and underlying academic values.

Organization and Governance

One pivotal issue is the organization and governance of universities. Japanese universities are organized as collections of individual faculties (*gakubu* or "academic division"). Each faculty corresponds to an academic discipline; it is the organization to which faculty members and students belong, and at the same time it is the basic unit of research and teaching. The faculty meeting is the basic governing body, determining academic regulations and allocating resources.

This organizational form creates serious problems in establishing exchange programs. Large-scale exchange programs will have to encompass more than one faculty, perhaps even all the faculties at an institution. Coordination with counterpart universities and the design and implementation of courses for incoming students must be undertaken at the institutional level. As it is, the ultimate authority to design curriculum, issue credits, and recognize diplomas rests with individual faculties. Internationalization in this sense runs counter to the principle of governance by faculty.

As the scale of international exchange grows, this problem will become more salient. It will ultimately lead to a discussion about the reformulation of internal governance, which has been on the agenda of university reform in the recent years.

Resources and Incentives

The issue of organization and governance is closely related to the collection of revenue and distribution of resources. This aspect of the internationalization of the university has not been explicitly discussed by the government or in the higher education community.

In anglophone countries, there are strong financial incentives for institutions to receive foreign students. In the United Kingdom and Australia, tuition levels for domestic students are strictly controlled by the government, while those charged to foreign students are set at much higher levels. In the United Kingdom, tuition revenue from foreign students had accounted for as much as 9 percent of total institutional revenue before the introduction of tuition for domestic students. As for Australian institutions, tuition revenue from foreign students accounted for 17 percent of total revenue in 2009. In fact, the revenue from these services—that is to say, the tuition paid by foreign students—made education Australia's third largest "export." There is a significant economic aspect to promoting the internationalization of higher education through national policy. In the United States, foreign students in the public sector of higher education are charged out-of-state tuition rates, which are substantially higher than in-state rates. Thus, in many countries there are significant financial incentives to receive foreign students.

East Asian institutions must face a completely different reality. The pools of potential students willing to come from other parts of the world and pay high tuition are substantially limited compared to the situation of anglophone countries. If the institution is only sending out students without any financial arrangements, it will lose potential tuition revenue. If the institution receives students, tuition revenue from those students may cancel out this loss. Realistically, however, this case will be difficult to realize. Moreover, even in this case, the institution must pay for additional hours worked by teachers and professional staff. Obviously, both in inviting foreign students and in sending Japanese students out, professional staff members are indispensable. Also, in order to provide extra courses for foreign students, a university must secure a significant amount of faculty hours, either by asking for additional teaching hours from existing faculty members or by employing new faculty members. As the number of exchange students grows, this cost becomes increasingly significant.

It should also be noted that in any event the students have to bear a fairly significant financial burden. Besides travel expenses and living costs, they are charged tuition and fees. As noted, institutions in the anglophone world charge especially high tuition for out-of-state students.

The grant program by the Ministry of Education is meant to compensate for some of the costs for the period that the grant covers, but thereafter the institutions are left to secure sufficient funds.

Teaching Practices and Underlying Values

A more fundamental issue is the teaching of foreign students. Even though the Japanese higher education system was reformed after World War II under the influence of the American system, there remains a deep-rooted Humboldtian idea of academic exploration at the core of the universities. Teachers tend to talk about their own academic specialization in large lecture halls. This approach is presumably complemented by seminars and laboratories where a teacher and a small group of undergraduate and graduate students form an intimate group.

While this arrangement has provided a favorable environment for academically motivated students, it may not be as effective in promoting deep learning among a large number of average students. In fact, our survey shows that the average time spent by Japanese students for learning over the duration of study falls far behind the norm extrapolated by the National University Standard (Kaneko 2014a).

The same structural characteristics of Japanese undergraduate education, relatively unstructured lectures presumably compensated for by the intimate personal relations of seminars and laboratories, make it difficult for Japanese universities to admit a large number of undergraduate students from overseas for exchange programs. On the other hand, seminars or laboratories at the graduate level, which lead to relatively close personal relationships, may match the needs of foreign students better. Nonetheless, the environment fails to produce more extensive and dynamic communication with foreign researchers and must be partially responsible for the slow increase in publications with internationally joint authorship (NISTEP 2011).

Ultimately, the challenge boils down to the values shared by faculty members. Insofar as faculty members insist that it is their specialized academic knowledge that has to be conveyed to students, international activities are given a secondary place among their priorities. It is when the values of international exchange in expanding the scope of education and learning are recognized that academics will more effectively participate.

Such a transformation of basic beliefs will not take place overnight. There will be gradual shifts in values amid the transformation of organizational arrangements and financial incentives. We are observing just the beginning of such a process.

Prospects for Transformation

While government initiatives create an environment for universities to proceed to expand student mobility, the effect of these policies on the internal structure of universities is not trivial. The most signifiant obstacles to internationalization are deeply embedded in institutions of higher education. In order for the internationalization of Japanese universities to gain momentum, some of their fundamental characteristics should be reexamined and eventually transformed. The challenges are formidable. How can Japanese universities overcome them?

Rather than viewing internationalization as a relatively insignificant trend, I have tried in this chapter to recognize its reality in Japan and the underlying structural problems that impede it. I believe that only by recognizing these problems will bringing about structural change be possible. One thing that is clear is that in the long run, internationalization may yield substantial benefits to Japanese universities. The need to accommodate a large number of foreign students will provide an excellent opportunity to reevaluate current educational practices. The involvement of young researchers in international research networks necessarily requires a change in the pedagogy of graduate education and research, which has been criticized as too narrowly focused. Exposing undergraduates to foreign culture will be effective in enhancing motivation to learn not only about foreign culture, but also to learn in general.

In this sense, internationalization may become a valuable driver of the institutional transformation of Japanese universities into more dynamic and effective entities. I should also note that internationalization is only one aspect of the pervasive innovation that Japan is about to engage in. At the same time, it is a vital step to achieving innovation in society as a whole. The challenge is not an easy one, nonetheless it is one that must be addressed.

References

Kaneko, Motohisa. 2013a. *Daigaku Kyouiku No Saikochiku* [Reconstructing college education in Japan]. Tokyo: Tamagawadaigaku-Shuppankai.
———. 2013b. "Japanese Higher Education and the State in Transition." In *Higher Education and the State*, edited by Roger Goodman, Takehiko Kariya, and John Taylor, 171–98. Oxford: Symposium Books.
———. 2014a. "Undergraduate Education in Japan: Observations from Student and Faculty Surveys." *Higher Education Forum* 11 (March): 21–35.
———. 2014b. "Higher Education and Work in Japan: Characteristics and Challenges." *Japan Labor Review* 11 (spring): 5–22.
National Institute of Science and Technology Planning (NISTEP). 2011. Benchmarking Scientific Research, Japan-NISTEP. 2011. *Bibliometric Analysis on Dynamic Alteration of Research Activity in the World and Japan.*
OECD. 2015. *Education at a Glance.* Paris: OECD.
United Nations Educational and Scientific and Cultural Organization and UNESCO Bangkok. 2013. *The International Mobility of Students in Asia and the Pacific.* UNESCO.
Zgaga, Pagel, Ulrich Teichler, and John Brenna, eds. 2013. *The Globalization Challenge for European Higher Education.* Frankfurt am Main: Peter Lang.

References

7 Transnationalizing and Internationalizing Higher Education in China

IMPLICATIONS FOR REGIONAL COOPERATION
AND UNIVERSITY GOVERNANCE IN ASIA

Ka Ho Mok

Over the past decade or so, we have witnessed the rise of transnational higher education and a call to internationalize higher education in Asia. In an increasingly borderless world, some Asian countries have begun the quest to become regional educational hubs by establishing university cities and inviting overseas universities to implement offshore programs or set up offshore campuses (Chapman, Cummings, and Postiglione 2010; Mok and Yu 2014). Perceiving education as both a trade and an industry, a few Asian economies, along with other economies in the Middle East, have embarked on their hub projects in India, Singapore, Hong Kong, Malaysia, and South Korea (Shields and Edwards 2010; Knight 2014). The emerging regional education hubs in Asia have inevitably transformed international student mobility patterns and induced intense competition among universities in the region vying for students. (Rivza and Teichler 2007; Mok and Ong 2012).

The internationalization of higher education and increasing student mobility are not new social phenomena. According to Knight (1997), the internationalization of higher education is "the process of integrating an international/intercultural dimension into the teaching, research, and service functions of the institutions." Similarly, Van der Wende (2007) understands the process of internationalizing higher education as "a strategic response to the demands and challenges of social, economic, and labor market

The author thanks Xiao Han and Genghua Huang for their assistance during the writing of this chapter, parts of which were adapted with revisions from Mok (2012), Mok and Chan (2012), and Mok and Ong (2012).

globalization," whereas Kerr (1994) simply refers to such a process as the global flow of people, information, knowledge, technology, programs, education services, and financial capital. To enhance their students' global competitiveness, governments around the world, particularly in Asia, are placing more emphasis on internationalizing student learning to foster the global knowledge, skills, and languages necessary for their graduates to perform professionally and socially in international, multicultural environments (Kuang et al. 2012; Stiasny and Gore 2012; Mok and Yu 2014).

Unlike patterns of international student mobility in the 1970s and 1980s, which were characterized by study destinations in Europe, the United Kingdom, and North America, since the late 1980s more students have begun studying in the Asia-Pacific region, especially since the 1996/97 Asian financial crisis (Mok and Ong 2012). We have analyzed changes in international student mobility patterns in light of Phillip Altbach's conceptual framework (Altbach 1989) and have witnessed a fundamental shift in which students who were moving from the periphery (developing economies) to the core (developed economies) for overseas learning experiences have instead begun to travel from the periphery to the semi-periphery (emerging economies). Meanwhile, Hawkins and Xu (2014) widen the perspective on the internationalization of higher education and consider how mobility and migration are paving the way for innovative universities throughout the Asia-Pacific region. According to the British Council, two-way travel has begun, with a growing number of students from developed economies in the West pursuing their educations in less-developed economies while students from Asia diversify their destinations for overseas study. The expansion of higher education in the Asia-Pacific region in recent years has resulted in more of its students choosing to stay home or attend local universities when pursuing a higher education (Brown 2012; Mok 2012).

In this chapter, we examine, in the context outlined above, what major policies and strategies the Chinese government has adopted to enhance student learning through engagements that promote transnational higher education and the internationalization of higher education, especially after China's accession to the World Trade Organization (WTO) in 2001. More specifically, we critically examine the Chinese government's serious attempts to transnationalize and internationalize higher education, with particular focus on the implications for higher education development and regional cooperation in Asia, given the increasing number of Chinese universities.

Policy Background: China's Quest to
Internationalize Higher Education

Realizing the importance of enhancing the quality of education and of recruiting/retaining and grooming talent that further sustains the nation's social, cultural, and economic development, the Chinese government has identified the internationalization of higher education as a strategic direction to improve the quality of graduates in general and enhance the global competitiveness of its higher education system in particular. In the last few decades, the Chinese government has not only increased its investment in higher education, but has also encouraged more students to study abroad to enhance the state capacity through knowledge transfer when graduates return from overseas universities. The internationalization of higher education in China began in the early 1980s and has developed rapidly in the past decade under strong state directives. In the early 1980s, studying abroad was mainly supported by the state-sponsored model and self-financed studying overseas was not common. In 2001, after fifteen years of negotiations, China successfully joined the WTO. Education is one of the twelve basic service items under the General Agreement on Trade and Services (GATS) framework. As a WTO member, the Chinese government has had no choice but to gradually open its education market to overseas players. Since then, the internationalization of higher education in China has entered a new phase of development driven by the increase in transnational higher education programs and the launching of campuses in China by overseas universities (Mok and Chan 2012; Mok and Han 2014). In this study, we examine how China has begun to open up its market to encourage overseas institutions to offer academic programs, facilitating the development of offshore campuses by cooperating with oveaseas universities to enhance international learning.

Recent Transnational Higher Education
Developments in China

In the past two decades, the Chinese government has encouraged the development of transnational higher education (TNHE) by promoting cooperation between universities in mainland China and overseas institutions and by establishing academic programs or even branch campuses in China (Zheng 2009, 36). In the 1980s, right after initiation of economic reforms and China's open-door policy, higher education was regarded as a priority by the state for realizing the four modernizations—industry, agriculture, national defense, and science and technology—by addressing the desperate need for professionals and new technologies. Students and scholars were sent by the state for overseas studies as a short-term measure to tackle this problem. The TNHE programs implemented during this period were scattered throughout the coastal provinces, such as Shandong and Jiangsu, and in big cities, such as Shanghai and Beijing. However, many of these institutions were unregulated and informal within the national education system.

By the 1990s, several factors had dramatically advanced TNHE development in China. There was the pressing need to boost the enrollment rate for Chinese tertiary education to sustain its soaring economic growth and meet the challenges posed by globalization. TNHE programs, in this regard, could be very helpful both in terms of internationalizing Chinese universities' curricula and in their quest for world-class status. In addition, concerns about "brain drain"—the outflow of Chinese human capital and the financial capital spent on overseas education—also prompted the government to rethink its monopolistic approach of governance over education, which has resulted in a more cautious and yet encouraging attitude toward TNHE (Wang and Liu 2010).

In July 2010, the State Council of the People's Republic of China (PRC) published the National Plan for Medium and Long-Term Education Reform and Development (*Guojia zhong chang qi jiayu gaige he fazhan guihua gangyao*, also known as and hereafter referred to as Education Blueprint 2020). One of the major goals of Education Blueprint 2020 was to further internationalize the higher education sector in the mainland by engaging in collaborations with leading universities overseas or within the region. In order to to transform the country from an economically strong nation to a country with strong human capital, the Chinese government is very keen to invest more in education and welcomes collaborations with overseas higher education institutions in terms of offering joint programs, venturing in high-level professional and research training programs, and engaging in international research projects to advance the country's knowledge and draw state-of-the-art technologies (State Council 2010).

It is within this wider context that transnational higher education in China has evolved from an informal, incidental, and rather laissez-faire activity into a systematic and regulated endeavor. In 1993, the Notice on Cooperation with Foreign Institutions and Individuals in Running Schools in China (*Guanyu jingwai jigou he geren lai Hua hezuo banxue wenti de tongzhi*) was issued, followed by the promulgation of the Provisional Stipulation on Chinese-Foreign Cooperation in Running Schools (CFCRS) (*Zhongwai hezuo banxue zhan xing guiding*) by the then State Education Commission on January 26, 1995. The Provisional Stipulation on CFCRS was particularly significant in the sense that it symbolized the formal inclusion of CFCRS activities into the management of state bureaucracy. It clearly specified the necessity of initiating CFCRS in China, its coverage, its application procedure, the defining authority over its program appraisal and approval, managerial framework for its institutions, and the awarding mechanism of its degrees/diplomas.

On December 11, 2001, TNHE experienced another momentous promotion in China prompted by WTO membership. China consequently promised to open up its education sector for commercial activities in the five subitems of primary, secondary, higher, and adult education and other educational services, encouraging TNHE under the legal framework of the international agreement. Foreign partners were now allowed to secure a majority ownership of the CFCRS institutions concerned, yet they remained prohibited from independently establishing and running an institution. In addition, the privilege of enjoying "national treatment" may not be granted to them as an entitlement during this process (Mok and Chan 2012).[1]

On March 1, 2003, the State Council, based on the above-mentioned WTO commitments, finally promulgated the Regulations of the PRC on CFCRS (*Zhonghua Renmin Gongheguo Zhongwai hezuo banxue tiaoli*, hereafter the 2003 CFCRS Regulations) to further regulate related activities and assert the legal rights of the stakeholders involved (Wang 2005, 188–89; Zhang 2005, 130). This was undoubtedly the most significant CFCRS regulation thus far, and the Ministry of Education subsequently released a set of corresponding measures in June 2004 to deal with more specific issues relating to CFCRS implementation. The 2003 CFCRS Regulations not only revealed the state's blessing in developing CFCRS, but more importantly, they did not forbid foreign institutions from profiting from such activities. TNHE development in China thus far can be broadly divided into three main phases in accordance with the shifts in national policies (Wang 2005, 189–90):

    1 Foreign universities planning to establish offshore campuses on the Chinese mainland have to work under the legal framework governing Sino-foreign cooperation in co-launching educational institutions, whereby foreign education institutions have to work with local institutions to mount their cooperative academic programs or education institutions. The major reason for such a governance arrangement is so the Chinese government can ensure that running academic institutions or programs are under the scrutiny of the Ministry of Education, so as to protect the "educational sovereignty" of China. For details, see Mok and Chan (2012). But once the Chinese government grants approval to the collaborative project, the local institution and the local government collaborating with the overseas partners are given strong support in running their Sino-foreign institutions or academic programs, as revealed by the case studies like Nottingham University in Ningbo and East China Normal University-NYU cooperation in Shanghai (see Han 2015).

- Laissez-faire exploration (before the promulgation of the Provisional Stipulation on CFCRS in January 1995);
- Progressive standardization initiated by the state (from 1995 to the promulgation of CFCRS Regulations in March 2003);
- Progressive legalization and regulation advanced by the state (from March 2003 to the present).

According to a recent study related to TNHE in China, there were about 712 programs and collaborative projects across twenty-eight cities and provinces in the mainland by the end of 2002 (Garrett 2004). Comparatively, by 1995, TNHE had increased ninefold. By the end of 2007, thirty-one countries and regions on different continents had reached agreements with the Chinese authorities for collaboration on joint programs or to offer TNHE programs on the mainland. In the latest list of approved CFCRS institutions and programs from the Ministry of Education regarding higher education (including both undergraduate and postgraduate levels), among twenty-seven approved CFCRS institutions currently operating in China, only two—the University of Nottingham-Ningbo in Zhejiang Province and the Cheung Kong Graduate School of Business in Guangdong Province[2]—were not established through collaboration between foreign institutions and local public higher education institutions. The University of Nottingham-Ningbo was founded in 2004 by the United Kingdom's University of Nottingham and the privately owned Zhejiang Wanli Education Group, and legally became the first CFCRS University in China. Intriguingly, the Cheung Kong Graduate School of Business was founded in 2002 in Beijing by Hong Kong's most successful tycoon and entrepreneur, Li Ka Shing. Its "local partner" is not even mentioned in the school's introductory statement, and on its official website, the school identifies itself as "China's first private, non-profit, and independent business school."[3]

Table 7.1 shows the major Sino-foreign cooperation programs, second-tier colleges, and cooperative universities established in mainland China to internationalize student learning. Up to early 2014, there were 930 Sino-foreign cooperative institutions and projects approved by the Ministry of Education, with 1,049 Sino-foreign cooperative institutions and projects approved by provincial governments and local departments of education,

2 Cheung Kong Graduate School of Business has been headquartered in Beijing ever since its establishment in November 2002. Currently, it has campuses in Beijing, Shanghai, and Guangzhou. In June 2010 a location was chosen in a Beijing suburb for its new main campus.

3 http://www.cheungkong-gsb.com/AboutUs/tabid/86/Default.aspx.

TABLE 7.1

Transnational cooperative higher education activities in China, 2015

Cooperation type	Number
Sino-Foreign Cooperation Programs	1,050*
Sino-Foreign Cooperation Second-tier Colleges	52
Sino-Foreign Cooperation Universities	8

Source: Ministry of Education 2015b.

Note: *There were originally 1,052 Sino-Foreign Cooperation Programs, but two of them in Hebei were dissolved by the MOE in 2014.

for a total of 1,979 cooperative institutions and projects. According to recent statistics, the number of students enrolled at all levels in all types of Sino-foreign cooperative educational institutions was about 550,000 in 2014, including 45,000 college students. With the rapid development of these TNHE activities, there were more than 1.5 million graduates from Sino-foreign cooperative educational institutions recorded in 2014 (CFCRS 2014). These figures clearly show the growing importance of Sino-foreign cooperative education projects in mainland China. Education Blueprint 2020 explicitly states that the Chinese government welcomes overseas universities to engage with local universities in China not only to diversify students' learning experiences but also to enhance the research and academic capacities of local institutions through the creation of TNHE programs and branch campuses in mainland China (Mok and Han 2014; see also table 7.2). The major countries having cooperation with China in terms of transnational higher education include the United Kingdom (252 out of 1,116[4]), the United States (220), and Australia (148). Figure 7.1 offers a breakdown of the partnering countries.

We must also note that the rapid growth of TNHE in China mainland has also caused significant challenges for educational governance. If we put the rapid development of TNHE into the wider context of the growing marketization in higher education since economic reform in the 1980s, especially when different kinds of private (*minban*) or quasi-*minban* (such as second-tier colleges or independent colleges in affiliation with national universities) higher education institutions have increased in number, we would argue that the proliferation of higher education has inevitably challenged the conventional governance model of higher education (see Lin et al. 2005; Mok and Ngok 2008; cited from Mok and Xu 2008, 406). The problems that

4 According to the data promulgated by the MOE in 2015, there are four programs or second-tier college collaborations between Chinese public universities and more than one foreign partner (in Chongqing, Jiangsu, Hubei, and Jilin).

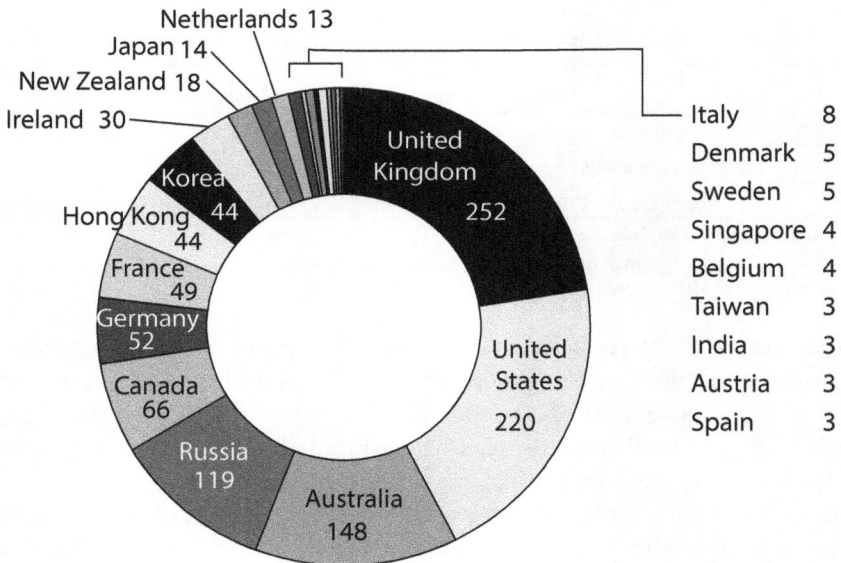

FIGURE 7.1 Sino-foreign higher education collaborations in China by number and national partner, 2015

Source: Ministry of Education (2015b).

emerged during the process of rapid development of TNHE in China—such as the unclear share of profits, the undefined quality assurance agency, the excessive use of overseas partners' brand names, and the blurring boundaries between public and private of TNHE—can be largely ascribed to the failure of regulatory frameworks, particularly when the existing legal and regulatory framework(s) were inappropriate and ineffective in governing these newly formed institutions. One of the challenges that confronted the operation of TNHE in mainland China was related to the academic quality of these programs, especially the difficulties some institutions faced finding sufficient high-quality lecturers teaching students in English. The problem is related not only to the shortage of high-quality teachers with English language proficiency but also to whether students would have sufficient English proficiency to study (see Mok and Han 2014). As Mok and Xu (2008, 406) observed,

> The Chinese government attempts to maintain a state-oriented regulatory
> regime in governing this increasingly complex and diverse higher education
> sector, [which blocks] the formation of a new regulatory state by adopting a
> corporate regulatory framework, civil society-led regulatory systems or inter-

national benchmarking evolving in governing the highly diversified sectors or markets.

Having examined TNHE development in China, let us now turn to examine how students are studying abroad and discuss the Chinese government's efforts to assert its global position by recruiting overseas students to study in China and by reaching out to the global community through the establishment of Confucius Institutes that promote Chinese culture and language.

Recent Developments in Students Studying Abroad

Studying Abroad with Government Scholarships

Chinese students studying abroad are not a new phenomenon. According to Huang (2003), mainland China has experienced two major phases in which the internationalization of higher education in post-Mao China was achieved by sending students overseas. The first phase was a restoration following the chaos that resulted from the Cultural Revolution (1966–76), during which the Chinese government tried to reinvent its higher education system by sending students to study abroad to make up for the lost decades. Realizing the urgent need for professionals and experts to help China master advanced scientific knowledge and modern technology, the Chinese government selected, financed, and dispatched scholars, faculty members, and students for advanced studies abroad, particularly in the fields of science, engineering, agriculture, and medicine (Ministry of Education 1978). The second phase of internationalizing higher education was driven by the call for world-class universities to address the growing competition driven by globalization in the 1990s. In 1996, the China Scholarship Council was established to handle student selection and execute the government-sponsored study abroad policy. After China's accession to the WTO, government-sponsored study abroad was not affected by the liberalization tendencies of the education service trade. In fact, it developed quickly. In 2001, the number of Chinese government-sponsored students abroad was 3,495, while in 2005 it increased to 3,979 (Welch and Hao 2014).

During this phase, the major features of the government-sponsored study-abroad policy were that the key government-sponsored fields of study were defined under the principle of cultivating talent to meet the state's desperate needs and catch up to the world-class university movement. It is in this context that the Senior Scholar program was developed in 2003 to nurture professionals and experts in developing an innovation-oriented nation and cultivating top-notch innovative talents. To turn mainland Chinese

universities into world-class institutions, the Chinese government formu-
lated and implemented the Government-Sponsored Postgraduates Studying
Abroad Program in 2006, (*Guojia jianshe gao shuiping daxue gongpai yanjiu-
sheng xiangmu*) with financial sponsorships for Chinese students to study
abroad at leading universities. These two projects clearly show that the key
government-sponsored fields were in strategic areas such as energy sources,
resources, environment, agriculture, manufacturing, and information, and
strategies related to life, space, the ocean, new materials, humanities, and
applied social sciences. The destinations for government-sponsored study-
abroad programs were mainly developed countries—the United States and
European nations. For instance, from 2007 to 2010, of the 18,482 students
the Government-Sponsored Postgraduates Studying Abroad Program sent to
study overseas, 43.5 percent (8,045 students) went to the United States, 8.85
percent were sent to England, 9.1 percent to Germany, 7.55 percent to Japan,
and 6.7 percent went to Canada. Figure 7.2 shows the increase in Chinese
students studying abroad on government scholarships from 2001 to 2012; it
is not surprising that the majority of Chinese students were sent to developed countries such as the United States, England, and Germany to study
best practices and advanced technologies at globally ranked universities.

Students were sent abroad for higher education not only to nurture
their talents, but also to enhance human capital through the return of these
highly qualified people once their studies were completed. These returning

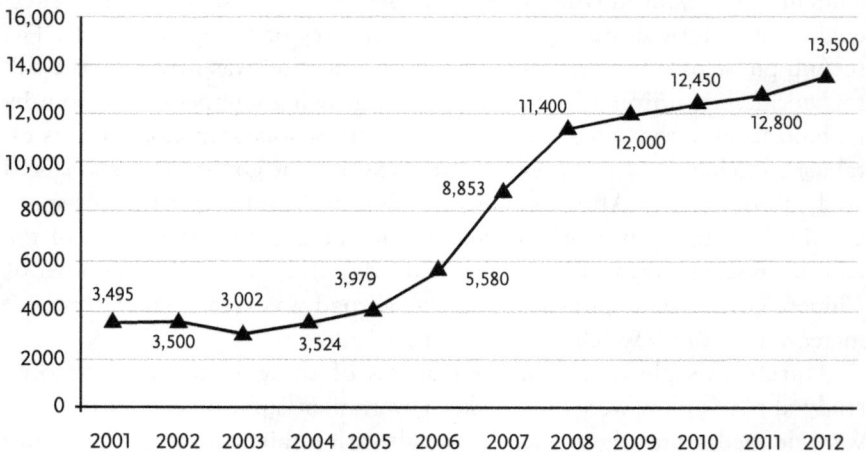

FIGURE 7.2 Chinese students studying abroad via government sponsorships, 2001–12

Source: Educational Statistics Yearbook of China, and China's Ministry of Education website. 2010 data are
estimated by the author.

students, also referred to as *haigui*,[5] have been important to China's human resources development. In 2007, the Ministry of Education and the Ministry of Finance issued the Policy Document regarding Provisions of Government-Sponsored Postgraduates Studying Abroad, which required government-sponsored postgraduates studying abroad to come back and work in China for two years. If they were to refuse, they would be required to return the subsidy and pay another 30 percent as liquidated damages. This provision restrained students abroad through financial reimbursement, legal accountability, and reputation punishment. The Chinese government also encouraged students abroad to come back by providing extra help and privileges in terms of professional titles, competitive wages and compensation packages, and job placement assistance for spouses. In 2001, the ministries of Personnel, Education, Technology, and of Public Security cooperated to issue a document entitled "Some Opinions on the Encouragement of Students Abroad to Return to Serve in Various Forms" (*Guanyu guli haiwai liuxue renyuan yi duozhong xingshi wei guo fuwu de ruogan yijian*). It proposed that the state would provide funds and intellectual property as safeguards for students abroad who chose to return and serve. In 2003, the First National Talents Work Conference (*Quanguo rencai gongzuo huiyi*) was proposed to attract high-level talents studying abroad to return home for employment. Subsequently, relevant policies were produced annually encouraging the placement of returning students. Regarding the dual effects of these binding and encouraging measures, in recent years the returning rate of government-sponsored students abroad has remained above 98 percent (Xiao 2012).

To attract *haigui*, the Chinese government has launched different incentive schemes, multiplied at the national, provincial, and institutional levels, especially among the most developed regions in eastern China. Under national plans such as the 12th Five-Year Plan and Education Blueprint 2020, by 2014 the range of high-level overseas talent recruitment programs numbered almost a dozen, implemented by various ministries and government agencies. The Thousand Foreign Experts Scheme (*qianren jihua*), together with other prestigious national chair professor/professor schemes such as the Changjiang Professor Scheme, brought home more than two thousand returnees in 2012 (Kirby 2014). Figure 7.3 shows the increase in number of returnees from 1978 to 2013, suggesting that China's talent pool has been significantly enhanced (Welch and Hao 2014).

---

5 "Returning from overseas," and a homophone for "sea turtles."

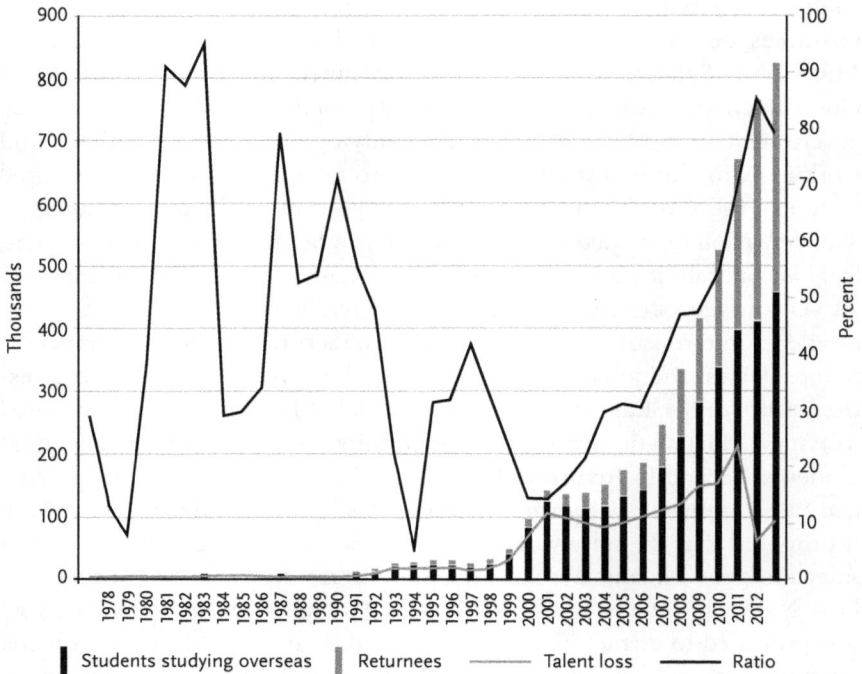

FIGURE 7.3 The increasing number of returnees, 1978–2013

Source: National Bureau of Statistics (http://data.stats.gov.cn/workspace/index;jsessionid=BC22523F-C8726E1040D36B51ED907A6E?m=hgnd).

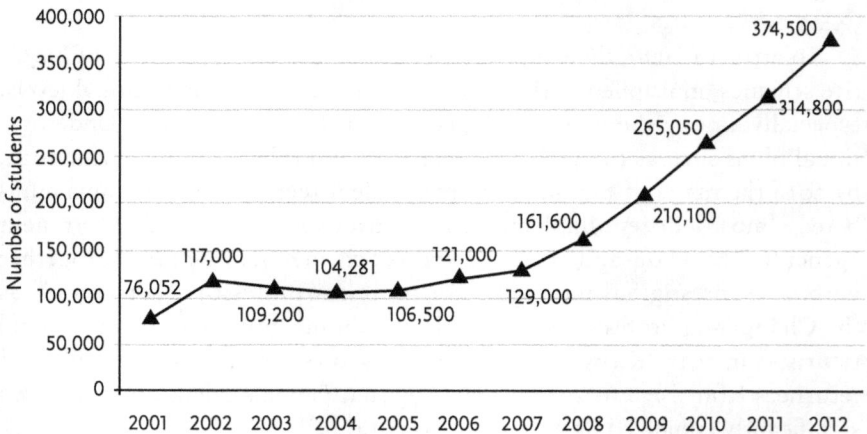

FIGURE 7.4 Chinese students engaged in self-financed study abroad, 2001–12

Source: Educational Statistics Yearbook of China, and China's Ministry of Education website. 2010 data are estimated by the author.

Self-Financed Students Studying Abroad: A Growing Trend

In addition to the growing number of students studying abroad through government sponsorships, there has also been a steady increase in self-financed Chinese students pursuing higher education in different parts of the globe. After the reform and opening-up, especially after 1992, when China had embedded itself not only in the process of economic marketization but also in the privatization and marketization of education, health, and housing (Mok 2006; Mok et al. 2010), the government began to encourage students to study abroad using their own financial resources. In particular, China's accession to the WTO in 2001 further encouraged self-financed students to pursue education overseas. To conform to GATS rules, China adjusted the related study-abroad policy. In 2003, the Ministry of Education announced that the approval process for self-financed study abroad for college degrees would be simplified, and advised colleges and local governments not to apply "higher education cultivating expenses" to or require qualification examinations of self-financed study-abroad applicants or those with associate degrees or above. At the same time, the Ministry of Education set up the Chinese Government Award for Outstanding Self-Financed Students Abroad (*Guojia youxiu zifei liuxuesheng jiangxuejin*) in 2003 to sponsor students who studied in developed countries such as America, Japan, England, Germany, and France. It was the Chinese government's first financial aid policy for self-financed students abroad. Figure 7.4 illustrates the growing trend in self-financed students pursuing education overseas.

The increase in students self-funding their education abroad is not only a result of this favorable policy environment, but also can be attributed to the steady economic growth enjoyed by a growing number of families in mainland China. China's gross domestic product (GDP) in 2001 was 129 times greater than in 1978, when the reform and opening-up began, and seventeen times greater than in 1992. Specifically, the average annual growth rate of China's GDP exceeded 10 percent right after the WTO accession (*China Statistical Yearbook*, various years). Rapid economic growth dramatically increased personal incomes, resulting in a significant number of families and individuals becoming capable of paying for their children or relatives to study abroad. The popularity of studying overseas was also closely related to the one-child policy adopted in China in the 1980s, as it allowed (or forced) most families to concentrate attention and resources to offer the best learning environment for their sole child. Although the higher education sector in mainland China has experienced massification in the past few decades, which has created more learning opportunities, many Chinese parents have not been satisfied with the university education offered by local institutions, believing that sending their children to study abroad will enhance their future global competitiveness. This explains why an increasing number of families are willing to pay high fees to send their children to study abroad (see figure 7.3).

Recruiting International Students and Promoting Cultural Diplomacy

Another major development related to internationalization strategies is the Chinese government's practice of establishing Confucius Institutes in different parts of the world to reach out to the international community and promote Chinese culture and language, while also asserting China's presence in an increasingly global world. It has been noted that education can be considered the fourth layer of diplomatic policy, increasing a country's influence in international society (De Wit 2002, 85). International cooperation in education, especially in higher education, which has always been regarded by politicians as an important form of diplomatic investment in various countries, has a specific diplomatic function. In the example of Germany, Roeloffs claims the educational exchanges and cooperation between Germany and France have mainly been for the recovery and development of their diplomatic relationship (Roeloffs 1994). In 2008, the Association of International Educators of America (NAFSA), the world's largest non-profit association dedicated to international education and exchange, issued a report arguing that

> [i]nternational education forms the foundation for addressing . . . challenges [facing the United States], and it is an indispensable component of the revived public diplomacy that must begin to rebuild America's global reputation. Yet the United States today lacks the policy instruments to realize international education's potential. It is time, as a nation, to be purposeful about international education. . . (NAFSA 2008)

After its accession to the WTO, China began to deliver on its promise to open up its education market. Perhaps most importantly, the control on foreign students studying in China was gradually relaxed and the number of foreign students studying in China increased annually, with most seeking higher education. It was also in 2002 that *China's Educational Statistics Yearbook* began to record related data about the number of foreign students. In that year the number of foreign students in China was 37,338, and in 2012 it increased to 102,991 (276 percent growth, see table 7.3). The significant increase in foreign students can be attributed to two forces. The first was the international education market. After its accession to the WTO,

China opened its doors to foreign students, and under the influence of the market, an increasing number of foreign students independently came to China for education. The second force was the Chinese state—as discussed above, China realized that education had diplomatic functions and could increase the country's influence, so it tried various methods to attract more foreign students. One such method was to offer foreign students different types of scholarships for study in China. In 2002, the Ministry of Education offered Chinese government scholarship quotas to 153 countries. In 2005, the Ministry of Education cooperated with some major corporations in China to set up scholarships for foreign students in China. For example, China Development Bank, Huawei Technology Limited Company, and China Oil Company all agreed to set up international student scholarships to attract overseas students. Meanwhile, local governments in Beijing, Shanghai, Tianjin, Chongqing, Yunnan, Hubei, Jiangxi, and Inner Mongolia also created local government scholarships, for an annual gross amount that exceeded seventy million yuan (China Education Press 2008, 457). By then, China had established a scholarship system mainly composed of central government scholarships and supplemented by local government, college, and enterprise scholarships. In 2003, the Ministry of Education even set up a special health insurance system for foreign students. Table 7.2 shows the increase in international students attending universities in China from 2002

TABLE 7.2

International students admitted to study in China, 2002–12

Year	Total	Receiving Chinese government aid		Self-supporting
		Number	Percent	
2002	37,338	2,310	6.19	33,152
2003	40,165	2,442	6.08	34,803
2004	50,603	3,000	5.93	45,000
2005	60,904	3,106	5.10	54,298
2006	62,612	3,947	6.30	52,198
2007	66,509	5,299	7.97	55,124
2008	71,294	7,325	10.27	57,659
2009	73,266	11,988	16.36	53,536
2010	80,846	13,591	16.81	56,886
2011	94,692	14,041	14.83	68,975
2012	102,991	15,730	15.27	73,204

Source: Educational Statistics Yearbook of China (various years 2002–12).

to 2012, as well as the breakdown between those who received Chinese government aid and those who were self-supporting.

More importantly, the Chinese government has made students from Asian and African countries its main targets, developing special scholarship schemes to draw them to study in China. In recent years, the Chinese government has signed agreements with Singapore, Thailand, Pakistan, Vietnam, Rwanda, and Tanzania to offer full scholarships to their students willing to embark on learning journeys in China. On November 4, 2006, Hu Jintao, then PRC president, declared that China would increase the annual government scholarship quotas from two thousand to four thousand to promote a new strategic partnership between China and Africa at the opening ceremony of the China-Africa Cooperation Forum Beijing Submit Meeting. On August 16, 2007, at the 7th Conference of the Shanghai Cooperative Association Chief Executive Council, President Hu further promised to establish Study in China Scholarships for Shanghai Cooperation Organization Members. In addition, China announced it would provide twenty more government scholarship quotas every year to member countries, for a total of one hundred quotas. In 2012, for example, 60 percent of foreign students studying in China came from Asia, 9 percent from Africa, 20 percent from Europe, 9 percent from North America, and 1 percent each from South America and Oceania (*Educational Statistics Yearbook of China* 2012). The main source countries in Asia were Korea (30.59 percent), Japan (10.18 percent), and Thailand (8.03 percent) (Ministry of Education 2013). More recently, 2014 data show that foreign students studying in China came from Asia (59.8 percent), Africa (11.05 percent), Europe (17.9 percent), America (9.58 percent), and Oceania (1.33 percent). The 2014 breakdown for overseas students coming from Asia includes Korea (27.91 percent), Thailand (9.44 percent), and Russia (7.63 percent) (Ministry of Education 2015a).

For the first few years after Chinese accession to the WTO, the increase in the number of foreign students studying in China was mainly the result of the opening up of the Chinese market. After 2007–08, the Chinese government increased scholarships to attract more foreign students. The above figures clearly suggest that the Chinese government's incentive methods played an important role in the recruitment of overseas students. Before 2007, the proportion of foreign students aided by the Chinese government lingered at around 6 percent, whereas in 2008 it exceeded 10 percent and even reached 16.81 percent at its highest (see table 7.2). In 2009, the vice minister of the Ministry of Education, Hao Ping, speaking at the twentieth anniversary celebration of the China Association for International Education, noted that "in the current financial crisis, all countries have tried very hard to attract and recruit international students by offering them scholarships." Minister Hao continued, "for this reason, we should carry out the Studying in China Project to increase the number of foreign students to more than five hundred thousand by 2020, and make China the biggest target country for Asian students abroad" (Hao 2009).

To attract more overseas talent, the government has developed scholarships with the aim of fully covering foreigners' expenses during their studies in China. The scholarships providers are diverse, including the central government, local governments, Chinese higher education institutions, and enterprises. Financial support has targeted a wide range of foreign students, from undergraduates to PhD candidates. With reference to the report published in 2009, the Chinese government proposed 18,245 scholarship schemes to 174 countries and regions globally, except for two grants that were targeted at specified source nations.[6] In 2009 16.36 percent of international students received aid from the Chinese government for degree courses, short-term education, and training programs. The origin of these recipients breaks down into 8,409 Asian (46.1 percent), 4,824 African (26.4 percent), 3,022 European (16.6 percent), 1,599 American (8.8 percent), and 391 Oceanian (2.1 percent) (CAFSA 2009).[7]

Students coming to China for an education are primarily ones highly competitive in their own countries, and they are keen to take senior and leadership positions upon returning after graduating from Chinese universities. When these future leaders later in their careers make business and/or policy decisions in their own countries, the financial support they received and their own educational experiences may make them more likely to be sympathetic toward China in these decisions. Thus, in this light, the provision of scholarships for overseas students to study in China can be seen as an act of cultural diplomacy. "Soft power," as coined by the American scholar Nye (1990), is an important concept in international relations. Nye emphasizes that soft power is cooperative, and its main source is culture.

6 The Confucius Institute Scholarship has stated that undergraduate scholarships in International Chinese Education (hanyu guoji jiaoyu) are open only to students from Asia (excluding Japan, Korea, Singapore, Israel), Africa, and Latin America; grants for "1+1" students (one year of advanced studies and one year to pursue a master's degree) are available only to African and Latin American applicants. See China Scholarship Council (2015).

7 The brief report by the China Association for International Education (CAFSA 2009) provides statistics for government scholarship schemes including financial aid for different types of programs, both degree and non-degree courses. The number is larger than shown in table 7.2, which focuses on statistics for international students attending universities.

With its unique seepage force and penetrating power, soft power affects diplomatic decisions among states.

China's rise in the global arena has occurred in tandem with a far-reaching transformation in international relations. The above discussion of the Chinese government's attempts to attract overseas scholars does provide some evidence of the regime's assertion of soft power. For the past two decades, a country's power has been perceived to encompass not only the traditional hard components of power but also, increasingly, its "soft face." Nye (1990) criticizes the traditional approach of defining power based on physical attributes and military capability, arguing that in this era of globalization, the intangible attributes of soft power—resources such as cultural attractiveness, institutions, good governance, political values, and foreign policies—have become more significant aspects of a country's power (Mok and He 2014). The Chinese government's investment in Confucius Institutes worldwide has offered additional evidence of its use of soft power. Leung and du Cros (2014), in their recent research examining how the rapid development of Confucius Institutes worldwide has accelerated learning through cultural exchange programs and Chinese language and culture programs, note that such efforts have served to foster mutual trust between China and the institute host countries. Beijing's ambitious expansion plan to establish hundreds of Confucius Institutes across the world is probably one of the most prominent initiatives in its global outreach agenda in recent years (see table 7.3). As Beijing has no intention of exporting its revolutionary past with its ideologically driven propaganda, the increase in students sent to study overseas and in attracting overseas students to study in mainland China, together with concerted efforts to promote global cultural and educational exchanges, do provide strong evidence that China is globalizing and internationalizing through various cultural diplomacy projects.

Similarly, China's engagement in Africa has been increasingly reported in the media over the last decade. However, most commentators have focused on China's growing influence in Africa through its engagements in economic activities and aid projects, while less attention has been given to educational aid. In fact, China has actively provided developmental aid to poorer countries over the years, even when its own economy was in deep crisis during Mao's reign. Although this irrational agenda was abandoned by Deng Xiaoping, who drastically reduced the volume of China's foreign aid and made it contingent on the country's real capacity, China's aid has produced tolerable outcomes overall and, more importantly, it has been greatly welcomed by recipient nations. Yuan's (2014) recent work centers on the operation of the Chinese Government Scholarship Scheme (*Zhongguo zhengfu*

TABLE 7.3

Cultural institutes worldwide

Country	Institute	Year founded	Existing institutes	Countries/ territories
Turkey	The Yunus Emre Institute	2009	18	Data not available
China	Confucius Institute	2004	322 Confucius Institutes; 369 Confucius Classrooms	96 countries
Romania	Institutul Cultural Roman	2003	16	16
Poland	Adam Mickiewicz Institute	2000	Data not available	Over 22 major cities
Portugal	Instituto Camões	1992	Data not available	Data not available
Spain	Instituto Cervantes	1991	Over 70	Across four continents
Korea	The Korea Foundation	1991	6 overseas offices	5
Japan	The Japan Foundation	1972	2 domestic institutes; 23 overseas offices	21
Germany	Goethe-Institut	1951	149 Goethe Institutes; 10 Liaison offices	92
Denmark	The Danish Cultural Institute	1940	Offices in 11 countries	11
UK	British Council	1934	191 offices	110 countries and territories
Italy	Dante Alighieri Society	1889	Over 450	Established in most countries and major cities
France	Alliance Française	1883	1040	136

Source: Leung and du Cros (2014, 73).

jiangxuejin) in Africa—one of the flagship programs in China's overseas education aid. It reveals the contrasting "donor logic" underlying Chinese and Western ways of providing foreign aid. While the West tends to impose conditions and emphasize a "catching up" logic, China upholds the principle of "non-interference in internal affairs" and regards educational aid as mutually beneficial instead of as a one-off donation. Yuan shows that the win-win strategy has indeed helped China gain the political trust of African recipient nations, and that higher education has become a significant source of soft power generation for China.

Discussion: China's Rise and Implications
for Regional Cooperation in Asia

Above we have suggested that China's higher education has undergone significant transformations not only in reforming its management and governance styles but also in diversifying the learning experiences of students and the modes of delivering higher education. Many Chinese university leaders realized that depending on universities based in mainland China to transform their structures and systems to enhance student learning experiences would delay the national goal, and that the transformation from within would create structural barriers that would further delay the reform processes. For this reason, the Chinese government has made serious attempts to engage local education institutions to work with overseas partners to inject new energy and ideas through changes to higher education in China. Given the importance of transforming the Chinese economy from manufacturing to engagement in knowledge-based production activities, the call to transnationalize and internationalize higher education reflects a significant historic mission for the country, not only in education but also in nation-building and the assertion of soft power in a global world (Mok and Chan 2012; Mok and Ong 2014).

In addition, our analysis shows that China's higher education system has transformed from highly elitist to massive in nature (Hayhoe et al. 2011), with the strategies adopted by the Chinese government significantly internationalizing higher education, as clearly reflected by the growing number of Chinese students studying abroad and foreign students studying in mainland China. The establishment of Confucius Institutes worldwide, together with the development and educational aid contributed by the Chinese government to the developing world, has made China a growing global influence. The country's rapid economic growth and its increasing numbers of highly educated people through the internationalization and transnationalization of its higher education have generated publications with titles such as *China's Rise, The Rise of China*, and *China's Ascent*. Some have even dubbed the twenty-first century the "Chinese century" (Kirby 2014). Given China's growing influence in economic and global issues, University of Illinois president James Stukel said in 1997 that "[e]very great nation in the world will inevitably be drawn into more or less intimate relations" with a rapidly changing China (cited in Kirby 2014, 147). More importantly, Stukel conceived of a China that would rise because of its international educational alliances.

With just a few decades of investment and expansion, China has more university graduates than the United States. According to Education

Blueprint 2020, 20 percent of China's working-age population (aged 20–59) will have a higher education degree by 2020. By 2020, the Chinese government expects 40 percent of young adults in this age cohort to have higher education qualifications. One point that deserves attention here is that this surge has been accompanied by a diversification of institutions offering a wide range of learning experiences. The Chinese government has realized its own limitations in nurturing talent through local universities; thus, the country has strategically internationalized higher education. As Kirby (2014, 149) observes, "[u]nlike the growth of American universities in the 1950s and the extraordinary expansion of European institutions that began in the 1970s, the development of higher education in China has been elitist as well as massive." The strategies being adopted by the Chinese state in transforming its higher education have earned the country better university rankings globally. In the 2012–13 Quacquarelli Symonds (QS) World University Rankings of more than eight hundred institutions worldwide, Peking University and Tsinghua University were ranked 44th and 48th, respectively. Similarly, the 2012–13 Times Higher Education Global University League ranked these two universities 46th and 52nd, respectively. In the most recent rankings, Peking University was ranked 48th globally by the Times Higher Education World University Rankings (2014) while Tsinghua University was, again, ranked comfortably high in Asia and the world. Tsinghua was regarded as the most reputable Chinese university by the Times Higher Education World Reputation Rankings (2014), where it ranked 36th globally. According to the QS BRICS University Rankings (2013), it was ranked highly in this newly launched independent regional league. Similarly, it was ranked 23rd in the Times Higher Education rankings by subject for engineering and technology, which were its strengths in 2013–14. If we include the university rankings of Hong Kong and Taiwan, it is clear that higher education institutions in the Greater China region have performed well in different university leagues.

With the rise of Chinese universities in regional and global contexts, what are the implications for Asia and beyond?

Analyzing the rise of Chinese universities and its global effect, Kirby (2014, 151) believes that

> [o]pportunities for foreign universities in contemporary China exist everywhere, but perhaps especially in three realms. First, the over-centralization of Chinese research universities in Beijing and the greater Shanghai region has led other cities to be highly entrepreneurial in recruiting international partners. Second, the Chinese government has committed to stunning levels of investment in the STEM fields (science, technology, engineering, and medicine) and

to international partnerships in these realms. Third, leading Chinese universities are developing American-style programs of general education and in the process have sought international advice, support, and models.

By strengthening cooperation with their Chinese counterparts, Asian universities could take advantage of these three areas of potential growth.

Nonetheless, to further enhance their capacity to contribute to the nation's future development and to the world, Chinese universities really need more than the areas outlined by Kirby (2104). What Chinese universities really need are the soft aspects—appropriate ways to exercise university governance, particularly in empowering university administrators and faculty members to enjoy a certain degree of the academic freedom enjoyed at other world-class universities. In preparing future generations to become far more adaptive to an ever-changing global environment, the elements missing in the Chinese university curriculum are creativity, innovation, and entrepreneurial spirit. Asian universities, sharing a similar cultural orientation but different development experiences, should engage in regional cooperation with their Chinese counterparts. The rise of Chinese universities should not be seen as a zero-sum game. Deeper regional cooperation that encourages students from China to mingle with their counterparts from Asia and beyond could offer comparative and international perspectives for understanding the changing world. Given the growing importance of regional cooperation, Asian universities should work closely to develop new theoretical models of education that reflect Asia's unique attributes, supported by serious comparative and empirical research. Those who have coined the twenty-first century the "Chinese century" must acknowledge that a strong China requires comprehensive cooperation among Asian countries and regions, not only in the fields of science and technology, but perhaps more importantly in the humanities, social sciences, creative arts, and culture.

Given the rapid expansion and improvement of higher education in East Asia, particularly the prosperity of the region's TNHE network together with a gradual convergence of the modes of higher education governance, this trend in East Asian regulatory regionalism is expected to persist (Hawkins, Mok, and Neubauer 2012; Neubauer, Shin, and Hawkins 2013). Moreover, China may gradually become the center of this regional drive to reposition higher education due to its remarkable size, its aggressive strategies for achieving world-class status, and its application of higher education as a means of exerting its cultural soft power. The most probable platform for further integration, in this respect, may be the ASEAN Plus Three (APT) process.

As argued in recent research, regional cooperation has not been confined to education but also has included cultural and social developments among different countries in the Asia-Pacific. Apart from the APT process involving China, Japan, and South Korea, other forms of regional cooperation have emerged, such as the ASEAN-sponsored East Asian Summits (EAS) and the added participation of India, Australia, and New Zealand in the APT (Arase 2011). ASEAN further extends beyond East Asia by organizing multilateral consultations through participation in the twenty-one-member Asia-Pacific Economic Cooperation (APEC) meeting. ASEAN also sponsors the twenty-seven-member ASEAN Regional Forum (ARF) to promote dialogue and consult on political and security issues of common interest in the Asia-Pacific region (Mok 2012).

The rise of Chinese universities should not be seen as a threat to Asia, but rather as an opportunity for deep cooperation in the region. Compared with what has been achieved in Europe toward establishing a common academic/qualification framework for promoting student mobility, the mechanisms to promote East Asian integration in higher education have not yet been fully developed (Robertson 2008). However, there have been signs of regulatory regionalism in related collaborations via certain regional organizations, or in the institutional interactions undertaken within a wider framework of ASEAN Plus One or APT. For example, ASEAN's formation as a regional collaborative framework is a case in point. Recent research on how regional cooperation has emerged not only in economic but also in educational and cultural aspects has clearly suggested that new modes of higher education governance are emerging in Asia, characterized by evolving features of "regulatory regionalism" (Mok 2013). Based on Ravenhill's (2005) definition of regionalism as a formal intergovernmental collaboration between two or more states, Robinson (2008, 720) further enhances this definition by arguing that regionalism should be viewed as an outcome of integration processes involving a coalition of social forces such as markets, private trade, investment flows, policies, and decisions of organizations and state-led initiatives. ASEAN—as an organization with formal collaboration between ten member countries and involving coalitions with the East Asia Big Three and other forms of regional cooperation—clearly indicates not only the growing stature of this regional international organization but also the emergence of regional forces fostering a more consolidated regional cooperation platform.

One point that deserves particular attention is that when analyzing regional cooperation or competition among Asian universities in general, and governmental cooperation in particular, we must not treat such processes as mutually exclusive. They should be seen as the regional platforms in which

Asian governments have become involved, such as ASEAN and other regional cooperative frameworks that closely interact with the regional cooperation venues spontaneously emerging from academic and research organizations, including different forms of academic and research associations, societies, or consortia. Government-driven regional cooperation efforts such as ASEAN and APEC should be conceptualized as "hard" approaches, whereas the regional collaborations initiated by individuals and universities or other research or academic organizations are soft approaches to regional cooperation. The central characteristic of the hard approach is that it is top-down, normally driven by the nation-state, and thus the governance style is much more centralized. In contrast, the soft approach is bottom-up, normally driven by local forces and organic in nature, with emphasis on network governance. We may argue that the hard approach shapes national policy directly, but the soft approach also influences national strategy and policy. Meanwhile, we must also note that neither non-governmentally nor governmentally driven cooperation is entirely exclusive, but rather complementary.

Deepening regional cooperation in the context of an increasingly competitive environment requires both a structural and a soft approach to maximize the political capital generated by governmentally driven cooperation frameworks and the network capital generated by the organically formed regional cooperation platforms. Empirical evidence can be found in support of the interactive relationship between hard and soft approaches when analyzing regional cooperation in Asia. Taiwan, for instance, which has encountered difficulty in asserting its national status due to the "one China" issue, has discovered different ways to assert its influence through engagement along a variety of regional/international cooperation venues such as academic/research consortia, associations, and societies. Mainland China has also taken a more active approach in asserting its regional and global leadership by participating in different forms of regional organization spontaneously evolving from local/regional communities (Chen 2011).

Another major observation that needs to be highlighted here is that when analyzing regional cooperation, we must note that regionalism is not a single phenomenon, but rather a complex and complicated process in which subregionalism emerges from regionalism. This requires us to closely examine the different forms and nature of regional cooperative frameworks. The emerging and deepening regional cooperation in educational and cultural domains suggest that there is plenty of room for China to benefit from a wide range of experiences offered by neighboring Asian nations. For instance, Korea's success in asserting its hard and soft power by reinventing its manufacturing industries into a high-technology-driven economy, together with its fascinating development of creative arts and culture into creative industry, could certainly provide China with valuable information, especially when China has been searching for good practices to transform and reinvent its own systems.

Historical evidence clearly shows that the presidents of Chinese universities have taken their U.S. counterparts very seriously by identifying good practices for China to follow in enhancing its higher education system, for example, the introduction in recent years of "general" and "liberal" educations to liberalize higher education curricula (Kirby 2014). After critical reflection, some Chinese university leaders may have found it difficult to truly adapt their higher education curricula to the U.S. model. However, many more of them have sought alternative models from Singapore and Hong Kong to reform their higher education sectors. This development provides an important clue for other Asian countries/economies regarding the enormous opportunity for cooperation. Strengthening regional cooperation in education and culture among Asian countries would be exciting, as they share similar cultural orientations and traditional practices. Engaging academics and students in regional comparative research to search for any Asian models capable of conceptualizing development in Asia would not only benefit China, but also significantly contribute to theory-building for the international academic community. Given these observations, more regional cooperation and engagements between China and its neighboring countries in education and related areas should be encouraged.

Conclusion

We have in this chapter reviewed the major policies governing the transnationalization and internationalization of higher education in China, critically examining the different phases and unique features of the TNHE and the trends of students studying abroad or of recruiting overseas students to study in China. We also discussed how the Chinese government has attempted to assert its soft power by offering scholarships and educational aid to attract overseas students. Moving beyond transnational programs, major universities on the mainland have engaged in various forms of international research cooperation, student and staff exchanges, and a variety of academic programs to enhance student learning experiences. Finally, we critically reflected on the rise of Chinese universities and its implications for future higher education development in Asia. Drawing on the European experience, engaging in deep regional cooperation would create more opportunities not only for China but also for counterparts in the region to advance research and development while diversifying student learning. Analyzing the above Chinese case from a comparative perspective from East Asia, we have witnessed significant improvements in terms of student mobility across different parts of Asia, especially when Korea, Japan, Taiwan, and Hong Kong are actively promoting the internationalization of higher education by not only sending out students but also recruiting inbound students to create a more international learning environment on campuses. With a steady growth of both inbound and outbound students, these Asian countries will discover the benefits resulting from the mix of domestic and overseas students. Even as some domestic students stay overseas for residence and work after studying abroad, we have to develop public policies conducive enough to support and attract these graduates staying abroad, making them function as ambassadors, or as "bridges" to their own countries. We must adopt a new perspective in reviewing brain drain, brain gain, and brain circulation matters when handling increasingly complex student mobility issues in the future (Shin and Choi 2015).

References

Altbach, Philip G. 1989. "The New Internationalism: Foreign Students and Scholars." *Studies in Higher Education* 14 (2): 125–36.

Arase, David. 2011. "Korea, ASEAN, and East Regionalism." *Joint U.S.-Korea Academic Studies* 21: 33–52.

Brown, Christopher K. 2012. "Asian and Arabian Gulf Futures: Reshaping Globalized Higher Education." In *Going Global: The Landscape for Policy Makers and Practitioners in Tertiary Education,* edited by Mary Stiasny and Tim Gore. Bingley: Emerald Group Publishing.

Chapman, David W., William K. Cummings, and Gerard A. Postiglione. 2010. *Crossing Borders in East Asian Higher Education.* Dordrecht: Springer.

Chen, Shengju. 2011. "Convergence or Divergence? The Asian Way in Internationalizing Higher Education." Paper presented at the 2011 Regional Symposium on Asian Education and Development Studies, National Chung Cheng University, Taiwan, November 5.

China Education Press [Zhongguo jiaoyu chubanshe]. 2008. *Zhongguo jiaoyu nianjian 2008* [China education yearbook 2008]. Beijing: Zhongguo jiaoyu chubanshe.

China Scholarship Council [Guojia liuxue jijin guanli weiyuanhui]. 2015. "2015 niandu kongzi xueyuan jiangxuejin zhaosheng benfa" [How to enroll for the 2015 annual Confucius Institute scholarship]. *China Scholarship Council*, March 10. http://www.csc.edu.cn/laihua/scholarshipdetail.aspx?cid=217&id=2727.

China Statistical Yearbook [Zhongguo tongji nianjian]. Various years. Beijing: China Statistics Press.

Chinese Association for International Education (CAFSA). 2009. "2009 foreign student statistical profiles" [2009 nian laihua liuxueshent tongji jiankuang]. *Zhongguo gaodeng jiaoyu xuehui waiguo liuxuesheng jiaoyu guanli fenhui.* http://www.cafsa.org.cn/research/show-193.html.

Chinese-Foreign Cooperation in Running Schools (CFCRS). 2014. "Jiaoyu gui-hua gangyao shishi san nianlai zhongwai hezuo banxue fazhan qingkuang" [The development of chinese-foreign cooperation in running schools]. http://www.crs.jsj.edu.cn/index.php/default/news/index/80.

De Wit, Hans. 2002. *Internationalization of Higher Education in the United States of America and Europe: A Historical, Comparative, and Conceptual Analysis.* London: Greenwood Press.

Educational Statistics Yearbook of China [Zhongguo jiaoyu tongji nianjian]. Various years. Beijing: People's Education Press.

Garrett, Richard. 2004. "Foreign Higher Education Activity in China." *World Education News & Reviews*, July 1. http://wenr.wes.org/2004/07/wenr-julyaugust-2004-foreign-higher-education-activity-in-china/.

Han, Xiao. 2015. "A Study of Transnational Higher Education in China: Challenges and Prospects." PhD diss., Hong Kong Institute of Education.

Hao, Ping. 2009. "Jiefang sixiang, kaita chuangxin: tuidong lai Hua liuxue gongzuo kexue fazhan" [Emancipating the mind, development and innovation, promoting international students studying in China]. http://www.cafsa.org.cn/pdf/2010/09-D3.pdf.

Hayhoe, Ruth, Jun Li, Jing Lin, and Qiang Zha. 2011. *Portraits of 21st Century Chinese Universities: In the Move to Mass Higher Education.* Dordrecht: Springer.

Hawkins, John N., Ka Ho Mok, and Deane E. Neubauer. 2012. *Higher Education Regionalization in Asia Pacific: Implications for Governance, Citizenship, and University Transformation.* New York: Palgrave Macmillan.

Hawkins, John N., and Jing Xu. 2014. "Mobility, Migration and the Road to the Innovative University: Implications for the Asia-Pacific Region." In *Internationalization of Higher Education in East Asia: Trends of Student Mobility and Impact on Education Governance,* edited by Ka Ho Mok and Kar Ming Yu. London: Routledge.

Huang, Futao. 2003. "Policy and Practice of Internationalization of Higher Education in China." *Journal of Studies in International Education* 7 (3): 225–340.

Kerr, Clark. 1994. *Higher Education Cannot Escape History: Issues for the Twenty-first Century.* Albany, N.Y.: State University of New York Press.

Kirby, William C. 2014. "The Chinese Century? The Challenges of Higher Education." *Daedalus: The Journal of the American Academy of Arts & Sciences* 143 (2): 145–56.

Knight, Jane. 1997. "Internationalization of Higher Education: A Conceptual Framework." In *Internationalization of Higher Education in Asia Pacific Countries,* edited by Jane Knight and Hans de Wit. Amsterdam: European Association for International Education.

———. 2014. *International Education Hubs.* Dordrecht: Springer.

Kuang, Ping, Richard Gatward, Ian M. Marshall, and Yang Dai. 2012. "Metrics for the Internationalization of Higher Education: A Pilot Test in China." In *Going Global: The Landscape for Policy Makers and Practitioners in Tertiary Education,* edited by Mary Stiasny and Tim Gore. Bingley: Emerald Group Publishing.

Leung, Chi-Cheung, and Hilary du Cros. 2014. "Confucius Institutes: Multiple Reactions and Interactions." *China: An International Journal* 12 (2): 66–86.

Lin, Jing, Yu Zhang, Lan Gao, and Yan Liu. 2005. "Trust, Ownership, and Autonomy: Challenges Facing Private Higher Education in China." *The China Review* 5 (1): 61–82.

Ministry of Education. 1978. *Jiaoyubu guanyu zengxuan chuguo liuxuesheng de tongzhi* [Notice concerning increasing and selecting overseas students by the MOE]. Beijing: Hainan Press.

———. 2013. "2012 nian quanguo lai hua liuxuesheng jianming tongji baogao" [2012 statistics of overseas students in China]. *Zhonghua renmin gongheguo jiao yu bu,* March 7. http://www.moe.edu.cn/publicfiles/business/htmlfiles/moe/s5987/201303/148379.html.

———. 2015a. "2014 nian quanguo lai hua liuxuesheng shuju tongji" [Statistics of overseas students in China]. *Zhonghua renmin gongheguo jiaoyu bu,* March 18. http://www.moe.edu.cn/publicfiles/business/htmlfiles/moe/s5987/201503/184959.html.

———. 2015b. "Jiaoyu bu shenpi he fuhe de jigou ji xiangmu mingdan (2015 nian 6 yue 29 ri gengxin)" [List of Ministry of Education-approved/reviewed organizations and projects (updated June 29, 2015)]. *Ministry of Education.* http://www.crs.jsj.edu.cn/index.php/default/index/sort/1006.

Mok, Ka Ho. 2006. *Education Reform and Education Policy in East Asia.* London: Routledge.

———. 2012. "Cooperation and Competition in Tango: Transnationalization of Higher Education and the Emergence of Regulatory Regionalism in Asia." In *Higher Education Regionalization in Asia Pacific: Implications for Governance, Citizenship, and University Transformation,* edited by

John N. Hawkins, Ka Ho Mok, and Deane E. Neubauer. New York: Palgrave Macmillan.

———. 2013. *The Quest for Entrepreneurial Universities in East Asia.* New York: Palgrave Macmillan.

Mok, Ka Ho, and Xiaozhou Xu. 2008. "When China Opens to the World: A Study of Transnational Higher Education in Zhejiang, China." *Asia Pacific Education Review* 9 (4): 393–408.

Mok, Ka Ho, and David K. K. Chan. 2012. "Challenges of Transnational Higher Education in China." In *The Reorientation of Higher Education: Challenging the East-West Dichotomy,* edited by Bob Adamson. Dordrecht: Springer.

Mok, Ka Ho, and Xiao Han. 2014. "Response to the Call for Internationalization: Recent Development of Transnational Higher Education in China." Paper presented at the 2014 Senior Seminar of the Many Faces of Asia Pacific Higher Education in the Era of Massification, Hong Kong, October 17–19.

Mok, Ka Ho, and Jingwei He. 2014. "Introduction: The Re-emerging China and Its Implications in East Asia and Beyond." *China: An International Journal* 12 (2): 3–13.

Mok, Ka Ho, and King Lun Ngok. 2008. "One Country, Diverse Systems: Politics of Educational Decentralization and Challenges for Regulatory State in Post-Mao China." *China Review* 8 (2): 169–200.

Mok, Ka Ho, and Kok Chung Ong. 2012. "Asserting Brain Power and Expanding Educational Services: Searching for New Governance and Regulatory Regimes in Singapore and Hong Kong." In *The Emergent Knowledge Society and the Future of Higher Education: Asian Perspectives,* edited by Diane E. Neubauer. London: Routledge.

———. 2014. "Transforming from 'Economic Power' to 'Soft Power': Transnationalization and Internationalization of Higher Education in China." In *Survival of the Fittest: The Shifting Contours of Higher Education in China and the United States,* edited by Qi Li and Cynthia I. Gerstl-Pepin. Heidelberg: Springer.

Mok, Ka Ho, Yu Cheung Wong, Richard M. Walker, and Xiulan Zhang. 2010. "Embracing the Market: Examining the Consequences for Education, Housing, and Health in Chinese Cities," in *Social Cohesion in Greater China: Challenges for Social Policy and Governance,* edited by Ka Ho Mok and Yuen-wen Ku. New York: World Scientific.

Mok, Ka Ho, and Kar Ming Yu. 2014. *Internationalization of Higher Education in East Asia: Trends of Student Mobility and Impact on Education Governance.* London: Routledge.

NAFSA: Association of International Educators. 2008. "International Education, the Neglected Dimension of Public Diplomacy: Recommendations for the Next President." http://www.nafsa.org/uploadedFiles/NAFSA_Home/Resource_Library_Assets/Public_Policy/public_diplomacy_2008.pdf.

Neubauer, Deane, Jung Cheol Shin, and John N. Hawkins. 2013. *The Dynamics of Higher Education Development in East Asia: Asian Cultural Heritage, Western Dominance, Economic Development, and Globalization.* New York: Palgrave Macmillan.

Nye, Joseph S. 1990. *Bound To Lead.* New York: Basic Books.

Ravenhill, John. 2005. "Regionalism." In *Global Political Economy,* edited by John Ravenhill. New York: Oxford University Press.

Rivza, Baiba, and Ulrich Teichler. 2007. "The Changing Role of Student Mobility." *Higher Education Policy* 20 (4): 457–75.

Robertson, Susan. 2008. "'Europe/Asia' Regionalism, Higher Education and the Production of World Order." *Policy Futures in Education* 6 (6): 718–29.

Roeloffs, Karl. 1994. "Global Competence and Regional Integration: A View from Europe." In *Educational Exchange and Global Competence,* edited by R. D. Lamberts. New York: Council on International Educational Exchange.

Shields, Robin, and Rebecca M. Edwards. 2010. "Student Mobility and Emerging Hubs in Global Higher Education." In *Higher Education, Policy, and the Global Competition Phenomenon,* edited by Laura M. Portnoi, Val Dean Rust, and Sylvia S. Bagley. New York: Palgrave Macmillan.

Shin, Gi-Wook, and Joon Nak Choi. 2015. *Skilled Labor as Social Capital in Korea.* California: Stanford University Press.

State Council, People's Republic of China. 2010. *Guojia zhong chang qi jiaoyu gaige he fazhan guihua gangyao* [Outline for national educational development]. Beijing: State Council.

Stiasny, Mary, and Tim Gore. 2012. *Going Global: The Landscape for Policy Makers and Practitioners in Tertiary Education.* Bingley: Emerald Group Publishing.

Wang, Jianbo. 2005. *Kuaguo gaodeng jiaoyu yu Zhongwai hezuo banxue* [Transnational higher education and SFCRS]. Jinan: Shandong Education Press.

Wang, D. G. and X. Liu. 2010. *Achievements of Higher Education Development in China in the Last Three Decades.* Beijing: Beijing Normal University Press.

Welch, Anthony R., and Jie Hao. 2014. "'Hai Gui' and 'Hai Dai': The Job-seeking Experiences of High-skilled Returnees to China" In

Internationalization of Higher Education in East Asia, edited by Ka Ho Mok and Kar Ming Yu. London: Routledge.

Van der Wende, Marijk. 2007. "Internationalization of Higher Education in the OECD Countries: Challenges and Opportunities for the Coming Decade." *Journal of Studies in International Education* 11(3–4): 274–89.

Xiao, Yuanyuan, ed. 2012. "Guojia gongpai chuguo liuxue renyuan anqi hui guo lü baochi zai 98% yishang" [The returning rate of government-sponsored students abroad stays above 98 percent]. *Zhongguo xinwen wang* [China news], October 30. http://www.chinanews.com/edu/2012/10-30/4287705.shtml.

Yuan, Tingting. 2014. "Diploma Serves Diplomacy: 'Donor Logic' in Educational Aid." *China: An International Journal* 12 (2): 87–112.

Zhang, Xiaopeng. 2005. "Neidi Zhongwai hezuo banxue yu Xianggang fei bendi kecheng xiangguan fagui bijiao yanjiu" [A comparative study on the relevant laws and regulations of "Chinese-foreign Cooperation in Running Schools" in the Chinese mainland and "non-local courses]. *Jiaoyu xuebao* [Education journal] 33 (1–2): 125–47.

Zheng, Lin. 2009. "Chinese Universities' Motivations in Transnational Higher Education and Their Implications for Higher Education Marketization." In *Internationalising the University: The Chinese Context,* edited by Tricia Coverdale-Jones and Paul Rastall. Basingstoke: Palgrave Macmillan.

8 Internationalizing Higher Education and Negotiating Ethno-National Identity

THE PERSPECTIVE FROM SINGAPORE

Michelle Foong and Brenda S.A. Yeoh

As an emerging player in the field of higher education, East Asia is fast gaining significance as an important global driver of international education mobility. Traditionally a major sender of international students, countries in East Asia such as China, Japan, South Korea, Taiwan, and Singapore are now actively promoting their "world-class" universities and competing for "global talent" within East Asia and beyond. Though still dominated by major English-speaking destination countries such as the United States, the United Kingdom, and Australia, a British Council (2008, 5–6) report confirmed "a shift toward a stronger Asian influence in global international education student flows," attributing this phenomenon to societal factors such as the high value placed on higher education and international education by students and parents in East Asia, as well as Asian governments desiring to position themselves within the international education arena. Such a shared desire to gain visibility in the global arena was encapsulated in the 2013 APAIE (Asia-Pacific Association for International Education) conference theme, aptly titled "An Ascendant Asia-Pacific: International Higher Education in the 21st Century." Coupled with the emergence of region-specific university league tables, notably the Quacquarelli Symonds (QS) Asian University Rankings (since 2005), East Asian universities with globalizing ambitions are set to compete to attract more international student flows from within the region and beyond.

The authors thank all those who participated in this research for sharing their insights and providing information. The research which informed this paper was funded by a Ministry of Education (Singapore) Tier 2 Grant (R111-000-069-112).

As the international education market in Asia grows and develops, Chan (2012) observed a shift in student mobilities—from net outflows for traditional "Western" destinations to a trend toward regionalization and greater horizontal mobility within Asia. Sugimura (2012) is also confident that there will be greater East Asian integration through the proliferation of regional networks and universities' cooperation programs, although she cautions that complex issues will need to be ironed out, such as immigration control with regard to student mobility, choice of language for programs, and the need to retain national and institutional autonomy in the midst of collaboration. This said, it appears certain that new, innovative forms of partnerships, such as the prestigious S3 Asia MBA,[1] which capitalizes on the strengths of the three dynamic Asian cities of Seoul, Shanghai, and Singapore, will continue to feature prominently in these regional collaborations.

Transnational mobility fostered by such regional collaborations impacts students' concepts of self and their formation of national, regional, and global identities. Studies alert us to the nuances within students' heightened sense of national identity, particularly with respect to the complex interrelationships (ethno-historical, colonial, etc.) between host and home countries. For example, Dolby's (2004) work shows how American exchange students' concepts of self and nation are challenged by their cross-cultural experiences in Australia, particularly in light of the September 11 attacks. She reveals the multiple articulations of "America" that students embraced in their responses, which could range from outright rejection, fervent patriotism, to the formation of a post-national American identity. Her work (drawing on Calhoun [2002]) on ethnocentric ("thick") to cosmopolitan ("thin") senses of national identity alerts us to the fact that there is nothing linearly progressive in "national identity" under conditions of transnationalism, and international students are involved in creative identity-forming strategies to display complex allegiances, creating new forms of belonging that can be simultaneously national and global, or oscillating between different nation-states. This fluidity is evident in Ghosh and Wang's (2003) work, which highlights the shifting and fluid identities among international students.

1 In 2005 NUS formed the aptly named S3 University Alliance (S3 UA), a tri-university colloquium with Fudan University (Shanghai) and Korea University (Seoul). An Asia MBA Double Degree Program (the S3 Asia MBA) was started in 2008 as a key product of this alliance. Aiming to fill the growing demand for a pan-Asian MBA program, the S3 Asia MBA prides itself on its taglines "through the eyes of Asia," "Asia to the world," and "the world to Asia." The unique program offers a situated understanding of regional economy, culture and business, attractive employment/internship opportunities within Asia-Pacific, and an extensive network of colleagues/alumni in Seoul, Shanghai, and Singapore.

They employ self-reflexive narratives of their own distinctive experiences as Indian and Chinese students studying in Toronto, Canada. The authors trace their journey in three periods—the time prior to their departure, their daily routines in Toronto, and their thoughts during their first visit home. They raise interesting questions about the multiple, fluid, sometimes contradictory identities students take on in various spaces. Ghosh, for example, adopted a dual lifestyle in Toronto, where in public spaces she "wore trousers, drank coffee, ate pork and beef, spoke English all day," while privately in her room found solace in donning the *shalwar kameez* (a traditional Central/South Asian outfit) and listening to Bengali music (2003, 274). Wang reflected on her own bilingualism and the embedded tensions where her "mind reads and speaks two languages, regards two countries as homes, and forms a continuous dialogue between the two" (2003, 272). Together, they acknowledged their "multiple, hyphenated selves" and consciousness of being perceived as the "other" in Toronto.

With increasing configurations of identities among mobile youths seeking higher education opportunities in the region, we highlight the complexities in students' identity construction processes and the resulting tensions and negotiations in everyday spaces of encounters. We focus on the National University of Singapore (NUS), a key player in the race to internationalize in the Asian context.[2] In the first half of the chapter, we outline the particular context and rationale for the internationalization of higher education and the resultant increase in international student mobilities and diversification of campus life. In the second half of the chapter, we investigate how international students at NUS negotiate their ethno-national identities and (re)construct national imaginaries as a result of encountering sameness and difference in emerging "contact zones" where "cultures meet, clash, and grapple with each other" (Pratt 1997, 63). We focus on contact zones as productive social spaces that prompt students to rethink relations between home, host, and third countries, particularly where there has been long-standing histories of conflict within and between countries, sometimes continuing on to contemporary times. Locating their transnational selves in the midst of these tensions becomes an important project for some

2 This chapter draws on data collected for Globalizing Universities and International Student Mobilities in East Asia (GUISM), a multi-disciplinary research project that spans across nine universities in eight East Asian cities; NUS was a participating institution in the project. The three main methods of inquiry in this project include a survey administered to international students, formal interviews conducted with university officials, and in-depth biographical student interviews. This chapter primarily utilizes in-depth biographical interviews with twenty international students from NUS conducted between September 2010 and June 2011.

international students. Such reflections play an integral role in shaping their performances and articulations of their identities abroad, which in turn affects their experience of contact zones.

The "Singapore Brand": Fashioning a "Leading Global University Centered in Asia"

Unlike universities in countries such as Australia, where internationalization is primarily driven by the need to increase student revenues in the face of declining state financial support (Altbach and Knight 2006, 28), the East Asian experience is shaped by two goals. First, East Asian flagship universities are given additional resources by the state on the premise that university-industry research collaborations will drive the country's economic development; and second, in light of the significant, and most likely irreversible, fertility decline in East Asia, international students are seen as a vital inflow of foreign talent to energize the economy upon graduation (Ho 2014, 164). Singapore's ambition to be a "home for talent" in Asia and globally[3] is hence based not only on aspirations to capture a larger slice of the lucrative global education market, but also in recognition of the limitations of a small and open economy where human capital is the most valuable resource. In short, ushering in the new knowledge-based economy was marked by a shift from "industrial development to education reform" (Olds and Thrift 2005, 7) and this in turn required internationalizing Singapore universities for talent augmentation and human resource development (Lee 2012).

To spearhead "education reform," Singapore's Economic Development Board pushed for the Global Schoolhouse initiative in 2002, with the aim of promoting Singapore's position as a "a hub of educational excellence" (MTI 2003). At the tertiary level, a select group of top international universities were invited to set up branch campuses in Singapore through various incentive schemes, including generous research funding and land for building the Singapore campus at a fraction of the market rate.[4] The imperative to build a strong international education system also necessitated an overhaul of Singapore universities. As outlined by Ho (2013, 229–32; see also Wong, Ho, and Singh 2007), these changes included financial and operational autonomy, which enabled restructured universities to become more nimble without checking with the Ministry of Education, rationalizing academic recruitment and the promotion and tenure systems to attract personnel

3 Economic Development Board. 2016. "Home for Talent." https://www.edb.gov.sg/content/edb/en/why-singapore/about-singapore/strategy/home-for-talent.html.

4 Sidhu's (2009) analysis of two failed Global Schoolhouse projects demonstrates the challenges of transplanting foreign university systems into Singapore soil.

internationally, providing new avenues of research funding to strengthen university research capacity, building international status and visibility, attracting foreign researchers and academics, and building on university-industry relations in order to enable the exploit of commercial applications of university research. The initiative also sought to remodel all levels of Singaporean education to nurture students who are creative and entrepreneurial (MTI 2007) and, at the same time, attract 150,000 international students to study in a wide array of educational institutions in Singapore by 2015. The goal of internationalizing higher education was to provide the globalizing city-state with an important avenue for attracting high-caliber talent to Singapore to supplement its labor capacity.

In line with this priority, Singapore universities such as NUS have given "primacy . . . to attracting overseas talent" (Sidhu, Ho, and Yeoh 2011) and have embarked on concerted marketing efforts (through overseas recruitment drives, attractive scholarships, etc.) to draw international students, particularly from China, India, and neighboring Southeast Asian countries. Daquila (2013, 635) notes that "the potential to become PRs [permanent residents] and ultimately citizens of Singapore" has continued to draw large numbers of international students from these source countries. To retain international graduates to contribute to the local economy, Singapore has instituted an international student bond that allows students to obtain generous tuition grants and loan schemes in return for a commitment to work in Singapore for three years upon graduating from university.[5] This is in stark contrast to traditional study destinations in the West, as well as those in more mature Asian markets such as Japan, where it is increasingly difficult for international students in host countries to secure employment upon graduation. More recently, however, there has been public dissatisfaction in Singapore at foreign scholars who were granted scholarships but failed to dispense their bonds, with some seeking out greener pastures in other countries. The state has in response emphasized that "more than eight in ten scholars have been working in Singapore and are contributing

---

5 The Immigration & Checkpoints Authority's (ICA) student pass entitles international students to seek part-time jobs and internships in Singapore while studying. Upon completion of their courses, international students who require a longer period of stay to look for jobs may also apply for a one-year (non-renewable) long-term social visit pass. Under the Service Obligation Scheme, international students participating in a government-subsidized program can apply for it in order to pay reduced tuition fees. In return, they are required to undertake a service bond to work for a Singapore-based company for three years upon completion of their degree. The rationale for this is so that they may "discharge some of their obligations to the Singapore public for the high subsidy to their graduate education" (NUS 2015a).

to our economy . . . [while others] may have deferred their bonds to pursue postgraduate studies" (Yee 2012). With the tightening of labor laws in the last few years resulting in companies facing lower quotas to hire foreigners as well as raised salary requirements for employment passes, more foreign graduates are finding it increasingly difficult to secure a job in Singapore upon graduation. Tightened hiring policies have also resulted in some foreign graduates leaving Singapore before discharging their bonds (Tan 2014). To counter this, bonds may be suspended for a year if students are unable to secure jobs upon graduation, or if they lose their jobs before the bond period is over.

Efforts to internationalize Singapore's universities have met with several challenges, including increasing local discontent against the state's policy of attracting and retaining foreign talent (Daquila 2013, 635). Competition for limited university places, scholarships, and jobs (including at the professional levels), and pressure on transport systems and housing continue to exert political pressure on the Singapore government. This led to the fine-tuning and tightening of immigration policies in 2009, resulting in a drop in the number of new permanent residents from an average of 58,000 per year from 2004 to 2008, to 28,500 per year from 2010 (Phua and Chuan 2012). Similarly, on the education front, the Ministry of Education announced in 2011 that the number of foreign students in Singapore's universities would fall from 18 percent to 15 percent in 2015 (Davie 2012). In line with this shift in policy, the number of student pass holders (including foreign students enrolled in private and public institutions—secondary schools, polytechnics, and universities) dropped from 84,000 in 2012 to 75,000 in 2014 (Lee 2014).

The National University of Singapore

As the pioneer institution of higher learning in Singapore, tracing its roots back to colonial institutions (King Edward VII College of Medicine set up in 1905 and Raffles College established in 1929), NUS was (at least for the first few decades of nation building after Singapore became independent in 1965) originally tasked with educating locals to fill workforce requirements to support its industrialization programs. Poised to celebrate its 110th anniversary in 2015, the university has since grown to house sixteen faculties and schools, boasting an enrolment of 28,000 undergraduates and 10,000 graduate students (2015/16 figures) (NUS 2015b). Keenly aware of the need to be "global" in reach and vision but grounded in a rising Asia, NUS in the most recent decade has branded itself as "a leading global university centered in Asia," emphasizing its global approach to education and research as well as its situated expertise in Asia (NUS 2015c). In the words of Lily Kong, former vice president for university and global relations, "internationalization is so much a part of NUS's DNA that it is difficult to conceive of any dimension of our university's work that is not, in some way, international" (NUS International Relations Office 2011).

The NUS student community is highly diverse, with "international students making up 20 percent and 60 percent of the undergraduate and graduate student populations, respectively" (NUS Corporate Brochure 2010).[6] This is a relatively high figure, even compared to more established Western universities.[7] Additionally, the campus annually attracts large numbers of exchange students from one hundred countries.[8] NUS's internationalization efforts have been recognized by global ranking exercises such as Quacquarelli Symonds (QS), which attributed NUS's strong performance in world rankings to its high proportion of international faculty and students, as well as its academic and employer reputation. Since 2009, when the rankings were first compiled for Asia, the university has rapidly progressed up its charts from an initial tenth place to second in 2013 and an unprecedented first place in 2014. Separately, in the QS World University Rankings 2014, NUS was among the world's ten best universities for eleven subjects in engineering and technology, arts and humanities, natural sciences, social sciences, and management.[9]

6 There were about 25,000 undergraduates at NUS, of whom more than 5,000 were international students. The total graduate student population is 8,000, of whom more than half are from overseas. In total, of the 33,000 students on campus, 10,000 are international students and the rest are citizens or permanent residents of Singapore (Tan 2011).

As mentioned earlier, rising aspirations among Singaporeans for university education as well as a more politicized public sphere have raised questions about social equity and public accountability issues and put the spotlight on highly valued university places going to foreign students at the expense of local students (Ministry of Education 2013). Moving forward, the state-commissioned Committee on University Education Pathways Beyond 2015 (CUEP) recommended expanding university places (3,000 more places by 2020), raising the cohort participation rate from 26 percent (2014) to 40 percent by 2020, and "developing a new applied degree pathway that will provide more opportunities and choices in a diverse university landscape" (Ministry of Education 2012).

7 NUS was ranked 19th in the 2011 "QS Top 500 Universities" in terms of its international student population (Quacquarelli Symonds 2011).

8 In academic year 2013/14, there were 174 university-wide Student Exchange Programme (SEP) partner universities and 155 faculty-level SEP partner universities in 47 countries. A total of 1,966 NUS students went abroad through exchange programs in academic year 2013/14, while the university hosted 1,849 international students (NUS 2015d).

9 "NUS also moved one spot up to the twenty-first position in the World Reputation

As a relatively young university in Asia vying for a slice of the global higher education pie, NUS strategically does so by leveraging on the branding potential of internationally renowned universities to effectively catapult itself into the world arena. This is achieved through a variety of innovative partnerships that include more than sixty double- and joint-degree programs with top universities in the world, seven NUS Overseas Colleges (NOCS) in major entrepreneurial hubs, and, more recently, the Yale-NUS College, Asia's first liberal arts college.[10] A strong commitment to internationalization is also reflected in the expected education outcomes of its graduates. These were clearly articulated by President Tan Chorh Chuan, who expressed the hope that an NUS education would produce graduates who were "critical thinkers, creative, articulate, and globally effective" (Tan 2009). Creativity and entrepreneurialism are key skills that NUS identifies as indispensable for the current economy. We suggest that while this is in line with Singapore's efforts to engage with creative industries,[11] inculcating these skills may also be a reaction to challenge stereotypes of Asian students as rote learners. One way to inculcate cosmopolitan sensibilities is to encourage students to participate in exchange programs with partner universities. To this end, the International Relations Office (IRO) has been working with more than two hundred partner universities to develop these programs. Anne Pakir, IRO director, aligns this move with the university's mission to mold among its students "a global mindset, the ability to thrive in diverse cultural settings, and the willingness to embrace new opportunities" (NUS International Relations Office 2013). NUS students are encouraged to participate in at least one overseas program, "as learning to live in a different environment could transform their lives." The view that an overseas experience helps to develop both "hard" and "soft" skills is endorsed university-wide, as echoed in Provost Tan Eng Chye's point that "overseas exposure not only allows students to

Rankings 2014 published by *Times Higher Education* (THE). In the THE Asia University Rankings 2014, [NUS] ranked second, retaining [its] position as one of Asia's top two universities" (NUS 2015d).

10 NUS has established NOCs in Shanghai and Beijing (China), Israel, India, Stockholm (Sweden), and Silicon Valley and Bio Valley (USA). This is an innovative program that "targets NUS undergraduates with the academic ability and entrepreneurial drive. . . to be immersed as interns in startups located in leading entrepreneurial and academic hubs of the world. At the same time, they will study entrepreneurship related courses at highly prestigious partner universities. The aim is to cultivate and nurture them into enterprising, resourceful, independent self-starters and eventually blossom into successful entrepreneurs" (NUS 2015e).

11 See, for example, the speech by Ng Eng Hen, Minister for Education, at the Nanyang Academy of Fine Arts convocation ceremony on August 22, 2009. http://www.moe.gov.sg/media/speeches/2009/08/22/speech-by-dr-ng-eng-hen-at-the-31.php.

learn from the world, but to also gain international mileage by acquiring linguistic skills and developing cultural sensitivity" (NUS 2009).

Given that English is the working language in the city-state, the adoption of English as the language of internationalization and instruction at NUS was deemed as a natural and straightforward extension. In this respect, it has a strong advantage over other internationalizing universities in the region, where English is not the primary language of instruction (Yeoh, Foong, and Ho 2014). While capitalizing on its comparative geographical advantage to provide "global thought-leadership" as well as "special expertise" to "understand critical issues within Asia and to find suitable solutions" (Tan 2009), operating entirely in the English language medium is an infrastructural strength that plays no small part in "competing with leading universities [in Asia and the West] to recruit the best minds" (Tan 2010). According to the findings of Sidhu, Ho, and Yeoh (2011), an overwhelming 72.4 percent of international students surveyed chose to study at NUS because of its good reputation as a global institution, instruction in English, and teaching quality. As Prime Minister Lee Hsien Loong emphasized while commenting on the strength of the Singapore brand of education, "Among Asian countries, Singapore is probably the least dissimilar in ethos to Western societies" (Lee 2011). Coupled with an ethnically diverse population with ancestral roots in major countries in the region, NUS is well placed to attract international students from Asia who would like to combine an English-based, Western-style university experience while remaining in close proximity to Asian cultures and languages.

On the NUS campus, efforts to foster "an academically and culturally vibrant environment, where students from different nationalities and cultures will interact and study alongside one another" have become a major priority (NUS International Relations Office 2011). Intercultural understanding and appreciation of other cultures are encouraged through annual campus-wide events such as In-fusion, where international students at NUS set up booths that showcase their countries and unique cultures. Commenting on the event's theme of "Connections" in 2008, Shih Choon Fong, former NUS vice-chancellor, emphasized that "instead of focusing on differences as a means to divide, we should see our differences as a means to connect" (Koh 2008). In a similar vein, at an inaugural Diversity Symposium held in February 2013, former vice-provost for student life Tan Tai Yong likened the university to a microcosm of Singapore and urged students to accept diversity as a strength and not take it for granted (NUS 2013).

NUS also seeks to pioneer new ways of teaching and learning, as reflected in the establishment of the University Town (UTown), an innovative residential college partly modeled after those at Oxford and Harvard. With the opening of its third residential college in 2012, UTown aims to be an "iconic landmark . . . [that] redefines Singapore's higher education landscape" by providing "an integrated learning and living environment for up to 6,000 students from a diverse mix of different nationalities and cultures" (NUS 2008). The merging of learning and living spaces is aimed at promoting "informal learning" as students "attend seminars, take on projects, and have discussions where they reside" (Chia 2012). UTown is tasked to "nurture tomorrow's leaders for the global arena" through innovative pedagogy (for example, promoting interdisciplinary perspectives, rigorous inquiry, and creative problem-solving) that will develop "global minds," while having "a focus in helping students understand and engage Asia" (NUS 2008). Though NUS is clear about its desire to learn from the best practices of other world-renowned universities, it also seeks to build a new model for others, thus making a mark in the international arena. This ambition is articulated by Provost Tan Eng Chye, who hopes that UTown will be "admired, studied, and held up internationally as a model to be emulated" (Tan 2007).

Student Sample Profile

Both undergraduates and graduates were recruited for this study, with the majority of them pursuing full degrees, though a handful of short-term exchange students were included for contrast. The students were recruited through a variety of means, such as annual campus-wide events for international students, snowballing through contacts provided by respondents, online advertisements on Facebook groups, international student groups' message boards, and personal contacts. Our sample is reasonably diverse in terms of students' countries of origin and aimed to mirror the existing international student ratio at NUS. While a significant proportion of respondents originated from the Southeast Asian region, we also interviewed a selected number of students from other parts of the world to take into account the diversity of experiences. The respondents were enrolled in a mix of science and non-science courses, which reflected the existing ratio at NUS. They also differed in their year of study and time in the host country, ranging from six months to five years. We tried to obtain an equal ratio of female and male students. Their ages ranged from nineteen to thirty-five.

Given the individualized nature of interview schedules that emphasize students' biographies, we acknowledge that the data obtained are not meant to be representative of all international students' experiences in these universities. Rather, we hope to draw out broad themes from these biographies that inform experiences of studying at NUS.

(Re)-constructing Ethno-national Identities
in the Contact Zone

The rapid advancement of NUS's internationalization agenda has been a major instrument not only in "bringing NUS to the world," but also in "bringing the world to NUS" (in the words of President Tan Chorh Chuan), where the latter strategy has created diverse environments on campus comprising "interlaced spaces for learning, living, arts, culture, sports, and social activities" that "provide opportunities for students from a wide range of nationalities and backgrounds to interact, learn together, and develop friendships" (Tan 2015). As students embodying different geographies and histories encounter one another in a proliferation of contact zones, they often experience what Pratt (1997) calls the "joys and pains" of the contact zone, where, for the first time, a student can "see the world described with him or her in it." These "pains" may derive from hearing about how their country or culture is objectified, seeing their roots traced back to "legacies of glory and shame," or coming face-to-face with ignorance, incomprehension, and occasionally hostility, while the "joys of the contact zone" often stem from "exhilarating moments of wonder and revelation, mutual understandings, and new wisdom." These mixed feelings were experienced by Vietnamese NUS undergraduate Thi, who had been confronted with negative views of Vietnam and communism by her NUS friends. Being situated in the contact zone forced her to critically reflect upon the source of her Vietnamese identity:

> Being in NUS makes me question about more things, things I haven't been taught at home. . . . [There] you're taught that Vietnam is a great country. . . . We have a long history of victory, and being communist is something we should be proud of. . . . I have no doubt of being a communist because my grandparents were communists. They fought hard for the independence of the country. My granddad lost one eye because of fighting in the war. . . . I am very proud of being their grandchild. (Thi, Vietnam, undergraduate)

While recognizing the overt influence of a pro-communist education on the formation of her national identity, she also draws on familial ties such as her grandparents' legacy as the foundation of her Vietnamese identity. It is no wonder that she was shocked when she learned of prevailing negative constructions of Vietnam and communism through interacting with her friends at NUS.

> [Now] I have a broader perspective of how people perceive communism . . . [and] it's really not all good . . . so I did some research. It doesn't mean that

I change my mind about the past. . . . It's to understand what happened that made people think like that.

The incongruence Thi has experienced in the contact zone sets into motion a process of reconstructing her Vietnamese identity, as she actively takes ownership of her national identity by finding out more about Vietnam's history, in a personal project that attempts to piece together a coherent self from her past and present experiences. Thus, while it is an area where differences are amplified, the contact zone also often results in careful reflection on one's identity. To take a different example, Hana, a South Korean PhD student at NUS, tries to take an inclusive stance in the contact zone, by "seeing Korea through the eyes of others." Her interactions with classmates of various nationalities caused her to appreciate intercultural similarities, thereby strengthening her existing Korean identity:

> I see Korea through people from other countries, I think that's reflection. It gives me a stronger sense of [national] identity. Like I can see Korea through you, through Singaporeans and Malaysians, through how they talk about Korea. I am more affiliated to my Korean identity because of that. (Hana, South Korea, PhD)

In the above accounts, we see how sites of contact during the experience of studying abroad can become a conducive, at times emotional space where new information about students' home countries is encountered and processed. Contact zone encounters in the study abroad experience act as triggers that intersect space with particular points in students' life histories, conflating points in their past and present in the process of identity negotiation. At the same time, there is a danger of overemphasizing the value placed on historical and cultural connections, while overlooking mobile youths' looser and more fluid constructions of places and identities. With increased mobility, identities may become less attached to national boundaries, as shown in Jenny's (a Malaysian undergraduate student at NUS) conclusion that the search is still on for a place to "belong" to:

> I don't feel that I fully belong in Malaysia, nor do I feel that I fully belong in Singapore. It's just the process of finding where I feel comfortable in. (Jenny, Malaysia, undergraduate)

The above suggests that contact zones are fertile grounds that demand that international students critically reflect upon their ethno-national identities. They do so by engaging in identity (re)negotiations that take into account past influences and present mobility experiences. However, due to the political workings of the contact zone, this process is seldom smooth, and students continue to learn how to make sense of themselves and others as they traverse these spaces.

Confronting National Politics in the Contact Zone

The globalizing university campus represents a politically charged space where international students are made aware of, and learn to negotiate, existing power relations with regard to their home countries. As Wenjie, a Malaysian Chinese undergraduate student at NUS, traversed between Singapore and Malaysia over the course of his study, he became more aware of the demarcating boundaries drawn in each country, which in turn determined how he picked and chose the identities he took on. As a Malaysian Chinese, he questions his identity as an ethnic Chinese in light of the sensitive racial politics in Singapore and Malaysia. The fluid characteristics of these identities, and the play of political power, are exemplified in Wenjie's dilemmatic response:

> Back in Malaysia I'm more Chinese than Malaysian. Over here I'm more Malaysian than Chinese, because there are boundaries being drawn . . . . I think there's always the "other." (Wenjie, Malaysia, undergraduate)

When asked to describe an experience at NUS when he felt marginalized, he revealed that in his recent application for an overseas exchange program, though he had better results than his Singaporean classmate, he felt that he had lost out on the opportunity because he was not local. Despite being unhappy with the outcome, he responded with some resignation, saying that he was "used to it" because "I've lived in *that* kind of environment," drawing parallels to *bumiputra* policies in Malaysia:

> We know there's a quota system. We've come to accept it. We're not happy but have learned to live with it and get by, survive in that kind of environment.

Despite feeling caught in the web of boundaries drawn by racial and national politics, he is optimistic that studying in Singapore, and being in the contact zone, has helped him to be more adaptive to the harsh realities of surviving in an international environment:

> All the boundaries drawn, inside and outside, as [Chinese] Malaysians—we're used to being outside anyway, we're always "the other" . . . but I think it actually helped me to adapt to Singapore . . . not just Singapore but in an international community or just anywhere . . . . I've gotten used to it, be more accepting, don't get too caught up, learn to live on despite the circumstances.

In contrast, encountering the nationalist politics of the contact zone did not sit well with Mihika, a Sri Lankan graduate student at NUS. She was appalled by the deep-seated divide in Sinhalese-Tamil relations that she experienced even on the NUS campus.

> During orientation, I boarded the shuttle bus and some South Indian students smiled [at me] . . . so I said "Hi" and thought at least someone was friendly enough. . . . They asked me, "Are you from India Chennai?" and I said, "No, I'm from Sri Lanka". . . . They asked again, "So you're Tamil?" I said, "No, I'm Sinhalese." When I turned around, all of them were gone! That was the biggest cultural shock for me because I had taken for granted my Sinhalese identity, and suddenly I realized I am a minority in a Tamil majority country. It has its impacts [here] so I think I became more nervous about my identity when interacting with South Indians here. (Mihika, Sri Lanka, master's)

Here, the contact zone is not only characterized by local-international interactions, but also ridden with encounters among international students whose countries have histories of conflicts. In Mihika's case, the Sinhalese-Tamil conflict, unexpectedly, has been transplanted from Sri Lanka to the Singapore context. She became more sensitive to the space she inhabited, avoiding unnecessary contact with Tamil-speaking Indians whenever she could:

> If I'm lost, I'd ask directions from a Chinese [as opposed to Indians]. I've had bad experiences [with Indians]. . . . [They would say] "*Oh, you're from Sri Lanka*" *sneering tone*. . . . People even think I am lying because I look very South Indian. Even in Sri Lanka, people sometimes mistake me, but this is one place where I really felt it and it has worked to the negative. It was a huge shock for me.

In Mihika's case, interacting with South Indians in Singapore is a potentially fearful encounter that she would rather avoid. In the globalizing Asian university context, contact zones reflect ongoing sociopolitical tensions that force students to think in new ways about their home countries. Ethno-physical similarities among Asian students become a double-edged sword as Mihika struggles to assert her Sinhalese Sri Lankan identity in a Tamil-majority Singapore. However, in the midst of emotional identity struggles in the contact zone, many respondents in this study also seized the opportunity in an international campus environment to promote a positive image of their countries from the "ground up."

Being an "Ambassador" in the Contact Zone

In the contact zone, where differences are amplified, international students often encounter stereotypes and prejudices. Some see these encounters as opportunities to educate and actively correct these preconceptions. Thi recognizes that, as a Vietnamese student in Singapore, she plays an important role in changing her friends' negative perceptions of Vietnam, which she feels are often misrepresentations. In her three years at NUS, Thi made it a point to share with her Singaporean and exchange student friends the positive aspects of Vietnam:

> My Vietnamese friends and I try to make friends with people from all over. . . . We try to show them how the Vietnamese are, that they are friendly, nice, and gentle. They welcome you to their country. In fact, many of our friends are Singaporeans or exchange students, and they are very eager to visit Vietnam and explore the country. I have two UK exchange friends who just came back from Vietnam because of our recommendation. They said they love Vietnam and will definitely go back. That's a good reward for us. (Thi, Vietnam, undergraduate)

With regard to how communism is often viewed in a negative light, Thi explains:

> People have to know that a communist country is not a bad thing. They think that the communists will kill you if you don't obey them, but I said, "No, I have never heard that," because I grew up in that country and everything is good . . . unless you go against the government. . . . [e]ven in Singapore, if you do that, you'd be blacklisted. (Thi, Vietnam, undergraduate)

While the experience of studying abroad offers a pair of "reflective lenses" to re-encounter one's country, it can also evoke contradictory feelings and confusion. Even then, students such as Thi actively take it upon themselves to be "ambassadors" for their countries. Interestingly, being such an ambassador is not limited to promoting one's home country. For Wenjie (introduced earlier), studying in Singapore was a transformative experience, so much so that he agreed to become an ambassador for the Singapore brand of education in Malaysia:

> [Studying in Singapore] is a life-changing experience, and I've benefitted a lot. I've grown so much as a person, intellectual and maturity level. . . . It's not a decision I regret. It's something that I will encourage others to take up. In fact, the Singapore Ministry of Education roped me in to promote the ASEAN scholarship. . . . I returned to Malaysia to share my experiences and promote Singapore education at an education fair. It is something that I believe in. They even featured me on the Malaysian *Reader's Digest*. I genuinely believe that a Singapore education is a positive one, and we Malaysians should take advantage of it. (Wenjie, Malaysia, undergraduate)

In the course of promoting one's country in the globalizing university contact zones, being away from home also prompts students to inwardly reflect upon their ties to "home" and different geographies of return.

(Re)-thinking Homeward Obligation and Return

The struggles and challenges encountered in the contact zone act as a catalyst for students to formulate narratives of return, shedding light in turn on the contents of their national identities. Kim, a Vietnamese student majoring in psychology, actively sought out an opportunity to contribute to social science research in Vietnam through Vietnam 2020, an NUS alumni-led group based in Singapore, seeing it as a way to fulfil her obligation to her country:

> We formed a group to discuss how we can bring social sciences into Vietnam, because those of us who have graduated from NUS realized a greater need for graduates of social sciences to return to Vietnam. The development in Vietnam is changing very rapidly whereas the social science infrastructure is absent. There are a great number of things that we can do in Vietnam. It is now recognizing the need to pull back the talent to do social sciences . . . so we try to bridge the demand there and supply here. . . . I've always wanted to do service for myself and for my country, so I think this is a good chance to do it. (Kim, Vietnam, undergraduate)

Bridging Singapore and Vietnam, Kim's desire to contribute to strengthening the academic foundations of knowledge in her country does not necessarily mean that she intends to return to her homeland:

> I love my country—that's something everybody would say—but while you can love someone, you don't have to marry them. Even if you marry someone else, you can still say you love the other person. I rationalize that I love my country, and I want to contribute to my country, but that is not the place where I will shape my education, my future, my life. It must be somewhere else. (Kim, Vietnam, undergraduate)

Her artful response attests to the fluid nature of mobile youth geographies.

Apart from desires to contribute to home countries upon acquiring an education abroad, students' identities are also constantly bound up with familial obligations that continue to "follow" them in their study abroad experience. Far from the dominant footloose, strategic, and self-seeking discourses that are often invoked in discussing students' motivations for studying abroad, the experience of the contact zone is often influenced by a student's continuing role in the family. Though Wenjie enjoys campus life at

NUS, being in Singapore has also meant bearing the guilt and responsibility for his younger sister's poor academic performance.

> My sister's not doing well in school. I feel bad about it, because I am not there. . . . I wasn't there to encourage her. . . . As the elder brother, I've always been teaching and helping her with schoolwork. The year she entered secondary school, I came here to Singapore, so it was a transition for me and her, too. She didn't adapt well and has failed several subjects already. . . . This would be my biggest trade-off for coming here . . . because of my responsibility to my sister. . . . I missed out on her, especially when she went through puberty, adolescent, the teenage years; I missed out on all that while I was living my life here. So there is always this regret. (Wenjie, Malaysia, undergraduate)

The sense of having "lost time and space" due to not being able to fulfill his responsibility to his sister makes Wenjie more aware of the geographical tensions of "being here and not there" for his family in Malaysia. Familial ties are thus often tied to ideas of national belonging, as Wenjie explains through the "exodus" of local students from the hostel during weekends:

> There has always been this tension in me of being in Singapore versus being in Malaysia. . . . My parents are already past their fifties. . . . Over here [at NUS], there is no family life. My family is in Malaysia. Even in the hostel, the Singaporeans go back and have family dinners every week . . . whereas for Malaysians, our families are not here. . . . [For me] the biggest trade-off of studying here would have been family life.

Within the contact zones of experiences studying abroad, students become aware of their precarious positioning, straddling the divide between home and host countries. This compels them to (re)define and articulate their ties to nation and family as a function of their own mobility projects. This process, far from being static, is subjected to changes over time.

Contact Zones, Identities, and the Experience of Time

Apart from spatial contexts, time plays an equally important role in shaping students' ideas of nation and national identities in the contact zone, taking into account changing life courses and young people's evolving selves. Jeremy, an Indonesian-Chinese undergraduate at NUS, describes his national identifications as moving along a spectrum between Indonesia and Singapore. He was an ASEAN scholar (NUS 2015f) who had completed his junior college education in Singapore before entering NUS. He consciously reflected on the concept of national identity throughout his years of education in Singapore and concluded that through the passing of time, his sense of identity and belonging had changed. This sheds light on the role of time in influencing the way identity is negotiated through contact zone encounters:

> Four years ago, I drew a line, with Indonesia and Singapore on each end. I drew a point, of where I stand at that point in time. . . . [W]hen I drew that point, it was nearer to Indonesia. Now if I were to draw the same diagram, it will be more toward Singapore. (Jeremy, Indonesia, undergraduate)

He explains this shift:

> Because now my life is in Singapore, I've a lot to do here. First of all, I've to study here. Many of my activities and most of my friends are here. But back then [during junior college], I didn't feel that attachment because I didn't really know what to do and didn't have a lot of friends. But it's different now. So if I really had to go back [to Indonesia], I'd lose a lot of things.

The notion of belonging is fluid and dynamic for Jeremy, and is closely tied to place, activities, and social circle. Yet there is also the desire to settle and invest emotionally in a particular locality. Though acknowledging his current attachment to Singapore, Jeremy adds that he is still in the process of layering, not watering down, his Indonesian identity:

> Now, I still identify myself as an Indonesian, but more of an overseas Indonesian, but I am also a resident staying here in Singapore. It's hard to say where I am now [on the spectrum], but definitely I'm not forgetting my identity. . . . At the same time, I'm constructing my identity as someone staying in Singapore.

Age and maturity also play an important role in shaping Mihika's experience of contact zones at NUS. As a graduate student from Sri Lanka, she asserts that one's age is an important influence on how one experiences the contact zone, especially in terms of national identity negotiations. She compares her own proud display of her Sri Lankan identity through speaking Sinhalese to the behaviour of younger Sri Lankan undergraduates she had met on campus, who instead preferred to speak English among themselves.

> I've a strong feeling that had I entered NUS at a younger age, I would be quite stressed. [Now] I probably have a greater sense of who I am at this age than when I was an undergrad. . . . I see that in the Sri Lankan undergrads here, and some of them I really want to shake . . . like, "What's wrong with you!" When I meet other Sri Lankans here, we talk in Sinhalese . . . they [the undergraduates] don't. They speak in English. . . . This sort of alienates me from them . . . but after I thought about it, I realized I would have been like that too. . . . Being older, I've a greater sense of who I am, [and of] my country. (Mihika, Sri Lanka, master's)

According to this logic, Mihika's conversing in Sinhalese with fellow

Sri Lankan students is an important display of her Sri Lankan identity in Singapore and is proof that she is more mature and sure of her national identity than they are. While she expresses her frustration with her younger conationals, her response sheds light on the politics of language in Sri Lanka, which has been transplanted to the NUS campus:

> [I just want to say] come on! I finally meet a Sri Lankan after so many years, and I want to speak to you in Sinhala, and you little brat have to go on in English! *jokingly* There's a whole dilemma, it's not that they don't know Sinhala . . . but there's a catch, in Sri Lanka, we don't speak in Sinhala, whether it be in a restaurant, anywhere. . . . It's sad, Sinhala is always downgraded, and English is, oh my god, the vestiges of colonialism. You gain social capital just by speaking in English.

Conclusion

As demonstrated above, contact zones in study-abroad experiences become important sites that trigger students' complex negotiations and articulations of their ethno-national identities. Traversing transnational spaces, international students at NUS also become more aware of the politics of power exerted on the spaces they inhabit. Regional politics, both historical and contemporary, are often encountered in a new light and conferred new meanings as students make sense of them during their interactions in the contact zone. Even as globalized mobilities intensify among young people today, a sense of national identity continues to be important for these international students. This is often tied to obligations and duties to one's country and family, though it need not bind them to traditional homebound trajectories. Far from being static, young peoples' experience of time and "growing up" intersect with contact zone encounters in a process that continually impacts their identity negotiations.

Turning to Singapore's experience with internationalizing its universities, it would be fair to say that university development in Singapore is closely tied to various stages of Singapore's economic development and nation-building process. The internationalization of universities has been regarded as critical to the country's economic progress in the twenty-first century knowledge-based economy. In recent years, the influx of migrants (including educational migrants) has resulted in unhappiness and discontent among some Singaporeans. The government has been compelled to respond by reviewing immigration policies while concurrently building university capacity by increasing university places (Davie 2014). However, Singapore remains an open economy highly dependent on international labor flows and foreign talent, and it is necessary to continue to seek a balance between the needs of locals and talent augmentation. Expanding capacities and the inevitable massification of higher education need to be brought about without sacrificing the quality of education or diminishing the value of degrees (Ng 2010).

Singapore's experience of internationalizing higher education continues to be lauded as a successful model in the East Asian region. Together with Hong Kong, it is often seen as a "high flyer" among Asian systems, with top-tier universities able to "balance internationalization, sovereignty, and university autonomy" (Postiglione and Arimoto 2015). As the country's leading national university, NUS's path toward internationalization has often been emulated by emerging economies in the region. Moving in tandem with Singapore's economic goals, NUS has also aspired to move beyond simply meeting the educational needs of the local population, hoping to become a "global knowledge enterprise" that excels in research and teaching as well as an entrepreneurial university that encourages high-tech spin-offs and generates economic wealth through innovation. In comparing the internationalization experiences of NUS and the University of Malaya (UM), Mukherjee and Wong (2014) observe that "the NUS story provides UM and other universities in emerging economies an exemplar of development as a process of integration within the world economy" rather than one that follows a separate pathway.

Boasting a "small highly selective system" that is "anchored in the service economy," the Singaporean government is able to propel changes in higher education systems swiftly and in a coordinated manner. However, in terms of scale, the governments of the three regional "industrial giants"—namely, South Korea, Japan, and China—have been able to finance large-scale initiatives such as Brain Korea, Japan's COE21, and China's 211 and 985 plans, which have resulted in a "jump-start" in global university rankings (Postiglione and Arimoto 2015).

Within the larger context of the Asian region, Singapore's globalizing universities hence face increasing competition in attracting and retaining talented international students. Clearly, the key to success lies with remaining adaptable in the midst of dynamic changes globally and in the region, embracing innovation and openness while managing local sentiment, and creating new models of internationalization that strategically harnesses the strengths of the region.

References

Altbach, Philip.G., and Jane Knight. 2006. "The Internationalization of
    Higher Education: Motivations and Realities." *The NEA 2006 Almanac*

of Higher Education: 27–36. http://www.nea.org/assets/img/PubAlmanac/ALM_06_03.pdf.

British Council. 2008. *International Student Mobility in East Asia: Executive Summary*. JWT Education. http://www.britishcouncil.org/sites/british-council.uk2/files/international-student-mobility-in-east-asia.pdf.

Calhoun, Craig. 2002. "Imagining Solidarity: Cosmopolitanism, Constitutional Patriotism, and the Public Sphere." *Public Culture* 14 (1): 147–71.

Chan, Sheng-Ju. 2012. "Shifting Patterns of Student Mobility in Asia." *Higher Education Policy* 25: 207–24.

Chia, Stacey. 2012. "New UTown College's Community Spirit." *The Straits Times*, October 3. http://newshub.nus.edu.sg/news/1210/PDF/UTOWN-st-3oct-pB4.pdf.

Daquila, Teofilo C. 2013. "Internationalizing Higher Education in Singapore Government Policies and the NUS Experience." *Journal of Studies in International Education* 17 (5): 629–47.

Davie, Sandra. 2012. "Foreign Student Numbers Drop Sharply After Climbing Steadily." *The Straits Times*, October 10. http://news.asiaone.com/News/Latest+News/Edvantage/Story/A1Story20121009-376559.html.

———. 2014. "University Places Rise to 14,000 this Year." *The Straits Times*, March 29. http://www.asianewsnet.net/Spore-university-places-rise-to-14000-this-year-58616.html.

Dolby, Nadine. 2004. "Encountering an American Self: Study Abroad and National Identity." *Comparative Education Review* 48 (2): 150–73.

Ghosh, Sutama, and Lu Wang. 2003. "Transnationalism and Identity: A Tale of Two Faces and Multiple Lives." *The Canadian Geographer* 47 (3): 269–82.

Ho, Kong Chong. 2013. "Peering Through the Dust of Construction: Singapore's Efforts to Build World-class Universities." In *Institutionalization of World-Class University in Global Competition,* edited by Jung Cheol Shin and Barbara M. Kehm, 225–36. Dordrecht: Springer.

———. 2014. "International Higher Education Ambitions and Regional Migration Supports." *TRaNS: Trans-Regional and -National Studies of Southeast Asia* 2 (2): 163–82.

Koh, Eng Beng. 2008. "Infusing Global Cultures in NUS." *Knowledge Enterprise Online* 7 (9). http://newshub.nus.edu.sg/ke/0804/articles/pg08.php

Lee, Hsien Loong. 2011. "Speech by Prime Minister Lee Hsien Loong at Launch of YALE-NUS College, 11 April 2011 at NUS." *Prime Minister's Office*, April 11. http://www.pmo.gov.sg/mediacentre/speech-prime-minister-lee-hsien-loong-launch-yale-nus-college-11-april-2011-nus.

Lee, Pearl. 2014. "Singapore Losing Allure as Hub for Education." *The Straits*

Times, September 20. http://www.straitstimes.com/news/singapore/education/story/singapore-losing-allure-hub-education-20140920

Lee, Tong Nge. 2012. "The Internationalization of Singapore Universities In a Globalised Economy—A Documentary Analysis." PhD diss., University of Leicester. https://lra.le.ac.uk/bitstream/2381/27814/1/2012leetnedd.pdf.

Ministry of Education. 2012. "Committee on University Education Pathways Beyond 2015." http://www.moe.gov.sg/feedback/2011/committee-on-university-education-pathways-beyond-2015/.

———. 2013. "Percentage of International Students in Undergraduate Programmes (Major) at NUS, NTU And SMU." Parliamentary Replies, July 8. http://www.moe.gov.sg/media/parliamentary-replies/2013/07/percentage-of-international-students-in-undergraduate-programmes-at-nus-ntu-smu.php.

Ministry of Trade and Industry (MTI). 2003. "Panel Recommends Global Schoolhouse Concept for Singapore to Capture Bigger Slice of US$2.2 Trillion World Education Market." https://www.mti.gov.sg/ResearchRoom/Documents/app.mti.gov.sg/data/pages/507/doc/DSE_recommend.pdf

———. 2007. "Developing Singapore's Education Industry." https://www.mti.gov.sg/ResearchRoom/Documents/app.mti.gov.sg/data/pages/507/doc/ERC_SVS_EDU_MainReport.pdf.

Mukherjee, Hena, and Wong Poh Kam. 2014. "The National University of Singapore and the University of Malaya: Common Roots and Different Paths." In *The Road to Academic Excellence: The Making of World-Class Research Universities,* edited by Philip Altbach and Jamil Salmi, 129–66. The World Bank: Washington DC.

National University of Singapore (NUS). 2008. "University Town: A New Era of Living and Learning." *Newshub,* January 31. http://newshub.nus.edu.sg/headlines/0108/utown_31jan08.php

———. 2009. "International Exchange Day Offers International Mileage to Students." *Newshub,* September 7. http://newshub.nus.edu.sg/headlines/0909/ied_07Sep09.php.

———. 2013. "Fostering Diversity on Campus." *Newshub*, February 25. http://newshub.nus.edu.sg/headlines/1302/diversity_25Feb13.php.

———. 2015a. "Service Obligation Scheme." *NUS.* http://www.nus.edu.sg/admissions/graduate-studies/service-obligation.php.

———. 2015b. "NUS at a Glance 2015/16." *NUS.* http://www.nus.edu.sg/images/resources/content/about/glance-en.pdf.

———. 2015c. "About NUS." *NUS.* http://www.nus.edu.sg/about.

———. 2015d. "Annual Report 2014." http://www.nus.edu.sg/annualreport/pdf/nus-annualreport-2014.pdf.

———. 2015e. "About NOC." *NUS Enterprise*. http://www.overseas.nus.edu.sg/about-noc.

———. 2015f. "ASEAN Undergraduate Scholarship." Office of Admissions. http://www.nus.edu.sg/oam/scholarships/freshmen/nsg/scholarship-nsg-aus.html.

NUS International Relations Office. 2011. *Yearbook 2010/11. NUS*. http://www.nus.edu.sg/iro/home/publications/annualreport/AY1011.pdf.

———. 2013. *Yearbook 2012/13. NUS*. http://www.nus.edu.sg/iro/home/publications/annualreport/AY1213.pdf.

Ng, Eng Hen. 2010. "FY2010 Committee of Supply Debate: 1st Reply by Dr. Ng Eng Hen, Minister for Education and second Minister for Defence on Strengthening Education for All." Ministry of Education. http://www.moe.gov.sg/media/speeches/2010/03/09/fy-2010-committee-of-supply-de.php.

Olds, Kris, and Nigel Thrift. 2005. "Assembling the 'Global Schoolhouse' in Pacific Asia: The Case of Singapore." In *Service Industries, Cities and Development Trajectories in the Asia-Pacific,* edited by Peter W. Daniels, Kong Chong Ho, and Tom Hutton, 201–16. London: Routledge.

Phua, Mei Pin, and Toh Yong Chuan. 2012. "Tighter Rules Lead to Fewer PRs Admitted from 2010." *The Straits Times*, September 11. http://www.straitstimes.com/breaking-news/singapore/story/tighter-rules-lead-far-fewer-prs-admitted-2010-20120911.

Postiglione, Gerard, and Akira Arimoto. 2015. "Building Research Universities in East Asia." *Higher Education* 70: 151–53.

Pratt, Mary Louise. 1997. "Arts of the Contact Zone." In *Mass Culture and Everyday Life,* edited by Peter Gibian, 61–72. New York: Routledge.

Quacquarelli Symonds. 2011. "QS Top 500 Universities." http://content.qs.com/supplement2011/top500.pdf.

Sidhu, Ravinder. 2009. "The 'Brand Name' Research University Goes Global." *Higher Education* 57 (2): 125–40.

Sidhu, Ravinder, Kong Chong Ho, and Brenda Yeoh. 2011. "Emerging Education Hubs: The Case of Singapore." *Higher Education* 61 (1): 23–40.

Sugimura, Miki. 2012. "Possibility of East Asian Integration through the Regional Networks and Universities' Cooperation in Higher Education." *Asian Education and Development Studies* 1 (1): 85–95.

Tan, Amelia. 2014. "Foreign Graduates On S'pore Govt Bonds Finding Job Hunt Tough." *The Straits Times*, April 29. http://www.stjobs.sg/career-resources/job-seeking-guide/foreign-graduates-on-spore-govt-bonds-finding-job-hunt-tough/a/162608.

Tan, Chorh Chuan. 2009. "State of the University Address 2009." http://www.nus.edu.sg/president/pdf/SoUA_2009.pdf.

———. 2010. "State of the University Address 2010: 'Reading the Water Well.'" http://www.nus.edu.sg/soua/2010/president.pdf.

———. 2015. "Bringing the World to NUS. Bringing NUS to the World." *National University of Singapore*. http://www.nus.edu.sg/global/president.html.

Tan, Eng Chye. 2007. "State of the University Address 2009: Realizing Our Dream." http://www.nus.edu.sg/soua/2007/soua_pvo.pdf.

———. 2011. "Leveraging on Diversity." *The NUS Provost Contemplates*, November 4. http://blog.nus.edu.sg/provost/2011/11/04/leveraging-on-diversity/.

Wong, Poh-Kam, Yuen-Ping Ho, and Annette Singh. 2007. "Towards an 'Entrepreneurial University' Model to Support Knowledge-based Economic Development: The Case of the National University of Singapore." *World Development* 35 (6): 941–58.

Yee, Jenn Jong. 2012. "Foreign Scholars, Parliamentary Reply by Mr. Yee Jenn Jong." *Ministry of Education*, January 9. http://www.moe.gov.sg/media/parliamentary-replies/2012/01/foreign-scholars.php.

Yeoh, Brenda S.A., Michelle Foong, and Kong Chong Ho. 2014. "International Students and the Politics of Language Among 'Globalising Universities' in Asia." *Knowledge Cultures* 2 (4): 64–89.

American Higher Education
TO BE INTERNATIONAL, ENTREPRENEURIAL, AND DIVERSE

Francisco O. Ramirez and Jared Furuta

Universities have their roots in medieval Europe. The medieval university was cosmopolitan insofar as it sought to conserve and disseminate universal knowledge. In the late twelfth and early thirteenth centuries, medieval universities did not have to contend with national states and national political agendas. Taken as a whole, medieval Europe was characterized by a low level of political centralization (relative to other civilizations) but was also increasingly culturally integrated as a Christian world. Western European dynamism is partly explained by the competitive processes made possible by political decentralization and cultural integration (Hall 1985). The latter provided some needed rules of the game that, together with the lack of a single dominant power, made it possible for competitive processes to lead to the more rapid diffusion of universities (and related institutions, such as science) throughout the West (Wuthnow 1980). Universities played a central role in the cultural integration of this earlier world; centuries later, universities would play a similar role in promoting nation-building in an emerging inter-state system (Reisner 1922). By the eighteenth and nineteenth centuries, universities were more clearly national institutions, though they retained their original mission of conserving, disseminating, and now producing, knowledge.

In the twenty-first century, universities appear to be embedded in what is often called "world society" (Marginson 2014; Ramirez and Meyer 2012), although they continue to be responsive to the demands of their national societies and states (Shin 2006). The globally embedded university is attuned to world standards of excellence, and these often call for world-class aspirations and benchmarking exercises. The latter, in turn, often emphasize international university rankings, and these rankings tend to favor those universities with more international students and with a greater international outlook. So, while one can examine the internationalization of higher education in this or that country and emphasize country-specific dynamics, it is important to keep in mind that there is growing global support for the internationalization of higher education.

The internationalization of higher education is linked to broader global models of progress and justice. With respect to higher education, these global models link internationalization to an idealized conception of the university that is both entrepreneurial and a source of local and national developments: the entrepreneurial university is supposed to energize the knowledge economy or society (Clark 1998). Furthermore, the idealized university is supposed to value diversity, both for the sake of fairness and justice but also because diversity is imagined to exert a positive influence on development. Thus, the internationalization of higher education in the twenty-first century is best conceptualized as a feature of a globalizing world that coexists with a world of nation-states. Marginson (2014, 7) puts it this way: "Research universities remain embedded in localities while subject at the same time to both national policy financing, and regulation, and also global linkages, movements, and comparisons." The globalizing world is characterized by a high degree of political decentralization (no world state) that fosters global market competition, which also contains a level of cultural integration that structures this competition within increasingly global frames of reference. Thus, we find a proliferation of conferences and articles on the "world-class university," a term that has grown exponentially in the twenty-first century (Ramirez and Tiplic 2013; see also the chapters in Shin and Kehm 2013).

In this chapter, we first briefly describe the internationalization of higher education in the United States in the post–World War II era. Next, we look at more recent developments, focusing on indicators of internationalization, entrepreneurship, and diversity. Lastly, we propose a research agenda to more directly study American universities and their aspirations to be international, developed, and diverse.

American Higher Education: Internationalization

American higher education expanded earlier and more extensively than in other industrialized societies. By the beginning of the twentieth century, an American advantage existed, as far as access to higher education was concerned (Rubinson 1986). The decentralized character of the American polity and its educational system facilitated competition between status groups that sought to promote their interests through educational attainment (Collins 1979). While European states dealt with class conflicts and related issues by constructing welfare states that offered security, in the United States an "opportunity" ideal emerged; expanded access to higher education, not social welfare services, became the favored path to social mobility in the United States (Heidenhiemer 1981). In some ways, the American polity was not unlike the medieval one: politically decentralized but culturally integrated. These characteristics made it easier for all sorts of interests to construct higher education institutions, but also made it more difficult to create a national university directly under the authority of the federal government: the Jeffersonian aspiration to make the University of Virginia the national university did not materialize. All sorts of universities, including private ones, could commit themselves to public and even national missions as well as seek funding from public sources. Public universities, in turn, could seek funds from private sources.

Thus, the distinction between public and private, a clear boundary in higher education in Europe, is blurred in the U.S. higher education system. To this day, commonalities across American universities are more a function of market forces and professional influences than state directives. A distinctive national educational ministry was not established until the late 1970s. And to this day, this department does not enjoy the authority and influence of similar departments in Asian countries. Educational decentralization continues to characterize the American landscape.

However, these political and cultural characteristics are no longer important triggers of expanded access to tertiary education. The worldwide expansion of tertiary education enrollments demonstrates that national commitments to expanded access are not contingent upon a particular type of political regime or a specific sociocultural configuration (Schofer and Meyer 2005). In fact, more universities have been established after World War II than throughout earlier human history. This reflects the proliferation of nation-states during the last sixty years and the degree to which expanded tertiary education is imagined to be of great value to people and their societies. The American enrollment advantage is no more, but the American vision of a mass credential society (as opposed to an elite "Mandarin" one) has globally diffused. An expanded system of tertiary education has become an indicator of the legitimate nation-state, quite apart from the benefits and costs of this system to individuals and their societies. Expanded access legitimates the university on equity and development grounds.

Keeping the decentralized character of the American political and educational system in mind, it is not surprising that no coherent national policy regarding the internationalization of higher education exists. Prior to World War II, some American professors visited German and British universities and returned with more cosmopolitan ideas about scholarship and teaching. But the internationalization of higher education was not a core feature of the patchwork of competing colleges and universities that characterized the American educational landscape (Labaree 2013). The more parochial character of American higher education in the late nineteenth century can be contrasted with the more cosmopolitan perspective of medieval universities exemplified by Henry III (in 1229):

> Greetings to the masters and the whole body of scholars at Paris. Humbly sympathizing with the exceeding tribulations and distresses which you have suffered at Paris under an unjust law, we wish by our pious aid, with reverence to God and His holy Church to restore your status to its proper condition of liberty. Wherefore we have concluded to make known to your entire body that if it shall be your pleasure to transfer yourselves to our kingdom of England and to remain there to study, we will for this purpose assign to you cities, boroughs, town, whatsoever you wish to select, and in every fitting way cause you to rejoice in a state of liberty and tranquility which should please God and fully meet your needs. (Daly 1961, 168–69)

By contrast, in a letter from future University of Chicago President Harry Judson to then president William Harper in 1891, Judson writes:

> I dislike the idea of a foreigner at the head of such a department in an American university. It seems to me that departments involving American history, American literature, and American politics should be under the charge of Americans. . . . I must confess that I don't fancy having to work for a German. I doubt if many American professors would. (Boyer 2003, 41)

The English king could contemplate acquiring and supporting a French university, because the political categories "English" and "French" were ill defined in the thirteenth century. Latin was the medium through which the English king attempted the first "faculty raid" ever recorded. But by the late nineteenth century, during the age of nationalism, the political categories "American" and "German" were more firmly established and more readily imagined as national boundaries in the nationalizing American university. German and American scholars functioned in their national tongues, though they may well have been conversant with the other languages.

The Cold War in the twentieth century marked the beginning of some important changes in American higher education (Altbach and de Wit 2015). Early interests in the international were clearly fueled by national security concerns. It was important to prepare American students to become ambassadors of American democracy, and also important to extend American education to students from other parts of the world. More generally, it was important to know more about the world: know your enemy and maximize your sphere of influence. These concerns led to both student exchanges and curricular developments that emphasized foreign language training and area studies (de Wit 2002), and also gave rise to the creation of the National Association of Foreign Students in 1948. In the United States and elsewhere, this early phase of internationalization primarily involved the mobility of people across national boundaries in pursuit of different kinds of educational degrees and experiences. Knight (2014) notes that the international student population worldwide has sharply expanded from 238,000 in the 1960s to 3.3 million in 2008.

As figures 9.1 and 9.2 illustrate, in the United States the total number of international students has tripled over the past few decades, from about three hundred thousand in 1980 to nearly nine hundred thousand in 2013 (Institute of International Education 2014b). During the same period, the percentage of international students almost doubled, from 2.5 to 4.5 percent. However, despite the fact that 50 percent of graduating seniors said that they planned to study abroad during college (American Council of Education, Art and Science Group, and Collegeboard 2008), just 1–2 percent of American students actually studied abroad in 2010–11. The trend, though is clearly one of growth: the Institute of International Education reports that approximately 62,000 students studied abroad in 1987; by 2012, this number had increased to nearly 290,000 students (Institute of International Education 2014b).

Nevertheless, it is clear that the United States is more of a receiving than a sending country. This pattern no doubt reflects the favorable status of American universities in the global higher education landscape, a status enhanced by the international rankings of universities. This pattern also reflects both the hegemonic status of the United States in the wider world as well as the establishment of English as a *lingua franca*. Four of the English-speaking "receiving" countries (United States, United Kingdom, Canada, and Australia) in the world host 38 percent of the world's students studying abroad (UNESCO 2014). Brain drain issues are less problematic in the United States, precisely because of its economic position in the wider world. However, in an increasingly integrated world within which economic opportunities arise in other countries, brain circulation dynamics may be increasing (see chapters 4 and 5 in this volume; see also OECD 2002). In particular, it is widely assumed that STEM (science, technology, engineering, and mathematics) field education is important for nations to establish and maintain

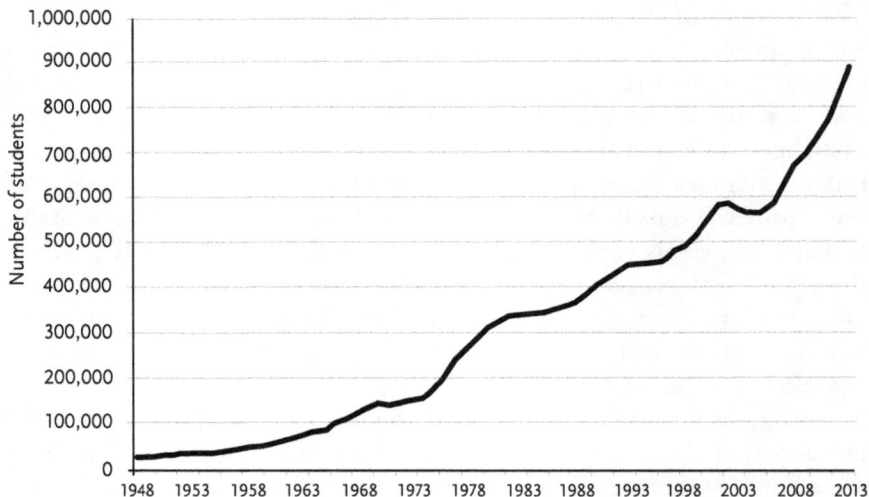

FIGURE 9.1   International students in U.S. higher education, 1948–2013

Source: Institute of International Education (2014a).

Note: International student enrollment measure includes both students enrolled in U.S. higher education and students in Optional Practical Training (OPT).

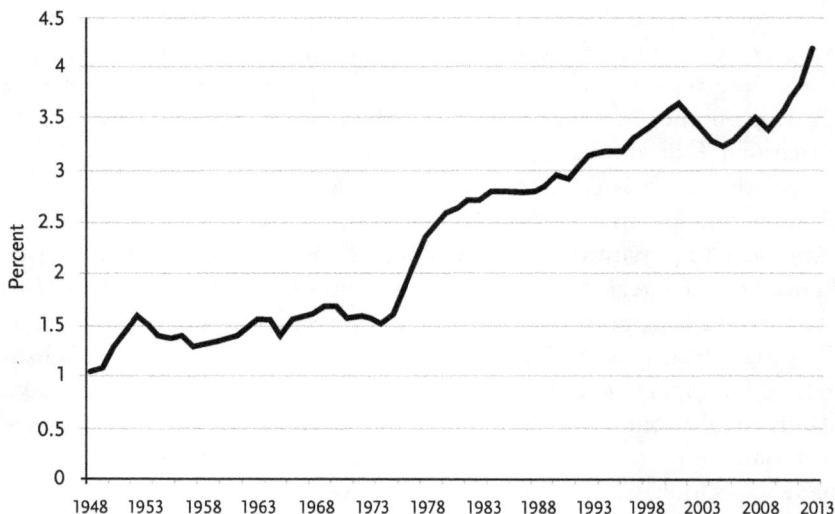

FIGURE 9.2   Percentage of international students (of total enrollment) in U.S. postsecondary education, 1948–2013

Source: Institute of International Education (2014a).

Note: International student enrollment measure includes both students enrolled in U.S. higher education and students in Optional Practical Training (OPT). Data on total student enrollments come from the National Center for Education Statistics.

the competitive status of their higher education systems. A commissioned report by the National Academy of Sciences (2007, 9) on the advancement of science and technology in the United States, for example, makes several recommendations to improve access and the attractiveness of the U.S. higher education system to international students, in order to "develop, recruit, and retain the best and the brightest students, scientists, and engineers from within the United States and throughout the world." It is especially worth noting that a substantial portion of international students in science and engineering in the United States, since the 1970s, have come from just four countries in Asia (China, India, Taiwan, and South Korea); these countries account for more than half of all science and engineering doctoral degrees given to foreign students (National Academy of Sciences 2007, 379).

By the 1980s, further developments in the internationalization of higher education were made. The Association of International Educational Administrators was created in 1981. The Alliance for International Educational and Cultural Exchange followed, lobbying the federal government to promote international education exchange programs. Universities, foundations, and other institutions were engaged in internationalization, though mostly through student exchange programs. The emergence of independent countries from Africa gave rise to cooperative ventures between universities and foundations, in efforts to train the future leaders of these countries. The Ford Foundation, for example, funded master's programs for African students in a number of universities, including Stanford University.

But these developments were not limited to scholarly exchanges. The Cold War gave rise to area studies funded by the federal government to create regional centers that would produce linguistically and culturally fluent scholars in regions of interest to the United States (Stevens and Miller-Idriss 2015). Earlier on, Eastern Europe was privileged, but by the 1980s many other parts of the world were targeted. Cold War area studies have been critiqued for creating too cozy a relationship between different federal agencies and these centers of scholarship (Wallerstein 1997). Their proliferation, in good part due to Title VI federal funding, contributed to the internationalization dynamics in American higher education.

To be sure, federal funding was not limited to area studies. The decades after World War II were unusual, since universities benefited from the extraordinary largesse of the federal government, directly and in conjunction with multiple foundations. An international sauce was added to the meat and potatoes of the American university. The teaching of history in American universities, for example, expanded beyond its traditional emphasis on American and British history (Frank, Schofer, and Torres 1994). New rationales for the internationalization of higher education emerged at the institutional and national levels. Human capital development and international economic competition rationales flourished. To be more international meant to more effectively position your students to compete in a global market. Their human capital would be enhanced by an increase in international knowledge, skills, and network ties. To be more international also meant to better harness international talent toward national development goals. Universities sought to internationalize for the sake of their students and their country. But the erosion of federal funding for higher education in the last two decades or so has led to the search for new revenue streams. This search can lead to international students, but also to what has been called the "second generation" of cross-border education: program and provider mobility efforts that internationalize the university (Knight 2014). Education City in Doha, Qatar, for example, currently hosts six branch campuses of American universities that offer a range of both bachelor's and professional degrees, the earliest of which was founded in the late 1990s (Lewin 2008). This new development suggests that the university also internationalized for its own sake, exploring new revenue streams and networking opportunities.

The more elite universities began to emphasize the broader virtues of internationalization in a globalizing world. These virtues were often cast as the valorization of "diversity": the ideal university incorporates a broad range of people and perspectives, and all are imagined to be culturally enriched in the process. Students and societies benefit from the realization of this ideal, but so does the university, as internationalization is linked to prestige and is rewarded in the international rankings. For example, Amherst College's website contains a page explicitly devoted to displaying its commitments to several varieties of diversity:

> Amherst College is proud of its efforts to achieve and sustain diversity in our community. Across many dimensions of diversity—geographic, racial/ethnic, socio-economic, academic, extra-curricular—Amherst has assembled an exceptionally vibrant student body and is one of the most diverse of all liberal arts colleges in the country. (Amherst 2015)

In discussing their geographic diversity, they further state that,

> our students come from 48 states, plus Washington D.C, Puerto Rico and the U.S. Virgin Islands, and more than 55 countries around the world. Approximately 10 percent of our students are international students with non-U.S. citizenship. Another 2 percent hold dual citizenship with the U.S. and another country and have lived or studied outside the U.S. (Amherst 2015)

While school websites did not exist in the 1980s, it is notable that the admissions section of Amherst's 1978 college catalog does not describe or contain any reference to racial, ethnic, or class diversity of the student population; it also does not contain a separate section (now common for many schools) specifically related to international student admissions.

Regardless of which type of rationale is involved, one should find, in the last thirty years in U.S. higher education, a greater societal and institutional interest in the internationalization of higher education. This overall shift from a more provincial to a more cosmopolitan university should lead to the development of university offices that focus on international students, for instance.

Table 9.1 reports the percentages of international student administrators in four-year colleges and universities in the United States. Approximately 21 percent of colleges and universities report having an international student director or administrator. While nearly twice as many public schools report having an international student advisor, these percentages are similar across all regions and among the four large states (California, Illinois, Texas, and New York) included in the descriptive table. It is important to note here that the data for foreign student administrators appear to be under-reported in the Higher Education Directory, and these percentages should be interpreted with caution: for example, schools such as Harvard University and Stanford

TABLE 9.1

Percentage of schools with foreign student administrators

Total for all schools	21.23
School type	
Private	16.34
Public	31.34
Region	
Northeast	23.67
Midwest	23.38
South	19.55
West	17.61
States	
California	21.19
Texas	20.83
Illinois	25.00
New York	20.47

Source: Higher Education Directory (2015); Integrated Postsecondary Education Data System (2013–14).

Note: Uses the Carnegie Classification (2010) of four-year colleges/universities.

University, which are known to have international student administrators, are not listed in the directory.

To summarize, higher education has greatly expanded worldwide, and both progress (development) and justice (equity) rationales are utilized to make sense of this phenomenal growth. Universities are imagined as engines of progress. In the American context (and increasingly in other national contexts), universities are expected to be entrepreneurial. Thus, universities are expected to contribute to local and national development, but to also be increasingly responsible for their own development. Furthermore, universities are expected to be fair in their admissions and curricular decisions. Fairness often leads to being more welcoming to different people and perspectives; thus, universities are expected to valorize diversity. Expanded higher education is increasingly an indicator of the legitimate nation-state. Earlier concerns about over-education (Dore 1976; Freeman 1976) carry little weight in current policy or public discussions. On the contrary, more and more countries move forward as if there were "no salvation outside higher education" (Shils 1971). The World Bank, once a skeptic, now champions higher education (World Bank 2002).

The internationalization of higher education is a more recent phenomenon, but it too appears to have gained worldwide traction. In the United States, multiple rationales have emerged to account for internationalization, and the latter involves multiple dimensions. It is important to remember that there is no coherent national policy on internationalization: a substantial amount of internationalization processes take place at the organizational or university level. However, there are two underlying ideas that both national and institutional leaders evoke: internationalization for development and internationalization for diversity. In the next section, we sketch some research directions to examine how American universities manage internationalization, development, and diversity.

Research Directions

To reiterate, American universities are expected to contribute to national development but also to manage their own development. This expectation in part reflects the history of fundraising for private colleges and universities in the United States. Harvard College was a first mover in this domain, seeking funds for its development as early as 1641 (Worth 2002). Other universities and colleges followed suit: an entrepreneurial spirit was added to the earlier religious zeal. Most interestingly, by the beginning of the twentieth century, these fundraising activities became more professionalized. Rational strategies emerged, and these included listing potential donors, publicizing the names of those who gave, and specifying fundraising goals and timetables. Harvard again led the way, launching a modern fundraising campaign between 1916 and 1921, a campaign explicitly designed to enhance its endowment (Cutlip 1965; Kimball and Johnson 2012). After World War II, paid professionals at the university increasingly undertook development work. The modern university development office would increasingly become an organizational feature of the American university. Armies of volunteers and consulting firms would continue to play a role in fundraising, but the university development office would become more central over time.

Foundations again played a key role in the establishment and diffusion of this organizational innovation. In 1958, a conference funded by the Ford Foundation sought to bring together university and alumni personnel to upgrade the quality of those engaged in non-academic tasks in universities. The conference led to the Greenbrier Report, which recommended the establishment of an administrator who would work with the university president to oversee alumni and public relations and fundraising. Though this recommendation may have made more sense to the leadership of private universities, the later demise of the "golden age" of public funding would lead to the rise of development offices in public universities. Moreover, though the revenue-seeking development office may make more sense in the competitive and decentralized American system, this organizational innovation has diffused to other countries. We explore both of these further developments below.

Table 9.2 shows the percentage of four-year American colleges and universities that have a development or advancement officer. More than three-quarters of these institutions report having a development administrator. Perhaps reflecting the demise of public funding, public institutions are more likely to have a development officer than their private counterparts. There is regional variation, but in every region a development officer is found in at least 60 percent of the institutions. There is also some variation across the four large states (California, Illinois, Texas, and New York) we selected for comparison. But here again, we find that the development officer is a common feature of higher educational organizations throughout the United States.

It is important to recognize that the Greenbrier Report laid the foundation for this development. It is also important to recognize the proliferation of associations, conferences, and scholarly journals promoting the professionalization of fundraising in the United States: the pivotal role played by the Council for Advancement and Support of Education (CASE) cannot be overlooked (Skinner 2015). What is striking, though, is that this peculiar

TABLE 9.2

Percentage of schools with development/advancement administrators

Total for all schools	76.13
School type	
Private	71.83
Public	85.04
Region	
Northeast	85.99
Midwest	74.68
South	77.36
West	61.62
States	
California	66.1
Texas	88.89
Illinois	78.12
New York	84.25

Source: Higher Education Directory (2015); Integrated Postsecondary Education Data System (2013–14).

Note: Uses the Carnegie Classification (2010) of four-year colleges/universities.

American innovation has diffused to a wide range of countries around the world. CASE now deals with over three thousand institutional members in over eighty countries; internationalizing the professionalization of development work in universities around the world is one of their strategic goals. CASE has regional offices in Europe, Latin America, and Asia, and is currently exploring Africa. CASE opened an Asian Pacific regional office in 2007 and has held conferences in several Asian countries. Increased fundraising has been advocated by a number of educational leaders in prominent Asian universities (Cheng 2011).

So, why has an American rhetoric that values shared expertise and practice in university development diffused across borders? First, there is a growing sense that universities must tap multiple sources of revenue in order to meet international standards. National and institutional leaders on different continents make this point. Second, the professionalization of the enterprise elevates it from a solely "hustling for dollars" business. Without enhanced resources, universities cannot contribute to local and national development, nor can they effectively prepare people who will succeed in the workplace, sometimes imagined in global terms. These understandings are enhanced by the professionalization of fundraising. Lastly, the new idealized university that is "free" to be entrepreneurial undercuts the older idea of the national state as the sole source of university funding. The international success of the American research university fuels the new idealized university. Thus, development offices and enhanced resources are linked to the internationalization of higher education.

American universities are also expected to be accessible. In recent decades, that expectation emphasizes diversity. One should hence expect to find that the diversity emphasis has grown in American higher education, and that this emphasis has also diffused. There are, of course, many different dimensions to diversity. One can look at the composition of university students. On a gender dimension, one can see the growth of women's share of higher education in America and globally (Bradley and Ramirez 1996). One can examine curricula and the rise of subjects such as women's studies, and here too there is evidence of growth nationally and globally (Wotipka and Ramirez 2008). In the American context, diversity concerns have often centered on race and ethnic issues, and continue to do so. One can analyze the rise of thematic centers and curricular content that focuses on race and/or ethnicity: these too have expanded over time (Rojas 2007; Olzak and Kangas 2008). More generally, and to parallel our earlier focus on development officers, one can examine the rise of diversity officers in American universities.

Table 9.3 cross-sectionally reports the percentages of diversity administrators in four-year colleges and universities in the United States. Over 30 percent of the schools in the data report having an administrator in this position. Nearly twice as many public schools contain diversity administrators as private schools, perhaps as a way for these schools to maintain legitimacy in response to public accountability pressures. Schools in the Northeast and Midwest regions, notably, report higher percentages of diversity administrator positions, when compared with those in the Western and Southern regions. It is also notable that, when the percentages of schools that report having a diversity administrator are broken down further into public and private sectors within regions (not shown here), these numbers increase: 46 percent of public schools in the West and 43 percent of public schools in the South report having a diversity administrator, while 63 percent of public schools in the Midwest and 38 percent of public schools in the Northeast also report having a diversity position. In Illinois, one of the "big" states included in this table with the highest percentage of schools with a diversity administrator, nearly 60 percent of public schools report having a diversity administrator.

To summarize, American universities have seen the growth of international students, and more universities have established international offices

TABLE 9.3

Percentage of schools with diversity administrators

Total for all schools	31.55
School type	
Private	24.26
Public	46.65
Region	
Northeast	37.44
Midwest	38.53
South	24.01
West	27.11
States	
California	31.36
Texas	27.78
Illinois	45.31
New York	36.22

Source: Higher Education Directory (2015); Integrated Postsecondary Education Data System (2013–14).

Note: Uses the Carnegie Classification (2010) of four-year colleges/universities.

and directors. The federal government played an early role in fostering the internationalization of higher education, driven in good part by the Cold War and national security concerns. In a decentralized educational system, however, universities themselves are mostly responsible for continued internationalization. The internationalization impetus is linked to ideas about the university as an engine of development and a place welcoming diversity. Thus, American universities have seen the growth of development and diversity offices and administrators in addition to international offices. American universities often act as if they aspire to be international, entrepreneurial, and diverse. But are these organizational developments related to one another?

To begin to answer this question, one could examine university mission statements and related institutional "presentations of self" over time to determine whether there has been a rise in internationalization aspirations. We expect such a rise in both public and private universities after World War II, but especially beginning in the 1990s. Further, one could examine whether there has been a discursive link associating the key terms "internationalization," "entrepreneurial or development oriented" and "diversity seeking and respecting" in American universities. One can ascertain whether this link has become stronger and is more pronounced in the more recent decades. The literature suggests that universities are more likely to be more self-consciously entrepreneurial and diversity-valorizing in the twenty-first century. The question is whether the earlier national security rationale for internationalization has become but one of many distinctive rationales. And more concretely, whether different kinds of universities use a more specific or a more diffuse rationale for their internationalization goals. We expect elite universities to emphasize a broader rationale for internationalizing, one that emphasizes the value of diversity. These questions call for some form of semantic network or cluster analysis.

A second line of inquiry more directly explores the ties between these different organizational offices. To what extent are the efforts of one office coordinated with those of the others? If internationalization is mostly designed to be a new revenue stream for the university, one would assume close working relations between internationalization and development offices. Admission officers, for instance, would be more attentive to the development impact of admitting more self-funded international students. Alternatively, if a more diffuse emphasis on diversity is in place, one would expect closer ties between the diversity and internationalization offices. Many universities proudly list the total number of countries represented in the student body or in the newly admitted cohort. Celebrations of diversity and the global reach of the university are displayed, as the examples above demonstrate. In this domain, one can also use archival data to estimate how much interaction there is across these offices. Just as one would assume that the discourse gets thicker over time, one would expect a thickening of activity at the organizational level.

Lastly, one could expand on the cross-sectional data provided in this paper and directly analyze the timing and founding rates of each of these organizational developments (international, development, and diversity offices in American universities). Using an event history analysis framework, one could ascertain whether universities with a longer history with development offices established international offices earlier. Or, perhaps the rate of international office formation is accelerated by the rise of an overall interest in the value of diversity, a rise that is in part reflected in the establishment of diversity offices. Perhaps the acceleration rate is mostly due to a period effect. Longitudinal data will also allow us to gauge whether the founding rates are influenced by university characteristics: elite versus non-elite, for example.

Conclusions

We live in a world in which higher education is not only expanding worldwide, but is also increasingly globally legitimated. "Higher education for all" and "all for higher education" are triumphant visions endorsed globally. More recently, research and policy questions have turned to matters of quality, increasingly influenced by the presence of transnational rankings. The legitimate nation-state must act as if it is committed to the growth of high-quality higher education. To be sure, uncertainty exists about what constitutes high-quality higher education, but the "world-class" mantra has become global. Bolstered by the international rankings, American research universities have become the benchmarks against which universities elsewhere gauge their standing and their progress. Universities in the United States increasingly aspire to be international, entrepreneurial, and diverse. Organizational developments in American higher education reflect these aspirations: development, diversity, and international offices emerge and diffuse. These developments appear to be linked to each other and to an idealized university template of excellence in the United States.

Not all features of American research universities easily cross national boundaries. The importance of intercollegiate athletic competition, for example, is not theorized as crucial to becoming a world-class university, though one can imagine the role of athletics in university fundraising. The low value assigned to "service" in the elite American university would be appalling to Asian university leaders who may see a connection between service and internationalization efforts. More research is needed to ascertain whether the internationalizing, entrepreneurial, and diverse university becomes a core feature of a global university template of excellence. Research is also needed to determine which of these dimensions is more readily adapted in different countries and different universities therein.

References

Altbach, Philip, and Hans de Wit. 2015. "Internationalization and Global Tension: Lessons from History." *Journal of Studies in International Education* 19 (1): 4–10.

American Council on Education, Art and Science Group, and the Collegeboard. 2008. *College-Bound Students' Interests in Study Abroad and Other International Learning Activities.* https://www.acenet.edu/news-room/Documents/2008-Student-Poll.pdf.

Amherst College. 2015. "Amherst College: Admission Office Diversity Programs." Accessed July 2015. https://www.amherst.edu/admission/diversity.

Boyer, Ernest. 2003. *Judson's War and Hutchins Peace: The University of*

Chicago and War in the 20th Century. Occasional Papers on Higher Education XII. Chicago: College of the University of Chicago.

Bradley, Karen, and Francisco O. Ramirez. 1996. "World Polity and Gender Parity: Women's Share of Higher Education, 1965–1985." *Research in Sociology of Education and Socialization* 11: 63–91.

Cheng, Kai-Ming. 2011. "Fundraising as Institutional Advancement." In *Leadership for World-Class Universities: Challenges for Developing Countries.* New York: Routledge.

Clark, Burton. 1998. *Creating Entrepreneurial Universities: Organizational Pathways of Transformation.* UK: Emerald Group.

Collins, Randall. 1979. *The Credential Society: A Historical Sociology of Education and Stratification.* New York: Academic Press.

Cutlip, Scott. 1965. *Fundraising in the United States: Its Role in America's Philanthropy.* New Jersey: Rutgers University Press.

Daly, Lowrie. 1961. *The Medieval University: 1200–1400.* New York: Sheed and Ward.

de Wit, Hans. 2002. *Internationalization of Higher Education in the United States of America and Europe: A Historical, Comparative, and Conceptual Analysis.* Connecticut: Greenwood Press.

Dore, Ronald. 1976. *The Diploma Disease Education, Qualification, and Development.* Berkeley: University of California Press.

Frank, David John, Evan Schofer, and John Torres. 1994. "Rethinking History: Change in the University Curriculum, 1910–90." *Sociology of Education* 67 (4): 231–42.

Freeman, Richard B. 1976. *The Overeducated American.* New York: Academic Press.

Hall, John. 1985. *Powers and Liberties: The Causes and Consequences of the Rise of the West.* Massachusetts: Basil Blackwell.

Heidenheimer, Arnold. 1981. "Education and Social Security Entitlements in Europe and America." In *The Development of Welfare States in Europe and America*, edited by Peter Flora and Arnold Heidenheimer, 269–306. New York: Oxford University Press.

Higher Education Publications, Inc. 2015. *Higher Education Directory.* Falls Church, VA: Higher Education Publications.

Institute of International Education. 2014a. "International Student Enrollment Trends, 1948/49–2013/14." *Open Doors Report on International Educational Exchange.* http://www.iie.org/Research-and-Publications/Open-Doors/Data/International-Students/Enrollment-Trends/1948-2014.

———. 2014b. "Open Doors Data: U.S. Study Abroad." http://www.iie.org/Research-and-Publications/Open-Doors/Data/US-Study-Abroad.

Kimball, Bruce, and Benjamin Ashby Johnson. 2012. "The Beginning of 'Free Money' Ideology in American Universities: Charles W. Elliot at Harvard, 1869–1909." *History of Education Review* 52: 222–50.

Knight, Jane. 2014. "Three Generations of Crossborder Higher Educaton: New Developments, Issues, and Challenges." In *Internationalisation of Higher Education and Global Mobility,* edited by Bernard Streitwieser, 43–58. UK: Symposium Books.

Labaree, David. 2013. "The Power of the Parochial in Shaping the American System of Higher Education." In *Educational Research: Institutional Spaces of Educational Research*, edited by Paul Smeyers and Marc Depaepe, 31–46. Dordrecht: Springer.

Lewin, Tamar. 2008. "U.S. Universities Rush to Set up Outposts Abroad." *New York Times*. February 10.

Marginson, Simon. 2014. "Foreword." In *Internationalisation of Higher Education and Global Mobility*, edited by Bernard Streitwieser, 7–10. Oxford: Symposium Books.

National Academy of Sciences, National Academy of Engineering, and the Institute of Medicine of the National Academies. 2007. *Rising Above the Gathering Storm: Energizing and Employing America for a Brighter Economic Future*. Washington, DC: The National Academies Press.

Olzak, Susan, and Nicole Kangas. 2008. "Organizational Innovation: Establishing Racial, Ethnic, and Women's Studies Programs in the U.S." *Sociology of Education* 81: 163–88.

Organisation for Economic Co-operation Development (OECD). 2002. *International Mobility of the Highly Skilled*. Washington, DC: OECD. doi: 10.1787/9789264196087-en.

Ramirez, Francisco, and John W. Meyer. 2012. "Universalizing the University in World Society." In *Institutionalization of World Class Universities in Global Competition*, edited by Jung Cheol Shin and Barbara Kehn, 257–74. New York: Springer.

Ramirez, Francisco O., and Dijana Tiplic. 2013. "In Pursuit of Excellence? Discursive Patterns in European Higher Education Research." *Higher Education* 67: 439–55.

Reisner, Edward. 1922. *Nationalism and Education since 1789: A Social and Political History of Modern Education*. New York: Macmillan.

Rojas, Fabio. 2007. *From Black Power to Black Studies: How a Radical Social Movement Became an Academic Discipline*. Maryland: Johns Hopkins University Press.

Rubinson, Richard. 1986. "Class Formation, Politics, and Institutions: Schooling in the United States." *American Journal of Sociology*, 92 (3): 519–48.

Schofer, Evan, and John W. Meyer. 2005. "The Worldwide Expansion of Higher Education." *American Sociological Review* 70 (6): 898–920.

Shin, Jung Cheol, and Barbara Kehm, eds.. 2013. *Institutionalization of World-Class University in Global Competition*. Dordrecht: Springer.

Shin, Gi-Wook. 2006. *Ethnic Nationalism in Korea: Genealogy, Politics, and Legitimacy*. Stanford: Stanford University Press.

Shils, Edward. 1971. "No Salvation Outside Higher Education." *Minerva* 6: 313–21.

Skinner, Nadine Ann. 2015. "The Professionalization of Development and Institutional Advancement in Higher Education." Unpublished manuscript.

Stevens, Mitchell, and Cynthia Miller-Idriss. 2015. *The Kaleidoscope: Universities and the Social Sciences in the Global Era*. Unpublished manuscript.

UNESCO Institute for Statistics. 2014. "Global Flow of Tertiary Students." Accessed August 15, 2015. http://www.uis.unesco.org/Education/Pages/international-student-flow-viz.aspx.

Wallerstein, Immanuel. 1997. "The Unintended Consequences of Cold War Area Studies." In *The Cold War and the University: Toward and Intellectual History of the Postwar Years*, edited by Andre Schiffrin, 195–232. New York: The New Press.

World Bank. 2002. *Constructing Knowledge Societies: New Challenges for Tertiary Education*. Washington, DC: The World Bank.

Worth, Michael J. 2002. "New Strategies for Educational Fundraising." In *New Strategies for Educational Fundraising*, edited by Michael Worth. Connecticut: American Council on Education/Praeger Publishers.

Wotipka, Christine Min, and Francisco O. Ramirez. 2008. "Women's Studies as a Global Innovation." In *The Worldwide Transformation of Higher Education*, edited by David Baker and Alexander W. Wiseman, 89–110. Amsterdam: Elsevier JAI Press.

Wuthnow, Robert. 1980. "The World Economy and the Institutionalization of Science in Seventeenth Century Europe." In *Studies of the Modern World-System*, edited by Albert Bergesen, 25–52. Academic Press.

Worth, Michael J. 2002. "New Strategies for Educational Fundraising." In *New Strategies for Educational Fundraising*, edited by Michael Worth. Connecticut: American Council on Education/Praeger Publishers.

Epilogue

AN INTERVIEW WITH YEON-CHEON OH

Translated and edited by Rennie J. Moon

On October 2, 2015, Gi-Wook Shin interviewed Yeon-Cheon Oh, a co-editor of this volume. Oh, former president of Seoul National University (July 2010 to July 2014) and president of the University of Ulsan (March 2015 to present), raises and addresses many of the issues, problems, and challenges that appear within these pages.

SHIN: How do you define internationalization?

OH: Internationalization is a diverse concept and people have a tendency to talk about it from their own perspective based on what they think it is. Working with this diversity of definitions, strategies, and directions was to me quite challenging. That is, without a clear, agreed-upon policy direction, different university stakeholders pursued their own goals and it became difficult to allocate and use resources efficiently. To me, internationalization policies can be divided into two broad categories: policies that focus more on the visible/tangible aspects of internationalization, such as geographical expansion and program reach, and policies that focus more on upgrading academic programs and research. But ultimately, both aspects of internationalization policies pursue similar goals and directions and move toward greater expansion and upgrading of standards. So I've thought that it would be useful to come to an agreement on what those standards are and what they should or should not include. Although we refer to internationalization as one concept, what it means differs depending on the particular situation of each higher education institution. Korea has about two hundred institutions of higher education. The major research universities such as Seoul

National University (SNU) or Yonsei tend to interpret internationalization as upgrading academic quality and standards, whereas the provincial universities tend to interpret it as expanding programs and their geographical reach. So the tendency to approach internationalization as one concept often causes confusion. We need to get used to thinking about it in terms of more categories, different levels, university-specific needs and targets, and different strategies. So when I was president, the office of international cooperation tended to emphasize the latter concept of the two: attracting foreign students, sending Koreans students on exchange, etc., while the academic departments thought of internationalization as raising academic standards, such as bringing in high-caliber faculty and the best students. One focuses on quantity and the other on quality.

There's also a cultural tendency to think that since Korea is an Asian country, a former colony, and a developing country, Korea entered late in the game in its efforts to upgrade itself toward a global standard. So there's a tremendous desire and momentum to compensate for these late beginnings. And this is mostly done through measures of quantity. Having those foreign students is seen to be a crucial part of the internationalization package and global standard. So in Korea internationalization is an indicator of and highly associated with concepts such as modernization, Americanization, and westernization. This perceived need to make progress and advance without limit has a very powerful momentum in Korean society.

SHIN: You earlier mentioned differences between major and minor universities. SNU is considered one of Korea's most prestigious universities while the University of Ulsan (Ulsan), although a reputable university, nonetheless is a provincial university. Could you discuss some of the differences between the two?

OH: At major universities such as SNU, there's an institutional base that does not necessarily require strong leadership initiatives are not really necessary, but in the case of Ulsan, the president or the executive leadership needs to push harder to make reforms. At the same time, Ulsan is quite distinctive because it is located in an industrialized area and centered around science and engineering, so the degree of internationalization is quite high.

SHIN: More so than other provincial universities?

OH: Yes, but even so the leadership needs to make a concerted effort. At SNU, not just for internationalization reforms but in other areas as well, the initiatives of the director of academic affairs will suffice. But at Ulsan, the president needs to take the initiative.

SHIN: You mentioned the distinction between quality and quantity. They are different but also mutually reinforcing aspects of internationalization. When you were president of SNU, which of the two did you focus on more?

OH: I would say I placed equal emphasis on both. For example, I was able to secure $20 million for a Global Human Resources project, where 15–20 Nobel laureates and top young professors were brought to SNU every year to help upgrade local professors to a global standard.

SHIN: So it seems that SNU stressed quality over quantity. Is internationalization deemed absolutely necessary? If so, how important is it?

OH: In one sense internationalization initiatives are considered to be a stimulant or facilitator. For example, we brought in a Nobel laureate in business and this cost us $1 million over two years. There's a lot of resistance from departments about such investment. They say that if SNU has that many resources, then it's better to give it to academic departments. Critics argue that such symbolic measures only have a marginal effect.

SHIN: Yes, and some in the media raise similar concerns. Do you personally think that such symbolic efforts have stimulating effects?

OH: Yes. At major universities such as SNU, Yonsei, and Korea University, making that amount of investment is necessary to let others know about your university's academic identity, that foreigners come to your university not just to teach but also learn from locals, and that has a significant stimulating effect. Our society and constituents need to understand that, but they strongly resist on the grounds of equity, and this I think is something that leaders have to be able to overcome. From my experience, even though university officials have to go to great efforts to secure such funding, academic departments aren't always appreciative of that effort and try to fight its use for hiring foreigners.

SHIN: Related to that is the practice of teaching in English. Courses in English have been significantly expanded in Korean universities in general. How do you view such courses? Is there still a controversy over this?

OH: There's a light and there's a shadow. Teaching and learning in English may translate into more internationalized learning, but for non-English speaking countries where the majority of English medium courses are being taught by non-native English speakers, the level of information delivery may be at a very low level. So teaching in English has become very formalized and mechanized in Korea. So as we discussed earlier, it's not the quantity or percentage of English-taught classes that should matter, but figuring out if teaching in English results in truly internationalized learning. So factors such as faculty selection, type of subjects taught, and student demand should be taken seriously to raise the quality and effectiveness of English-medium courses. Even when we teach in students' mother tongue, studies show that only two-thirds of the information is effectively delivered. But if Korean professors teach in English, then the professor has trouble delivering the content and the students don't learn as much as they should. This is more serious for Korean professors teaching subjects like history, Korean literature, and philosophy. But the policy goal for most Korean universities is to raise the percentage of courses taught in English because it's counted as one of the indicators for various kinds of national assessments, evaluations, and rankings.

SHIN: What are your thoughts about encouraging professors to publish in indexed international journals? Some say it is generally a good idea but others critically say it lowers the quality of publications because junior scholars publish in indexed journals regardless of quality, rather than aiming to publish in top journals, which usually takes longer. Young professors make this their goal in order to survive, sacrificing quantity for quality.

OH: I see this as a very positive development. The quality doesn't improve proportionally with quantity, but I see this as a virtuous cycle. However, I think journals published in Anglophone countries should relax their linguistic standards for non-Anglophone academics or at least provide an alternative route for academics whose first language is not English. Despite the difficulties, however, there's a general social consensus that publishing in indexed international journals contributes to internationalization.

SHIN: What main internationalization initiatives did you pursue as president of SNU?

OH: I created summer and winter study abroad programs such as SNU in Paris, SNU in Tokyo, SNU in Washington, etc. where our students could receive credit during their breaks. The school would subsidize part of the expenses from funds like the Global Human Resources project I mentioned earlier. SNU's international cooperation efforts mostly focused on Chinese universities. I believe I traveled to Beijing about thirty times while I was president. I also focused on revitalizing exchange between four Asian universities in particular—Beijing University, Tokyo University, Seoul National University, and the University of Hanoi. We also sponsored and hosted three-quarters of the cost for the Asian Presidents Conference over four years.

SHIN: Then what were some of the challenges you faced while trying to achieve such initiatives?

OH: The most challenging aspect was funding and coping with a rigid university budget structure.

SHIN: How much funding comes from public vs. private sources?

OH: About one-third each from government, internal university funding, and student user fees. But very few universities in Korea have this capability.

SHIN: SNU is a special case.

OH: Yes. For most national and private universities, internationalization is more inbound-oriented—attracting foreign students, especially from China and Southeast Asia. In many ways, it's about filling up student numbers. There needs to be a balance in inbound and outbound student numbers in order for internationalization to have an optimal effect, but there are not many Korean universities that can or have put in the necessary efforts to do so.

SHIN: When looking back, do you have any regrets about not being able to make improvements or do more? And if so, in what areas?

OH: One regret I have is not being able to create a more professionalized system for internationalization efforts. That is, an organizational structure that can manage such affairs in a systematic and sustainable way. Right now, the administrative positions and staff involved in internationalization are all part-time and temporary—very under-professionalized without any permanent career tracks. There needs to be sufficient funding, professionalized staff, a formal organization, and executive ability to mobilize a sense of mission and work responsibility. Finding and retaining English-speaking human resources is especially difficult since they are of higher value and find better positions in other fields like law or business. This type of system is also non-existent as you go further down to the level of departments. We've hired lots of foreigners but departments and schools do not have a system for managing and taking care of them. Deans and associate deans are often tied up with other responsibilities.

SHIN: How many foreign faculty are there at SNU, and how many are tenured?

OH: When I was there, foreign faculty numbers increased from 142 to 240. This includes all non-tenure track faculty. Each department has about two foreign faculty and many of them are Korean-Americans. In Korea, about 80–90 percent of tenure-track faculty make tenure. This is the same for foreign faculty and even perhaps more favorable for them, since we'd like to retain foreign faculty as much as possible. Foreign faculty, however, come to Korea with a "wait and see" attitude. So even though they are in many ways guaranteed tenure, they often go on the job market again and go to countries like Singapore or Hong Kong. So if you include all such foreign faculty, then the percentage of foreign faculty receiving tenure is low, but if you include only those foreign faculty who have plans to stay, then the percentage should be high. So it depends...

SHIN: Then SNU does not have a department like the Underwood International College of Yonsei University, where there are a large number of foreigners?

OH: Yes, since there is a Graduate School of International Studies, but not an international college at the undergraduate level like Underwood.

SHIN: Another important issue is whether Korean universities embrace such foreigners or if they are considered tokenistic or symbolic for internationalization. For example, is there even one foreigner who has taken on an administrative position at the dean level?

OH: No.

SHIN: Is that because they don't want to or they are not allowed to?

OH: It's because it is assumed that they will not be able to manage the local politics often required of such a position. I would say that one-quarter of Korean professors who have been around for twenty-plus years would not be able to successfully manage the position of dean.

SHIN: What is your opinion regarding global rankings? Even though the rankings are arbitrary and problematic in many ways, they still exert pressure on universities.

OH: There are positive and negative aspects to rankings. On the one hand, it is a business and the rankings themselves are artificial and limited, but from the point of view of university leadership, they are helpful because we can use them to push for reforms such as teaching and publishing in English. Rankings are not an absolute standard but they can be used to effect change.

SHIN: Are foreign faculty hired for their ability to publish in English?

OH: No. In general, Korean faculty are actually much more productive than foreign faculty in this regard. Foreigners are hired because of social pressure to be more "diverse" and "international" and they tend to be the most visible indicator. And more English on campus makes it seem like we're doing something. Japan used to be quite good about this but lately they have fallen behind.

SHIN: Do you feel that Korean universities make the best use of foreign faculty and students?

OH: As far as SNU is concerned, yes.

SHIN: According to one source, the foreign student employment rate in Korea is only about 1 percent. Reliable statistics are largely unavailable. Neither the government nor universities keep such statistics. Perhaps it is closer to 5 percent. But statistics also show that a far greater percentage of foreign students wish to find a job in Korea upon graduation [than are able]. Perhaps this is because Korea doesn't provide them with opportunities, but most return to their home countries. Couldn't this be viewed as a tremendous loss of human resources? If we are to achieve internationalization shouldn't Korea be able to embrace the talent that such foreigners bring to Korean society?

OH: Internationalization in Korea has not really addressed such "software" aspects of internationalization. It still focuses much on hardware. I myself fell short of addressing such aspects as president. That was beyond my realm of thinking.

SHIN: What currently are your main internationalization initiatives at Ulsan?

OH: The University of Ulsan is located in Korea's most industrialized area. So internationalization focuses on industry-university collaboration—attracting foreigners who can build experience in Korea's industrial settings, mainly through programs in the school of engineering. The industrial complex is quite impressive. That's why Ulsan attracts the largest number of Vietnamese students . . . over one hundred I believe.

SHIN: When those students graduate, is there a high chance that they will find jobs in the Ulsan area?

OH: Yes. This university-industry cooperation is a strength.

SHIN: Do you have any suggestions, just one or two, for Korean or other Asian universities regarding internationalization?

OH: Most urgent I think is governance. Also, clear goals and systematic management are needed at the outset to achieve desired results. A consulting system. That kind of system is very undeveloped. Everything is just left to the market. There needs to be specific goals, tools and systematic preparation to succeed. At the same time, compared to China and Japan, internationalization is still considered a major priority in Korea. There's a social consensus about it. There's no question that it's considered an important part of higher education development for Korea. This became evident when I attended international conferences when I was president. We would prepare a week in advance for such meetings, as many as four people would accompany me, we would proactively invest in reserving a room at the conference hotel so we could set up meetings and consult with other Asian university presidents for short meetings. We were always the busiest people there. Other university delegations didn't seem to have that level of interest.

Index

Karen Eggleston, ed. *Prescribing Cultures and Pharmaceutical Policy in the Asia-Pacific.* 2009.

Donald A. L. Macintyre, Daniel C. Sneider, and Gi-Wook Shin, eds. *First Drafts of Korea: The U.S. Media and Perceptions of the Last Cold War Frontier.* 2009.

Steven Reed, Kenneth Mori McElwain, and Kay Shimizu, eds. *Political Change in Japan: Electoral Behavior, Party Realignment, and the Koizumi Reforms.* 2009.

Donald K. Emmerson. *Hard Choices: Security, Democracy, and Regionalism in Southeast Asia.* 2008.

STUDIES OF THE WALTER H. SHORENSTEIN ASIA-PACIFIC RESEARCH CENTER (*with Stanford University Press*)

Thomas Fingar, ed. *The New Great Game: China and South and Central Asia in the Era of Reform.* 2016.

James Bourk Hoesterey. *Rebranding Islam: Piety, Prosperity, and a Self-Help Guru.* 2015.

Gi-Wook Shin and Joon Nak Choi. *Global Talent: Skilled Labor as Social Capital in Korea,* 2015.

Larry Diamond and Gi-Wook Shin, eds. *New Challenges for Maturing Democracies in Korea and Taiwan,* 2014.

Harukata Takenaka. *Failed Democratization in Prewar Japan: Breakdown of a Hybrid Regime,* 2014.

Gene Park. *Spending Without Taxation: FILP and the Politics of Public Finance in Japan.* 2011.

Erik Martinez Kuhonta. *The Institutional Imperative: The Politics of Equitable Development in Southeast Asia.* 2011.

Yongshun Cai. *Collective Resistance in China: Why Popular Protests Succeed or Fail.* 2010.

Gi-Wook Shin. *One Alliance, Two Lenses: U.S.-Korea Relations in a New Era.* 2010.

Jean Oi and Nara Dillon, eds. *At the Crossroads of Empires: Middlemen, Social Networks, and State-building in Republican Shanghai.* 2007.

Gi-Wook Shin. *Ethnic Nationalism in Korea: Genealogy, Politics, and Legacy.* 2006.

Andrew Walder, Joseph Esherick, and Paul Pickowicz, eds. *The Chinese Cultural Revolution as History.* 2006.

The authorized representative in the EU for product safety and compliance is:
Mare Nostrum Group
B.V Doelen 72
4831 GR Breda
The Netherlands

www.ingramcontent.com/pod-product-compliance
Lightning Source LLC
Chambersburg PA
CBHW020341270326
41926CB00007B/278